SCHILLER'S WOUND

Kritik: German Literary Theory and Cultural Studies
Liliane Weissberg, Editor

A complete listing of the books in this series can be found at the back of this volume.

SCHILLER'S WOUND

THE THEATER OF TRAUMA FROM CRISIS TO COMMODITY

Stephanie Hammer

WAYNE STATE UNIVERSITY PRESS

DETROIT

Library of Congress Cataloging-in-Publication Data

Hammer, Stephanie Barbâe.
Schiller's wound : the theater of trauma from crisis to commodity /
Stephanie Hammer.
p.   cm. — (Kritik)
Includes bibliographical references and index.
ISBN 0-8143-2862-8 (alk. paper)
1. Schiller, Friedrich, 1759–1805—Criticism and interpretation.   2.
Psychoanalysis and literature.   I. Title.   II. Kritik (Detroit, Mich.)
PT2492   .H36   2001

832'.6—dc21   00-010462

Producers of great art are no demigods but fallible human beings, often with neurotic and damaged personalities. On the other hand, if one were to dump the idea of genius entirely, aesthetics would be left with nothing but insipid uninspired craft knowledge on how to do things; it would sink to the level of mere stencilling. The concept of genius has an element of truth.

ADORNO

Contents

Preface

What This Book Does

The following study of German author Friedrich Schiller reads the playwright and his plays in terms of the psychological category known as trauma. Equally important, it argues that this canonical author forms a crucial link to contemporary cultural practices and issues of cultural life under late capitalism, particularly the ways in which we think about art and money and the ways in which we have come to understand the theater and other visual media as increasingly psychological displays of personal pain.

The present volume aims to be provocative and descriptive rather than exhaustive. Accordingly, this study outlines an overarching approach that applies to the dramas as a whole, and then undertakes in-depth readings of the plays that mark particularly important moments of crisis and transition in Schiller's career. These include Schiller's first and last plays—*The Robbers*, and the fragment *Demetrius*—as well as the transitional work *Don Carlos*, the seminal *WALLENSTEIN* trilogy and the less studied neoclassical play, *The Bride of Messina*.

While the performance of femininity was a key issue for Schiller's dramas, this book focuses on the ways in which Schiller's theater of trauma put masculinity on trial, and explores in particular the continuing resurgence of an angry, distraught son deprived of his mother. A future volume, *Schiller's Anima*, will address how Schiller theorized femininity and will explore the complex strategies involved in his use of female characters to represent alternative responses, therapies, and cures for the traumatized society that he observed and experienced.

Each of the following chapters situates one of Schiller's plays against a background of other materials: the author's letters as well as a twentieth-century text or series of texts. These texts include works of high modernist literature, psychoanalytic case studies, and artifacts from German cinema and American popular culture. This comparative, cultural approach provides scholars not only with new critical insight into this canonical author but also with innovative pedagogical strategies that can be successfully deployed in the university classroom.

Preface

Using the unorthodox intellectual gambits presented here (successfully enlisted in curricula at both Riverside and Irvine campuses of the University of California), college teachers in German, European, and comparative studies can fruitfully reintroduce this very important writer back into literary and cultural studies classrooms everywhere, but particularly here, in the United States. In order to meet the needs of scholar-teachers who may wish or need to work with Schiller in English, this book provides translations for all the relevant material, and gives American students contemporary cultural access points by which they can fruitfully encounter Schiller's texts—such as Neil Gaiman's graphic novel, *The Sandman*, the seminal German Expressionist film, *The Cabinet of Dr. Caligari*, and the recent American film, *The Thin Red Line*.

The reintroduction of Schiller into university curricula is of special concern because public awareness of the influence of German culture in America is weak and growing weaker, even while German-run companies such as Bertelsmann increasingly exert control over American book and print culture. Americans have always needed to understand Germans, they urgently need to do so now, and Schiller, as one of the founders of German *national* literature, offers an excellent starting point.

The idea for a book about Schiller and trauma arose in a Focussed Research Group on Male Love and Friendship convened by George Haggerty and funded by the Center for Ideas and Society at the University of California, Riverside, in 1996. Faculty members of the seminar also included Carole Fabricant, Richard Godbeer, and Linda Thomko. All of the seminar members contributed important ideas to this book. Research on the project was subsequently supported by sabbatical leaves and research grants from the University of California, Riverside.

My two departmental chairs who have been involved with this stage of my work, Jules Levin and Thomas Scanlon, have been most supportive of this research direction.

I appreciate and value the collegiality of the faculty in the departments of Comparative Literature and English at Riverside. John Ganim, Reinhold Grimm, Catherine Kinney, Zhang Longxi, Kathleen McHugh, Wendy Raschke, George Slusser, and Theda Shapiro merit particular thanks for their insights, which, in one way or the other, shaped the present effort. Colleagues from other campuses, Susan Gustafson, Simon Richter, Mark Katz, Alice Kuziniar, Ruth Klueger, Meredith Lee, Barbara Becker-Cantarino, Tom Saine, Hans Vaget, and Jill Kowalik made helpful suggestions and/or shared their own strong understanding of German, the eighteenth century, or both. Thanks also to the members of the 1999 UC Irvine graduate course on Trauma and Spectacle (Brigitte Bower, Jay Lorenz, Thilo Zelt, Chuck Hammond, Jennifer Bierich, and Nancy Cheng) for their questions and explorations of Schiller and to the

1998 class of World Literature 17B, who enthusiastically tackled *The Robbers* and who, in many ways, inspired the analysis of that text undertaken here.

My appreciation to Dr. Ellen McGrath for her generous sharing of her expertise on depression and trauma.

Christian Mahoney began the process of assisting me with tracking down research materials in three different languages, and this onerous task was taken over by the valiant Robert Van Cleave who proved to be the best (and the kindest) graduate assistant anyone could ever hope for.

From its outset this project was supported by the late Jean Pierre Barricelli—my mentor and friend. Other unflagging support has come from Robert Gross and Gail Hart. The former, an accomplished scholar on the theater, and the latter, a formidable Schiller scholar in her own right, were of invaluable assistance in innumerable ways. Both have helped me to write and think better about Schiller. My heartfelt thanks to them for their conversation, humor, and friendship.

My warm thanks to Kritik series editor Liliane Weissberg for her enthusiasm for this project, and to Arthur Evans, Director of Wayne State University Press; thanks as well to Adela Garcia, project editor, and to Tammy Oberhausen Rastoder, copy editor. My former teacher, the brilliant Elizabeth Harries of Smith College, not only read this manuscript but went over it with a fine-tooth comb. I am more grateful than I can say for her critical acumen and fine editorial eye. Anne Rothe of UCLA's German department proofed the Schiller quotations and made helpful suggestions. And my student Pam Kuhken of UCR ran a crucial last minute library errand. To all, my heartfelt appreciation.

Finally, my thanks to my family, especially, my beloved daughter, Lillian Behrendt, to whom this book is dedicated. She shares this dedication in part with her grandmother, Barbe Tirtov-Romanov Hammer. My mother died only a few weeks before the completion of this manuscript, but her love of German language and culture is present on every page. In particular, the reading of *The Bride of Messina* stems from a conversation held long ago, when I was a child, regarding a strange film my mother had seen as a child herself, about a necromancer and a handsome man held prisoner in a box. I dedicate "The Picture Palace of Dr. Schiller" to her in loving memory of the many cinema houses—large and small—that we frequented together in New York City. Appropriately, the last film we saw together in a movie theater was *Wings of Desire*, after which my mother—half in jest—promised to watch over us as faithfully as the stalwart angels of that unforgettable film.

Here's hoping.

Schiller and Trauma

The question with which Freud frames his text (Moses and Monotheism)
. . . is thus: in what way is the history of a culture, and its relation to a
politics, inextricably bound up with the notion of departure?

Cathy Caruth

My pain is the hidden side of my philosophy, its mute sister.

Julia Kristeva

I am not yet twenty-one years old, but I may tell you honestly, the world
holds no charm for me any longer, I take no delight in the world.

Schiller to Christian Daniel von Hoven, June 15, 1780

Ich bin noch nicht ein und zwanzig Jahr alt, aber ich darf es Ihnen frei
sagen, die Welt hat keinen Reiz für mich mehr, ich freue mich nicht auf
die Welt.

Schiller

DISPLACED PERSONS

Precipitous departure from home tends to be a given in the dramatic
productions of Friedrich Schiller (1759–1805). Many of the Weimar dramatist's most unforgettable characters are refugees, people forcibly driven or emotionally compelled to abandon their own domestic/national space. Personalities
as diverse as *The Robbers'* [*Die Räuber*] Karl Moor, *Intrigue and Love*'s [*Kabale
und Liebe*] Lady Milford, *Don Carlos*'s Elizabeth of Spain, the *Wallenstein* trilogy's
Max Piccolomini, Maria Stuart of the drama by the same name, *The Bride of
Messina's* [*Die Braut von Messina*] tragic siblings Beatrice, Don Cesar, and Don
Manuel, and even Schiller's last hero, Demetrius, as well as his presumed
mother, Marfa, are all exiled from the space they call home. Still other figures
envision a transformative departure in their immediate future: Ferdinand von
Walther, the romantic hero of *Intrigue and Love*, dreams of finding personal
freedom in the trackless deserts of nomadic existence; Don Carlos of Spain
plans escape to Flanders; and Wallenstein, the turncoat military leader of the

13

Thirty Years War, flirts with the notion of rebellion and independence from the emperor within the bounds of his own created empire—his army.

The act of crossing domestic or national thresholds in Schiller's dramas heralds social transgression, and the characters who dare to go out are inevitably perceived by others as criminal: Karl Moor leaves home and soon after becomes a delinquent and leader of a robber band; Don Carlos and Wallenstein are prospective and actual traitors, respectively; Ferdinand von Walter and Don Cesar are murderers; Maria Stuart is a conspirator and an accessory to murder; Lady Milford is regarded by others as a high-price prostitute. Johanna is accused of transgressing against God himself when she takes her place in the most public space of all—the crowning ceremony of the Dauphin. Demetrius is condemned as a treacherous impostor. Criminalization through departure applies even to Schiller's most unproblematic stage hero; by the simple act of leaving his house and attempting to conduct himself publicly as a free citizen, Wilhelm Tell becomes a wanted man.

Thus, in Schiller's plays, leaving home and homeland tends automatically to make the person leaving into an outlaw. Moreover, departure usually brings on annihilation. Repeatedly, and often tragically, these characters' attempts at self-liberation through departure prove abortive, effecting not the creation of a new personal destiny in a new place but rather the death of the would-be refugee protagonist. Departure from home and homeland proves disastrous for all but Wilhelm Tell.

On the other hand, Schiller shows his audiences that there are good reasons for wanting to leave, as testified by the characters who remain at home. Those left behind in Schiller's dramas often find themselves trapped within a domestic space that is as constricting as it is deadly. On Schiller's stage political struggles invest and infect the apparent pure space of the domestic from the outset, making home a prison rather than a haven. Not coincidentally, the characters contained within the home are almost always women in Schiller's dramas; their uncanny home may be the court—as it is for Elizabeth of Spain, the Princess of Eboli, Elizabeth of England, and Agnes—where matters of the heart and of politics inevitably clash—or the troubled hearth of the aristocratic, bourgeois, and agrarian homestead. Here too power struggles come into play: Amalia, Luise, Donna Isabella, and Hedwig inhabit such spaces. Over and over again, Schiller suggests that Home is not where the Heart is but where male, and specifically fatherly, privilege resides.

Elsewhere I have argued that Schiller's dramatized societies are always governed by what a character from *Wallenstein's Camp* [*Wallensteins Lager*] calls "the reign of the stick"—the phallic rule of men at war (Hammer, "Schiller, Time and Again"). Likewise in the private sphere of familial relations, patriarchal power holds sway and is rarely, if ever, beneficent. Consequently, it is no

14

surprise that such enterprising, androgynous female heroes as Johanna determinedly escape from a domestic space where they are held enthralled by the rule of fathers, while Schiller's most compelling female antagonists seek to flee equally patriarchal spaces—the ambitious queen Isabeau, and aspiring czarina Maryna of Schiller's last play.

Notably, only two men in Schiller's dramas actively choose to stay home, and both figure in his earliest dramatic attempts: Franz Moor attempts to assume the power of the father within the household and fails spectacularly, finding himself a prisoner of his own schemes. Fiesko remains in his homeland, which he, like Franz Moor, attempts to take over from within. The results are equally catastrophic; Fiesko murders his own wife by accident and is in turn killed by Verrino, the play's paternal representative.

Because of the problematic, patriarchal nature of the home, returning proves as disastrous as staying (or going): Karl Moor, Demetrius, Beatrice, Don Cesar, and Don Manuel attempt it, and make the deadly discovery that, in the words of American novelist Thomas Wolfe, you really can't go home again.

In this manner, Schiller's drama repeatedly poses the issue of departure as a triple-bind; it is fatal to leave, to remain, and especially to return. Yet most of his main characters are impelled to go—escaping the vicious circle of coming and going through death. What drives Schiller's characters again and again to go, to attempt frantically and impossibly to depart? What is at stake in these dramatizations of catastrophic leave-taking?

DEPARTURE/TRAUMA

In her groundbreaking essay on *Moses and Monotheism*, Cathy Caruth links Freud's theorizing of trauma with his own departure from Vienna in the wake of the National Socialist takeover. Trauma, according to Caruth, is a concept-event, which resonates at once with history and with the historian, with literature and with the interpreter of literature. *Experienced on both personal and cultural levels*, trauma inaugurates our very way of thinking about history at all. Ironically, according to Caruth, it is trauma that makes *history*—a series of radical departures—and *nation*—a people departing to declare a separate and God-given identity—*possible*.

Caruth's argument offers a powerful philosophical commentary on one of the most frequently invoked psychological terms of the late twentieth century. *Trauma* (from the Greek word for *wound*) refers to an experience so awful it cannot be properly remembered and dealt with by the psyche. In trauma, the event or series of events is repressed, so that the victim can survive the terror, but the repressed memory haunts the victim in dramatic and very specific ways. This psychological state has been studied intensively by psychiatric and

15

psychological communities in the United States since the Vietnam War, and trauma is currently being used to account for the ways in which atrocities as divergent as the Holocaust and contemporary domestic abuse impact on the individuals who suffer and sometimes survive them. Itself subjected to a complex process of historical forgetting, because of the disturbing issues that the category raised, the study of trauma is only now emerging as a fully valid and important field of inquiry.[1]

According to both medical clinician Judith Herman and psychoanalyst/ literary critic Julia Kristeva, trauma victims tend to live on the edge of an experience they have never truly digested or understood.[2] Eternally anxious, vigilant, alert, and disconnected, trauma survivors may remember bits and pieces of the cataclysmic event, but they remember it either as disconnected elements and/or they remember without emotion,[3] while the emotions themselves linger on, unattached, provoked by experiences from the present that trigger a post-traumatic stress response.[4]

Attempting to narrate or indeed even referring to information related to the unspoken past may serve as such a trigger, and thus for the trauma victim, to tell is to relive the experience in traumatic terms which are at once unapproachable and intimate (Kristeva, *Powers* 6), where pieces of vision and sensation stand in for the lost terror of the entire event.[5]

Trauma victims may mask their symptoms through neurotic behaviors and affects. In her work on the depression/melancholy cluster, Kristeva argues that people subjected to traumas may often be narcissists—withdrawn, resentful people secretly obsessed with grandiose self-images entailing enormous power and global fame. They may also be empty rather than angry—doomed lovers in love with sadness: an irreducible sadness, Kristeva argues, is one of the ultimate affects of the traumatized (*Black Sun* 21).

Thus, the trauma victim lives in a psychic no-man's-land between the present and the much feared traumatic past. Ready at any time to bolt from the present reality, the traumatized subject has, as one analyst puts it: "a special relation with the EXIT sign."

A THEATER OF WOUNDEDNESS

This book attempts to make sense of Schiller's plays through the use of the psychological term *trauma* in all of the senses discussed above. The readings that comprise this study argue that traumatic traces hide in plain sight throughout Schiller's dramatic corpus. These symptoms are to be found not only in the desperate departures that proliferate in the plays but also in the unbearable social and familial situations, which Schiller presents as natural or even ordinary in his dramas. These traces linger also in the things that he has his characters *almost* say. In the plays' interstices, Schiller's characters utter odd half-sentences that create curious gaps in their otherwise supremely articulate speech-acts.

These gaps reveal that many of Schiller's characters suffer from a strange complaint, which, though it barely names itself, lurks on the boundaries of his theatrical texts. Unlike Hamlet and so many other problematic heroes of the Renaissance and neoclassical stage, they do not suffer from simple melancholy but rather from something that resembles it, but which derives from a more complicated source and which is as hard to identify as it is to cure. They suffer from a psychic discordance, as Karl Moor puts it, of which they are only fleetingly aware and which they are at pains to describe, but which preys upon them all the same.

However, although these characters cannot name their pain, references to wounded minds and in particular to wounded *memories* repeatedly come to the fore in Schiller's plays. Certainly, terrible incidents from the remote past tend to invade the troubled present. These incidents often constitute abusive and/or annihilating childhood experiences involving the father; this is overtly the case for Franz Moor, Don Carlos, and Elizabeth I of England. More covert cases also exist; past neglect and/or abuse is strongly implied in the father-child relationship between the President and Ferdinand von Walter, while the annihilating language of Thibaut d'Arc toward his daughter in the opening scene of *The Maid of Orleans* [*Die Jungfrau von Orleans*] suggests that she is leaving home to escape him as much as to fulfill her holy mission. Likewise, a strong incestuous threat governs the boundless love of the Count von Moor for his troubled elder son, and the hysterical authority that musician Miller exercises over his daughter Luise. For still others, it is abduction—to protect the child from the father or else in the wake of the death of the all-powerful father—that is a hidden source of horror, as is the case for both Beatrice and Demetrius.

In keeping with the clinical and psychoanalytic theories of trauma just enunciated, the characters do not themselves announce the importance of traumatic origin in any direct way. Rather, invocations of a near forgotten and/or imperfectly remembered incident from the past "come up" in parenthetical statements or as throwaway transitional lines. For example, in the middle of a discussion about entirely different matters, Don Carlos unwillingly remembers horrifying, splintered images: one of humiliating corporal punishment by his father, and another the first "sight" of his father who has signed a death sentence. Likewise, in the middle of a speech articulating his materialist philosophy, Franz Moor refers cryptically to himself as crawling out of the inert body of his dead mother—a death, for which he is ostensibly to blame. He later refers en passant to his father's constant cruel mocking of him as a "wooden"

17

boy—a child without affect. Elizabeth I of England blocks the past from conscious memory altogether, and it is Talbot who in a few terse lines remembers her terrifying childhood for her (2.3). The mute Johanna gains and loses her voice again to the power of the father; she must retire to a forest where she combats and vanquishes a violent internal storm.

Demetrius, Schiller's final protagonist, is perhaps the most interesting example of traumatic memory; he suffers from what the playwright precociously understood as repressed memory—the contested psychological phenomenon employed so often in incest and domestic abuse lawsuits brought by adult survivors. The threat of death serves as a trauma trigger, bringing the entire—false, as it turns out—memory back to him.

Others suffer from symptoms brought on by cultural practices, which are inherently traumatizing. Such is the world both of war and of the court. Interestingly, both Milford and Wallenstein suffer from the periodic paralysis and kindling-effect rages that occur in burned-out veterans encountering battle fatigue in a war they cannot hope to win. Schiller offers his audiences a veritable panoply of women who are both wounded and angry—Milford, Elizabeth I, Isabeau, Marfa, Maryna—or silenced and sacrificial—Luise, Elizabeth of Spain, Maria, Johanna, Agnes, Beatrice. Through these characters, Schiller (at least in his plays) seems to have clearly understood that gender construction wounds women deeply, and often fatally. The dramas, which deal with war—in particular the *Wallenstein* trilogy—suggest that, despite their heroic overlay, these constructions are no less damaging and no less fatal to men.

In *Wallenstein* and elsewhere Schiller's plays seem to comprehend in advance Caruth's argument that trauma inflicted on individuals indeed "make" history and national identity (and masculinity) possible. It is notable that *Wilhelm Tell* features as its central scene a traumatic spectacle: a male child who submits to paternally inspired terror; Walther Tell experiences the real possibility of being killed by his own father, who commands him to hold completely still as he takes aim at his son's head in front of a crowd of onlookers—which include the actual audience of the play. The apparent ease with which this highly successful drama refocuses childhood terror *away from the child-victim* and toward the father, who is cast as a hero, indicates how often German, European, and Anglo-American cultures have used (and continue to use) and then glossed over the most obvious historical horrors in order to generate masculine mythologies of heroism and nationalism.

Schiller's pageant naturalizes trauma in the service of the state, and in this sense *Wilhelm Tell* is, almost purely, an ideological work of nationalist propaganda. But the final moments of the work seem to recognize that other truths and possibilities have been forcibly suppressed. The unwelcome appearance of the parricide, Duke Johannes of Swabia—clearly a double for Tell himself—reminds us of the violent and murky ways in which lands become nations,

and the means by which political revolutionaries achieve their ends. The difference between a national hero and a murderous demagogue seems uncomfort-
ably fragile in the final scenes of *Wilhelm Tell,* and Johannes' speedy expulsion
and departure from the stage do little to allay that tenuousness.[6]

SCHILLER'S DEPARTURES

The notion of departure as the physical manifestation of trauma resonates with the history of Schiller's own personal migrations: geographical, voca-
tional, and aesthetic. As a child Schiller was dragged away from home
unceremoniously to the detested Karlsschule, where he spent several miserable
years. Later, he was eventually forced to leave his home province—escaping
over the border as dramatically as some of his protagonists. Significantly, his
first play was the agent of that forced departure, and of others. In its incarnation as Sturm und Drang[7] tour de force, *The Robbers* represented stylistically
and formally a radical departure from the more staid (if equally psychologically
agonized) productions of German drama heretofore; in particular, this early
drama reacted against the procedures of Gotthold Ephraim Lessing, who exer-
cised a considerable influence on Schiller.[8]

Lessing's writing for and about the theater and the visual arts may be
seen as the culmination of a more general trend in European enlightenment
thought as a whole: an ongoing fascination with the aesthetics of pain and of
terror. In his impressive study *Angenehmes Grauen,* Carsten Zelle skillfully traces
the evolution of these interests through a massive array of texts in English,
German, and French; he sees a progressive valorization of a "pleasurable terror"
in aesthetic discourse of the period (75–76). This notion—and its correlatives
of ugliness, disorder, and evil—would gradually emerge as a compelling artistic
alternative to the normative classical goals of expressing the beautiful, rational,
and ordered. Moreover, Zelle argues, fear, terror, and horror become an increasing source of excitement and admiration for emerging bourgeois culture, at the
same time as these affective categories pose serious ethical problems for German intellectuals, in particular (for how could art that catered to such "negative" audience reactions be morally justified?). These debates are seen most
keenly in the discussions surrounding the theater in midcentury Germany, as
discussions such as the one between Lessing and Gerstenberg regarding Gerstenberg's tragedy about the cannibalistic father, *Ugolino,* testify (409–11).[9]

Certainly, the anatomy and aesthetics of pain fascinated Lessing, as
Simon Richter has observed (33), and he was also deeply influenced by the
concept of horror, as Dorothea von Mücke has noted.[10] But Lessing's dramatic
theory and practice ultimately insisted, as Susan Gustafson has argued, on the

19

radical suppression of the ugly, the horrifying, and the objectionable, and proclaimed the importance of audience sympathy with the beautiful and noble (and masculine).[11] Likewise, the eighteenth century as a whole tended to keep these new emotive and affective possibilities under tight control—a paradox that highlights the limitations of the century's ability to think about the very alternative aesthetics it raised (Zelle, *Angenehmes Grauen* 418).[12]

In contrast to this tradition, and to Lessing in particular, Schiller turned the procedure of containing the horrifying on its head in his first drama, bringing what Julia Kristeva has called *the abject* to the fore and forcing his audiences to contemplate the play's cowardly, conniving, and self-hating male villain as an awful kindred spirit to both the play's ostensible hero and to the audience members themselves. And even in his later plays, Schiller's characters do not embody the beautiful, "heroic" suffering of the Laokoon—a figure who fascinated German thinkers of this period.[13]

The emotional impact of *The Robbers* was no less a departure from the past. Lessing's notion of audience pity ("Mitleid," Gustafson, *Absent Mothers* 56) was transformed into a veritable explosion of violent empathy and identification that literally propelled viewers out of their seats. As though at a rock concert, Schiller's original audiences fell into a hysterical frenzy at the end of the first production of his first play. The German Theater would never be the same after *The Robbers,* and theater audiences would now expect an experience altogether different from those they had known before. Significantly, Peter Brooks credits *The Robbers* as being the originator of European melodrama—a genre that works by undoing and crashing through all mechanisms of repression in order to create an experience of raw emotional affect. And the affect that Schiller himself stresses in the first production's playbill is *horror* (Brandt 250–51).

But Schiller's career knew other departures: the tortured and jagged wanderings from Mannheim to Stuttgart toward Weimar; his sudden departure from the theatrical scene after the composition of *Don Carlos* to the profession of historian and philosopher; his departure to the university; his departure from bourgeois to noble status; his departure from prose to the verse play; and most notably his drastic departure from the Republican and high affect aesthetics of Sturm und Drang to the restrained and refined ranks of German neoclassicism. Fittingly, many of the days before his death were spent contemplating the financial feasibility of a possible move from Weimar to Berlin. Schiller appears to have resembled his characters insofar as he too was always on the move; he never stopped leaving or trying to leave.

Schiller's own correspondence (he never wrote an autobiography, in contrast to Goethe) indicates that his theatrical attempts at working with trauma may also have represented a means of self-therapy or even self-cure. The letters are often brilliantly written, emotional, and highly dramatic. As such, they may be fruitfully understood not only as communications but also as performative acts profoundly connected to the gesture of playwriting. The intimate performances of self that Schiller enacted for a number of close family members and friends—for Christophine Schiller, and eventually, above all, for Körner and to Wilhelm von Humboldt—reveal a great deal. Beneath the intellectual veneer that he cultivated, Schiller continually portrayed himself as a quintessentially tortured artist, for whom writing was difficult and increasingly painful. Accordingly, the letters dramatize the writer's huge anxieties, resentments, and inner struggles.

One of Schiller's youthful letters to his sister provides a useful template for the concerns that emerge in his plays and indicates the degree to which the emotional dynamics of the dramas derived from the emotional turmoil of the author himself, which he rehearsed in letters before actually staging it publicly. The letter reports the death of a beloved male friend in extravagant terms:

> Dearest Sister, I have often justly earned your reproaches for why I haven't written you, but this last one I did not deserve, my dear one. You do not yet know, that a dear, worthy friend was torn from me through an early death; I mean the young son of Captain von Hoven, and you can easily understand, how little room I could have to write, as I was occupied at the bedside of the dying man in my capacity as doctor but even more as an involved friend, and I even kept an entire night's vigil with the brother and his distressed mother. (Schiller to Christophine Schiller, June 19, 1780)

> Liebste Schwester, ich verdiente Deine Vorwürffe, warum ich Dir nicht schrieb, schon sehr offt, aber diesen letztren verdien ich nicht, meine Liebe. Du wusstest wohl damals noch nicht, daß mir ein theurer, werther Freund durch einen frühen Tod entrißen wurde, der junge Sohn des Hauptmanns v. Hoven, und nun begreifst Du leicht, wie wenig ich Raum zu schreiben haben konnte, da ich imer um des Sterbenden Bette als Medicine sowohl als auch und noch mehr als ein theilnehmender Freund beschäftigt war, und selbst eine Nacht durch mit seinem Bruder and seiner angefochtenen Mutter bei ihm wachte. (*Schillers Werke* 23:13)

Schiller excuses his—apparently consistent—failure to correspond with his sister with the account of his friend's death, a loss which he feels so keenly that he wishes he could take his place: "And I may tell you that I would happily die for him. For he was so dear to me, and life was and has become a burden to me" [Und ich darf Dir sagen, mit Freuden wär ich für ihn gestorben. Denn er war mir so lieb, und das Leben war und ist mir eine Last worden] (13). The homosocial attitude of the letter is clear; the dying adopted brother takes precedence over the needs of the biological sister, and Schiller unashamedly justifies neglecting his own family in order to take his place with this new, adopted one. Not content to bond with the young man (and the young man's brother), Schiller also actively pursues a relation with the deceased's father and reveals the result to his sister with no little satisfaction, "I have written the father of the noble deceased myself and the answer to my letter was very flattering. He writes that he wants to consider me a second son, and that he wishes to be my friend and my father" [Ich habe dem Vater des Verlorenen Edeln selbst geschrieben, und die Antwort darauf war mir sehr schmeichelhafft; er wolle mich für seinen zweyten Sohn halten, mein Freund, mein Vater seyn] (14). The wish to garner virtual adoption and to bond with the dead man's father results in an emotional and flattering exchange of letters between the two.[14] This move weirdly prefigures the seductive maneuvers of the Marquis von Posa vis-à-vis King Philipp and contextualizes the ongoing obsession with fathers and sons that dominates the dramas.

But throughout the letter to Christophine, Schiller's stance remains paradoxical and troubled. Tellingly, his role at the deathbed of his friend is a contested, double one; he is both doctor and friend, at once distanced, professional healer and emotionally involved, yet ultimately powerless witness. Schiller's language veers accordingly between factual detail ("an entire night's visit") [eine Nacht durch] and the language of personal bereavement and anguished loss ("a . . . friend was torn from me") [*mir* ein . . . Freund . . . entrißen wurde].

Furthermore, Schiller tells his sister that the many gifts of affection that he has received—including this latest one—cannot rectify or quell the nagging presence of a nameless, persistent and frightening pain:

> I have the good fortune (the unmerited good fortune) to have the *best father* in a thousand, and here another admirable man presents himself, who calls me his son. I have many friends in the academy who love me very much. I have you my dear and yet none of this can call any cheerfulness of any duration into my soul. You do not know, how very much I am changed, destroyed within. Also, *you should certainly never experience, what undermines the powers of my spirit.* . . . See to the underclothing soon, and also the shoes. Please, ask dear Papa if he will send me a book of paper and some pens . . . (to Christophine Schiller, June 19, 1780)

> Ich habe das Glück vor vielen Tausenden (das unverdiente Glück), den *besten Vater* zu haben, und hier findet sich ein anderer auch vortrefflicher Mann, der mich Sohn nennet. Ich habe viele Freunde in der Academie, die mich sehr lieben. Ich habe Dich, meine Theure, und doch kan dis alles keine Heiterkeit von einiger Dauer in meine Seele rufen. Du weist nicht, wie ich so sehr im innern verändert, zerstört bin. Auch sollst Dus *gewiß niemals erfahren, was die Kräfte meines Geists untergräbt.* . . . Die Wasche

besorge bald. Auch die Schuhe. Bitte den lieben Papa, daß er mir ein
Buch Papier schike und einige Kiele. (*Schillers Werke* 31:14)

Something that the author cannot explain keeps him from being happy,
and he remarks that something undermines his "powers," which comes up
from beneath them, buried, like the dead friend, who now seems to be more
of a double than a comrade or even adopted brother. The very enunciation of
this pain and its ability to corrupt and taint (*untergraben* also means to eat away
and to shatter) the powers of the soul is so frightening to the writer that
the thought is instantly broken off and repressed. Significantly, the supremely
articulate and often verbose Schiller is rendered speechless here; in this and
other key moments in the correspondence he resembles Herman's and Kristeva's fragmented teller of traumatized memory—the alternatively empty and
angry lover in love with sadness. At this point Schiller returns—abruptly—to
questions of material things that he desperately needs and, oddly, wants his
sister to provide for him. Repressing the earlier concerns, this early letter closes
by hinting at a struggle of a somewhat different kind—Schiller's very real and
ongoing struggle to earn a living.

This letter and others like it testify to Schiller's preoccupation with a pain
that he himself could not name. He wrote about it constantly and haltingly for
the stage and for friends and family. Increasingly, the writing linked a half-
spoken agony with a concern for material wealth. Goods and money are marshaled in this letter and in others not only as a necessity but as a stand-in for a
trouble that the author could not fully comprehend, but which he seems to
have sensed was crucial for him to make sense of, both as an artist and as a
medical man—a profession that, arguably, Schiller never ceased to practice.

MAKING PAIN PAY

As his career progressed and as he became a man of letters with a family
to support, Schiller eventually came to understand something else about
trauma that seems quite contemporary by early twenty-first-century standards;
he seems to have grasped that he had *to make trauma pay,* as his ongoing concern
with cash testifies. From the outset, Schiller's letters reveal that his aesthetic
ambitions were always tied both to agonized questions of self-validation and to
financial necessity. Again, an early letter makes this connection clear. In a letter
to Wilhelm Petersen written at the end of November 1780, Schiller poignantly
enumerates his three conflict-ridden reasons for wanting to be a writer:

The first and most important reason for wishing the publication is that
all-powerful Mammon, who never takes refuge under my roof—money

. . . The second reason is, as is easy to understand, the judgment of the world, that which I and a few other friends esteem with perhaps exaggeratedly positive eyes as the unimpeachable Judge, the public, . . . And then finally a third reason, which is completely genuine, is this: I have no other object in the world than to work in my field. . . . Writing from the domains of poetry, tragedies and so on, would present an obstacle to my plans to become a professor of physiology and medicine. *That is why I already seek to clear away these things here.* (Schiller to Petersen, end of November/beginning of December 1780, my italics)

Der erste und wichstigste Grund, warum ich die Herausgabe wünsche, ist jener allgewaltige Mammon, dem die Herberge unter meinem Dache gar nicht ansteht—das Geld . . . Der zweite Grund ist, wie leicht zu begreifen, das Urtheil der Welt, dasjenige, was ich und wenige Freunde mit vielleicht übertrieben günstigen Augen ansehen, dem unbestochenen Richter, dem Publicum, preißzugeben. . . . Und dann endlich ein dritter Grund, der ganz ächt ist, ist dieser: Ich habe einmal in der Welt keine andre Aussicht als in meinem Fache zu arbeiten. . . . Schrifften aus dem Felde der Poesie, Tragödien usw. würden mir in meinem Plane, Profeßor in der Physiologie und Medicin zu werden, hinderlich seyn. *Darum such ich sie hier schon wegzuräumen.* (*Schillers Werke* 23:15)

Already at this stage of Schiller's career, artistic creation presents itself to him as at once profoundly desirable and deeply suspect: as labor that should bring in money and as troubling writing to be dispensed with at the earliest possible opportunity. Again Schiller's doubleness emerges; he wants to be two different men: a professor and a popular artist. More important, his anxiety about artistic creation is so great that he almost wishes that his work would fail, so that the "poetry, tragedies, and so on" can be cleared away, like so much garbage. Poignantly, Schiller hopes to make his artistic powers pay or go away for good.

At first, they did neither. But eventually Schiller achieved the very goals he saw as contradictory in this youthful epistle. He actually became a professor *and* a poet, a philosopher *and* a playwright. However, Schiller's private writing repeatedly demonstrates an astute reading of the contradictory pressures exerted on him by the culture in which he lived. The German states—in particular, Weimar—were emerging societies of capital and capital's cultural complement, the "culture industry." This term, coined by Horkheimer and Adorno, aptly describes the culture of Weimar during the late eighteenth century, for Weimar took part in the general shift occurring in cultural practices during the course of the European Enlightenment. During this period, art and the artist gradually ceased to be shielded by aristocratic patronage and became increasingly dependent on and influenced by the complexities of marketing (Horkheimer and Adorno 157, Woodmansee 41).

Martha Woodmansee's study of aesthetics, artists, and the market in eighteenth-century England and Germany argues that this was a particularly bewildering transitional period in the German states. During the latter half of the eighteenth century, lowbrow literature sold like mad, with publishers taking the lion's share of the profits, popular books were often pirated and sold by unauthorized publishers, and the very understanding of an artistic creation as the copyrightable "property" of its creator was a long time in coming economically and legally (Woodmansee 39). Then, as now, the profession of artist was a profoundly contradictory one, but it became more so during this transition as idealistic, intellectual artists such as Schiller found themselves torn between a sense of spiritual calling and a pragmatic need to earn a living.

Significantly, Woodmansee sees Schiller as an especially striking example of an artist caught between changing paradigms of patronage of the arts. She notes, "Despite his productivity, however, Schiller barely succeeded in making ends meet; and when his health broke down in 1791, he followed in Lessing's footsteps and accepted a pension from a Danish admirer. . . . Serious writers like Schiller and Moritz who gave us the modern concept of art found it difficult to compete with the lighter literature that began flooding the market in the last quarter of the century" (41). Observing also that Schiller often found it "impossible to make the kinds of concessions" that the demands of unceasing dramatic productivity required (80), Woodmansee repeatedly emphasizes Schiller's predicament as an artistically ambitious and financially impecunious writer; in her view his gradual philosophical move away from notions of compromise with the public (do good work artistically but also get the public to buy it), toward the dubious claims for art's full autonomy from the public in the *Aesthetic Letters* (Woodmansee 81–85) must be seen against the backdrop of his personal economic struggles, as well as those of his fellow writers and artists.

But to his credit, Schiller's correspondence repeatedly and often honestly addresses the contradictions inherent in his position as bourgeois artist—as creative visionary on one hand and as moneymaker on the other. The plays themselves increasingly foreground questions of finance and acquisition and interrogate their relation to human worth and human suffering in incisive and disturbing ways.

Schiller's inability to resolve the paradox of the bourgeois artist may have been one of the significant pressures that contributed to his early demise. Yet, this failure, accompanied by the multitude of ailments that afflicted the author as he grew older, may be read as yet another expression of his resistance to the emerging cultural market. Significantly, cultural historian Mark Seltzer interprets the breakdown of a factory worker in Jack London's "The Apostate" in terms of a complex connection between nervous complaints and political rebellion: "But the result of his working at 'high tension' was that 'he grew nervous' and the result of this case of nervousness is his complete turning from work and turning apostate to the work ethic. Yet, this version of hysteria or neurasthenia is a kind of inverted work ethic: as Anson Rabinach has recently shown, neurasthenia is an 'ethic of resistance to work' " (Seltzer 13). Seltzer's reading of London implies that labor under capitalism may be traumatizing in and of itself, wearing the worker down in much the same ways that the experience of war wears down the soldier through constant, unceasing mental and physical demands, an imminent sense of danger, and the gradual exhaustion of the body. Although he was not a twentieth-century man, Schiller already felt (and resented) the peculiarities of his position within the early formation of consumer capitalism, which sets up contested relays between "an ascetics of production (self-discipline) and an aesthetics of consumption" (Bell in Seltzer 60).[15] In this way, Schiller's struggles with and around the dramas connect him and his theater to our own late capitalist moment, which makes of art an "intangible asset" (Seltzer 62), and which thrives on the display of personal pain—from soap opera to the traumatized guests on network and local talk shows. This displayed pain is at once real *and* commodified—something we feel and something we buy, sell, and *watch*. Schiller's work represents a radical departure from the theater of the past in its wounded acknowledgment of and often unwilling participation in that hurtful, yet lucrative, practice of staging personal pain for profit.

CHAPTER I

My Villain, My Self

Melodrama, Laughter, and Abjection in *The Robbers*

> Abjection . . . is immoral, sinister, scheming, and shady: a terror that dissembles, a hatred that smiles, a passion that uses the body for barter instead of inflaming it, a debtor who sells you up, a friend who stabs you.
>
> *Julia Kristeva*

> *"Your money or your life!"* If I choose the money, I lose both. If I choose life, I have life without the money, namely a life deprived of something. I think I have made myself clear.
>
> *Jacques Lacan*

> As for Mother, I don't care what's happened to her.
>
> *Sade*

Written expressly for young people, and for young men in particular, the graphic novel arguably provides the late-twentieth-century equivalent of the German Storm and Stress drama—itself an end-of-the-century phenomenon. Exaggerated, lurid, and rhetorically and visually over-the-top, such high-minded comic books as *Maus, The Watchman,* and *V Is for Vendetta* share both the violence and the idealism of Storm and Stress. These books propose a frame-by-frame performance of raw emotion—each cel representing a snapshot of a theater of the mind, to which the reader alone has access.

The graphic novel holds enormous sway over the contemporary reading audiences—American, European, and Asian—in no small measure because it seems a democratic medium; in comparison to a theater ticket, a movie ticket, or even a video rental (for which one needs a VCR), the graphic novel is still a good bargain, a private piece of theater you can own and continually revisit, without having to rewind. But, at the same time, both graphic novels and their authors are regarded with scant respect by makers and defenders of high art. Practitioners of a dubious aesthetic—rooted in the comic strip and comic book traditions of Peanuts, Dick Tracy, Little Orphan Annie, and Superman—graphic novel authors remain artistically suspect, and must struggle for cultural

27

legitimacy even as they are involved in a breakneck creative schedule to make their art pay.

The situation of the graphic novel writer exemplifies the contradictions that inform the construction of art and the artist in the late twentieth century West. The artist must be successful but not "commercial"; he must be accessible but not "popular" and not "low." He must not appear to "sell," although he is always in a hurry. Likewise, he can challenge society but only in certain ways, using certain forms. The graphic novel in particular offends by reintroducing the picture and the theatricality of *visible affect* back into literature. It is at once avant-garde and regressive, using the gambits of the Victorian children's book to sell very adult ideas. This suffices to make it an outrage.

In this chapter I argue that the contested, stressed placement of the graphic novelist and his work in late-twentieth-century America provides a useful historical point of comparison for the situation of the young Friedrich Schiller. From this place in the present, we can recognize traces of the position in which Schiller found himself, as he was composing the controversial Storm and Stress drama that would make him famous in the provincial territories we now know as the nation of Germany, and beyond.

RAISING CAIN

In the closing frames of volume two of Neil Gaiman's graphic novel series, *The Sandman,* a demon named Abel is killed for the umpteenth time by his brother Cain. After he has recovered from this latest murder, Abel confides a tearful tale to his pet gargoyle, and by extension, to us, "IT'S A *SECRET STORY.* IT'S A STORY ABOUT TWO *BROTHERS,* AND THEY UH . . . THEY *LOVED* EACH OTHER VERY *MUCH,* AND THEY WERE ALWAYS *NICE* TO EACH OTHER . . . AND THEY LIVED TOGETHER IN THE *SAME HOUSE,* AND THEY WERE . . . HNH, UHAH, TH-THEY WERE, UH, V-VERY *HAPPY.* I'M SORRY. I WASN'T—I'M N-NOT *CRYING.* I'M REALLY *NOT*" (24). As Abel tells this fantasy of brotherly love, he visibly weeps tears of blood.

Gaiman's Abel is certainly a pathetic character, and yet there is something odd about this sequence. Abel's bleeding tears are more repulsive than sad, and his dream of fraternal bliss seems silly under these dire circumstances, making him appear not innocent but stupid. Moreover, since these characters can never truly die, the endless repetition of killing takes on the quality of a game, at once horrifying and ridiculous.

Finally, behind Abel stands his fiendish but compelling elder brother, who, in Gaiman's rendition, turns out to be an artist: a "purveyor of penny dreadfuls, shilling shockers, blood and thunders and fust-rate nightmares" (49). Cain, first murderer and sadistic artist of the horrible, is surely more interesting

28

than is Abel, the meek, self-appointed "er-victim" (47). He is also, in his guise as creator-marketer of low culture, a stand-in for the author himself, for it is Gaiman who has made a successful career for himself precisely by telling "fust rate nightmares." Thus, Gaiman self-reflexively suggests that the comic book maker betrays the brotherhood of literary authors and necessarily becomes Cain: murderous, disobedient, and exiled son.

Significantly, the author situates the household of Cain and Abel on the border of the collective unconscious— the liminal space between waking and dream. This repositioning suggests that the brothers enact not a biblical story but a story of the psyche that features repetitive murder, anger never directly expressed but acted out, and a double vision of art as the performance of both horrifying destruction and the equally horrified narrative of pain. The deserted domicile of the brothers also implies parental absence; Cain and Abel resemble infantile orphans left to their own devilish devices in an empty house, through which Gaiman's hero, the dream king Morpheus, passes like a phantom father. Bereft, with only each other as mirror and double, the brothers have no recourse than to endlessly replay their deadly variation of Freud's *fort/da* game (Freud, "Beyond the Pleasure Principle" 145–47); the one sadistically throws away the other, who never fails to reappear.

In this manner, Gaiman's graphic novel *The Sandman* drastically revises one of the oldest and most famous myths of Western culture and transforms it into a self-conscious *danse macabre* where tragic pity and fear flip over into the pathos of melodrama and then into something else altogether, which uses both, but which is ultimately neither.

We will see that it is these dynamics that Schiller explores within the dreamscape of his first play, *The Robbers* [Die Räuber].

There are good reasons for interpreting the first drama within the context of the un- or partially conscious, as Christophine Schiller would explain:

> He composed his first play, "The Robbers" during the leisure hours and for the most part in the sickroom where he had to be confined often for weeks at a time from attacks of fever. It is therefore no wonder, that there would arise in the fantasy of a young man in this mood—still unacquainted with people, driven by the pull of relationships—such pictures as he depicted in the character of Franz Moor.

> Sein erstes Schauspiel "Die Räuber" entwarf er ebenfalls in den Nebenstunden und groessentheils im Krankenzimmer, dass er oft Fieberanfaelle wegen wochenlange hueten musste. Es ist also kein Wunder, wenn in dieser Stimmung, noch unbekannt mit dem Menschen, bei den Zwang der Verhaeltnisse in der Phantasie eines Juenglings solche Bilder entstehen muessen, die er im Charakter des Franz Moor darstellte. (*Schillers Persönlichkeit,* cited in Grawe 127)

Schiller's sister pointedly positions the creation of *The Robbers* within the boundaries of a fever-dream—a dream from whose deepest depths the villain Franz Moor emerges as the crucial figure. Christophine Schiller's focus on this character is not fortuitous; she understands clearly what and whom the play is really about. The play is ultimately about Franz, not Karl.

This chapter follows Christophine's lead and examines Franz Moor as a phantasm, as a representative of that which has been deeply repressed and which returns in dream form to consciousness. It also considers *The Robbers* in terms of the aesthetic contradictions enunciated by Gaiman's comic book: horror, pathos, and an intermittent disruptive comedic force, all of which work together to inaugurate a spellbinding collective entertainment. But this entertainment is itself problematic, as Gaiman signals through his ironic reference to himself and his own art. If Gaiman figures himself as the Cain of contemporary American literature, the man who murders high art and dismembers it into the fragmented cels of the comic book, Schiller is no less implicated in and tainted by the subversive work that, indeed, both began his career and inaugurated his own exile.

<h2>MELODRAMA/TRAUMA[1]</h2>

The Robbers is possibly Schiller's most influential play. It is also without a doubt his strangest, as Schiller himself seems to have recognized.[2] Containing, as he put it, at least three different plays smashed together into one, it is jam-packed with nonstop violent occurrences—making it an eerie precursor to the contemporary action film.

Awful, unwilling departures constitute the principal action of the drama: Karl leaves home for school, leaves school for the Bohemian robber band, leaves Amalia, leaves the band, leaves Amalia again, leaves the robbers, and leaves his own life behind, when he give himself up to the authorities. The other characters follow suit in an elaborate hall of mirrors (Hammer, *Sublime Crime*) involving agonized leave-takings. The students abandon school to become robbers, and they eventually abandon Karl, their beloved leader. Old Moor is forcibly removed from his house in a coffin, subsequently imprisoned in the mausoleum, never to return. Hermann leaves home, Kosinsky leaves home, while the faithful servant Daniel packs his bags and prepares to wend his weary way from the Moor estate.

Home is figured in no uncertain terms as a trap. Franz Moor paces around the perimeter of the estate like a caged tiger; having become the master he quickly discovers that none will obey his will and he is now the prisoner of his own failed plan. Amalia, Schiller's least developed female character, languishes around the house, a melancholy domestic angel waiting to be rescued in vain, for when she finally crosses the boundary marking the outside from the inside, she is run through by her fiancé's sword.

Exile too provides no amelioration, for the outside world of *The Robbers* exactly replicates the inside. Public mirrors private, and Karl's failure to control the robber band in the woods eerily resembles Franz's failure to control the household at home (Hammer, *Sublime Crime*). In the end, there is nowhere to go, for either of them, but to death.

In keeping with this drive toward death, *The Robbers* places enormous stress on the body in pain. Physical wounds and hurts abound in the play; the shattered characters drag themselves across a stage space increasingly littered with the dead and dying, those who have been burned, hanged, smothered, or cut. Roller's face is slashed, Schweitzer's forehead is covered with saber cuts, Karl's dog's leg has been amputated, he himself has a scar, Spiegelberg's foreskin has been mysteriously cut off although he insists—dubiously—that he is not a Jew, Franz's nose is smashed in, making him look African; according to a report an entire town burns down and a motherless baby is thrown into the fire.

In the final moments of the play, wounding culminates in a gruesome spectacle:

> THE ROBBERS: (*all together, tearing open their clothes*) Look, Look here! Do you recognize these scars? You belong to us! We bought you for our bondsman with our heart's blood. (5.2.157)[3]

> DIE RÄUBER: (*durcheinander, reissen ihre Kleider auf*) Schau her. schau! Kennst du diese Narben? Du bist unser! Mit unserem Herzblut haben wir dich zum Leibeigenen angekauft. (*Schillers Werke* 3:132–33)

The robbers disrobe in a ghastly striptease, displaying their scars to the distraught Karl, who would once again leave them. Refusing to be outdone, Karl responds by staging a horror show of his own; he fatally wounds Amalia with his sword and remarks sarcastically, "She is hit! This last convulsion, and it is over—Now see! What more can you demand?" (5.2.158) [Sie ist getroffen! Dis Zucken noch, und dann wirds vorbey seyn—Nun, seht doch! habt ihr noch was zu fordern?] (3:134).

As exemplified in this final, triumphant criminal gesture, the accounts of wounding in *The Robbers* tend to stress the masculine and the phallic—a tendency that indicates that masculinity is itself put on trial in the play.[4] Real and fantasized penetrations abound: an entire convent of nuns is raped and pillaged; Karl's ersatz death in battle is "proven" by the account of his demise, which includes his writing in blood on his own saber; Amalia is ripped open by Karl's sword rather than receiving his phallus; Franz dreams of digging his

31

spurs into the flesh of his tenant farmers. Violence, Schiller shows us repeatedly in this homosocial nightmare world, is the price paid by men who would prove masculinity.[5]

But these physical marks of injury are only part of the story that the play tells, for it is the mind itself that is repeatedly represented in *The Robbers* as wounded, empty, broken, poisoned, and split. Exclamations proliferate in the drama, as the characters are repeatedly bombarded by agonies they cannot even articulate; pained to the point of losing language, the figures of the play struggle to voice and explain the extremities that they undergo, often threatening to fall into mutism (Brooks 56–57).

The intensity of the proceedings in *The Robbers* has tended to link Schiller's first play with the evolution of the dramatic form we know as melodrama. Peter Brooks in particular credits Schiller's first play as exercising an influence on the development of melodrama in France (86). At first glance, the play seems to fit all of Brooks's criteria, which include moral polarization and schematization of good and evil; extreme states of being, situations, and actions; overt villainy; persecution of the good; inflated and extravagant expressions; dark plottings; suspense; breathtaking peripety (11–12). The enemy Moor brothers create a polarized world of good and evil, at either end of which the plays' other figures must arrange themselves.[6] On the face of things, Karl emerges as the "good" elder brother who is wrongfully tricked and manipulated out of his estate and virtuous fiancée by the younger brother, the calculating villain, Franz von Moor. Likewise, the other "good" characters—old Moor, Amalia, Daniel, Kosinsky—are all innocent victims of relentless persecution by the villain and his doubles—Spiegelberg, Hermann, and the Catholic priest. On the rhetorical level, both brothers speak in emotional, extravagant terms that clearly proclaim their opposing moral identities. Expressions such as the following identify Karl and Franz in their respective ethical roles:

> KARL: In the shady groves of my father's home, in my Amalia's arms a nobler pleasure waits for me. (1.2.41)

> Im Schatten meiner väterlichen Hayne, in den Armen meiner Amalia lockt mich ein edler Vergnügen. (3:24)

> FRANZ: Away then with this burdensome mask of gentleness and virtue! Now you shall see Franz naked as he is, and cringe in terror! (2.2.71)

> Weg dann mit dieser lästigen Larve von Sanftmuth und Tugend! Nun sollt ihr den nackten Franz sehen, und euch ensetzen! (3:52)

The plottings of the villain are dark indeed; Franz's projected malefactions include patricide, fratricide, rape, and tyrannical oppression of the underclass. Likewise, the events of the play devolve with fatal quickness in the final

32

scenes. These poles are reinforced by the other characters, who repeatedly reinforce the differences between the good and evil brothers.

Significantly, Brooks links the aesthetic of melodrama directly with the staging of *trauma*:

> [In melodrama] . . . we are paralyzed spectators of all possible threats to the self. *Evil's moment of spectacular power provides a simulacrum of the "primal scene." It is a moment of intense, originary trauma* that leaves virtue stunned and humiliated. In fact, the true primal scene may be in the past . . . and the breakthrough of evil in the play connects to it, offering a present horror fully explicable only in terms of a past horror, faithful in this to Freud's structure of pathogenetic trauma. . . . From . . . [the] full acting out [of emotions], the "cure" can be effected. Virtue can finally break through its helplessness, find its name, liberate itself from primal horror, fulfill desires. (35)

Melodrama, Brooks argues, is a theater that literally reenacts trauma, overwhelming audiences through the force of emotion and obliging them to vicariously live through the pain of the characters. Specifically, Brooks links melodrama with the traumatic outlines of the Freudian "primal scene"—the spectacle witnessed by the small child of the parents engaged in sexual intercourse (Freud, "Wolf Man" 195–97). The connection between trauma and the primal scene suggests in turn that the audience of melodrama regresses to some much younger childhood state; from this psychic position viewers can come face-to-face with their own mental wounds. Having effected this simulacrum of trauma, melodrama then offers audiences a therapeutic experience, in which traumas are re-presented, brought into symbolic order, and then cured.

Schiller seems to have consciously grasped at least part of this aesthetic. Both his playbill for the first productions and his many published and unpublished forewords to and commentaries on *The Robbers* emphasize the production of unbridled emotionality. In one unpublished foreword, Schiller comments on the superiority of theater to other modes of poetic representation because of its ability to exteriorize and cause audiences to share profound and mysterious inner realities, "because it [the dramatic method] displays for us the pains and the most secret movements of the heart in the very expressions of the characters" [da (die dramatische Methode) . . . uns . . . die Leidenschaften und geheimsten Bewegungen des Herzens in eignen Äußerungen der Personen schildert] (Kraft 2:503). Likewise, the playbill stresses the importance of shared emotions that are violent and horrifying:

> Here too you will, not without horror, glimpse the inner workings of vice and learn from the stage how all the gildings of fortune fail to kill the worm of conscience, and fright, anguish, remorse, despair follow hard on

its heels. Let the spectator today weep—and recoil—before our scene. (Schiller, quoted in Brandt 250)

Man wird auch nicht ohne Entsetzen in die innere Wirtschaft des Lasters Blicke werfen, und wahrnehmen, wie alle Vergoldungen des Glücks den inneren Gewissenswurm nicht töten—und Schrecken, Angst, Reue, Verzweiflung hart hinter seinen Fersen. (Kraft 2:510)

Interestingly, Schiller's playbill anticipates Brooks in its clear intention of provoking the paralyzing fear that grounds trauma (see Freud) and that forms the affective ground for melodrama. The play aims to horrify its audiences and at the same time enrapture them, forcing them to identify with its outlaw characters—effecting a kind of psychological purge, which really seemed to have deeply affected original audiences, as this famous eyewitness account attests:[7]

The theatre was like a madhouse—rolling eyes, clenched fists, hoarse cries in the auditorium. Strangers fell sobbing into each others' arms, women on the point of fainting staggered towards the exit.

Das Theater glich einem Irrenhaus—rollende Augen, geballte Fäuste, heisere Aufschrei im Zuschauerraum. Fremde Menschen fielen einander schluchzend in die Arme, Frauen wankten, einer Ohnmacht nahe, zur Türe. (original and translation in Sharpe 29)

FORBIDDEN LAUGHTER

But melodrama does not entirely account for the emotions generated in and by The Robbers. As is the case in Gaiman's The Sandman, there is also something vaguely funny about the play at times. Throughout The Robbers odd flashes of juvenile humor—filled with personal jibes and sarcasm—appear in the midst of the disastrous goings-on:

SCHUFTERLE: I'll be hanged if your plans aren't very much like mine. I was thinking to myself, what if you were to turn evangelical, and hold weekly classes in spiritual improvement?
GRIMM: That's it! If that was no good, turn atheist, blaspheme against the four gospels, have our book burnt by the hangman, and we should do a roaring trade.
RATZMAN: Or we could set up to cure the pox—I know a doctor who built himself a house on a foundation of mercury, so the motto over the door says.

34

SCHWEITZER: Moritz, you are a great man—or a blind pig has found an acorn!

SCHWARZ: Excellent plans! Most reputable professions! How great minds think alike! All that's left now is to turn into women and become bawds, or even sell our own virginity in the streets.

SPIEGELBERG: Nonsense! Nonsense! And what is to stop your being most of these things in one person? (1.2.44–45)

SCHUFTERLE: Zum Henker! ihr rathet nach zu meinen Projekten. Ich dachte bey mir selbst, wie wenn du ein Pietist würdest, und wöchentlich deine Erbauungsstunden hieltest?

GRIMM: Getroffen! und wenn das nicht geht, ein Atheist! Wir koennten die vier Evangelisten aufs Maul schlagen, liessen unser Buch durch den Schinder verbrennen, und so geing's reissend ab.

RAZMANN: Oder zögen wir wider die Franzosen zu Felde—ich kenne einen Dokter, der sich ein Haus von purem Queksilber gebauet hat, wie das Epigramm auf der Hausthüre lautet.

SCHWEIZER: . . . Moritz, du bist ein grosser Mann!—oder es hat ein blindes Schwein eine Eichel gefunden.

SCHWARZ: Vortrefliche Plane! honete Gewerbe! Wie doch die grossen Geister sympathisieren! Izt fehlte nur noch, daß wir Weiber und Kupplerinnen würden, oder gar unsere Jungferschaft zu Markte trieben.

SPIEGELBERG: Possen, Possen! Und was hinderts, daß ihr nicht das meiste in einer Person seyn könnt? (3:28)

Minor characters are exaggerated to the point of ridicule: the priest and pastor are nasty beyond belief, Razmann and Daniel are naïve to the point of stupidity, and Spiegelberg in particular is wickedly funny.

Eternally engaged in ironic word play, Spiegelberg consistently speaks the language of the comic. Filled with wild and crazy ideas, he is a fast-talking, sly deprecator reminiscent of both Shakespeare's Mercutio and Jonson's Mosca.[8] He mercilessly teases Karl Moor when the latter declares he has reformed, satirically invokes biblical imagery in the most inappropriate situations, and enacts awful but entertaining pranks.[9] His speech in act 2 begins with a story of how he got out of capture by fingering a quack doctor, and culminates with a gleeful depiction of the rape at the convent:

> On we go, one cell after the other, take all the sisters' clothes in turn, last of all the abbess' . . . ha, ha, ha! You should have seen the sport we had; the poor creatures fumbling around in the dark for their petticoats, and weeping and wailing, when they found the devil had taken them! and us upon them like a whirlwind, and them rolling themselves up in their blankets so surprised and scared they were, or creeping under the stove

like cats, and some of them wetting themselves with fright . . . and last of all the old hag of an abbess, dressed like Eve before the Fall. (2.3.73)

Wir gehn weiter von Zelle zu Zelle, nehmen einer Schwester nach der anderen die Kleider,[10] endlich auch der Aebtissin . . . hahaha!—da hättest du die Haz sehen sollen, wie die armen Thiergen in der Finstere nach ihren Röcken tappten, und sich jaemmerlich gebaerdeten, wie sie zu Teufel waren, un d wir indes wie alle Bestuerzung in Bettlacken wickelten, oder unter dem Ofen zusammenkrochen wie Katzen, andere in der Angst ihres Herzens die Stube so besprentzten . . . und endlich gar die alte Schnurre die Aebtissin, angezogen wie Eva *vor* dem Fall. (3:54)

Spiegelberg places the stress not on horror but on high jinks, and the boyish high spirits that attend them, as though the robbers were overzealous fraternity boys at a panty raid. The scene is horrible, but it is also comically rendered, and the narrator's embarrassed desire to hide the prank from Karl Moor only adds to this effect.

Spiegelberg is not alone in such capers. At the apex of Franz Moor's criminal triumph, the stage directions call for the villain to skip across the stage, gleefully crying "Now I am the master!" [Izt bin ich der Herr], as though he were a small boy who has secretly acquired a large carton of ice cream while his parents were out, rather than a frighteningly powerful villain stealing the hero's property.

Anticipating Gaiman's cheerful Cain as well as such contemporary fictional criminals as Alex from *A Clockwork Orange,* Franz proudly announces himself as a creative mind who is simply and purely bad. He proposes his own ironic medley of talents—philosophical rather than literary—which precociously anticipate Darwinian notions of the survival of the fittest morality, Nietzsche's critique of the slave morality in *Beyond Good and Evil,* and the manipulation of Nietzsche's Übermensch vision by German Fascism:[11]

Swim who can, and let sink who is too clumsy! . . . Might is right, and the limits of our strength our lonely law. It is true, there are certain conventions men have made, to rule the pulses that turn the world. . . . Yes, indeed, most admirable devices to keep fools respectful and to hold down the mob, so that clever people can live in better comfort. (1.1.33)

Schwimme wer schwimmen kan, und wer zu plump ist geh unter! . . . Das Recht wohnet beym Überwältiger, und die Schranken unserer Kraft sind unsere Gesetze. Wohl gibt es gewisse gemeinschaftliche Pakta, die man geschlossen hat, die Pulse des Weltzirkels zu treiben. . . . In der That, sehr lobenswürdige Anstalten, die Narren im Respekt und den Pöbel unter dem Pantoffel zu halten, damit die Gescheiden es desto bequemer haben. (3:18–19)

Franz uses poetic diction—rhythm, assonance, and consonance—to create speeches that shimmer with wit, a humor of hatred that uses elegant language to mystify, hypnotize, and convince, "We will have ourselves a conscience made in the latest style, so that we can let it out nicely as we grow. How can we help it? Go to the tailor!" (1.1.34)[12] [Wir wollen uns ein Gewissen nach der neuesten Facon anmessen lassen, um es hübsch weiter aufzuschnallen wie wir zulegen. Was können wir dafür? Geht zum Schneider!] (variant, *Schillers Werke* 3:357).

Thus, for all its literal Sturm und Drang, there is something giddy about *The Robbers*, as though pain and suffering were being invoked only to be turned inside out, producing not tragic catharsis but some thing more unspeakable, and more subversive still—a sense of horror that "laughs, then panics, and laughs again" (Gordon 3). Indeed, one of the least discussed aspects of Schiller's first play is its periodic use of disruptive, inappropriate, and profoundly subversive laughter. This deployment of ironic, "black" humor looks forward not to melodrama but to melodrama's dark twin, the grotesque, objectionable, violent, and immensely popular low culture theater of *Grand Guignol*.[13] Drama historian Mel Gordon could well be describing *The Robbers* when he defines the Grand Guignol as a theater genre that is "predicated on the stimulation of the rawest and most adolescent of human interactions and desires: incest and patricide; blood lust; sexual anxiety and conflict; morbid fascination with bodily mutilation and death; loathing of authority; fear of insanity; an overall disgust for the human condition and its imperfect institutions" (2).

It is important to remember that Schiller was interested in unorthodox uses of humor. Many years later, in *Naïve and Sentimental Poetry* [über naïve und sentimentalische Dichtung], Schiller was to emphasize the power of satiric poetry, and he would make the curious observation that Rousseau belonged to the great satiric tradition of Juvenal and Swift (*Naïve and Sentimental Poetry* 117–18, *Schillers Werke* 20:443). While the Rousseauian *The Robbers* cannot be said to be satire in any normative sense, it does use exaggeration and irony to intermittently perform a language of aggression and witty hatred that glitters against the play's somber moralistic backdrop.[14]

At once melodrama and Grand Guignol *avant la lettre*, Schiller's *The Robbers* reveals itself to be a play about doubles that is itself *double*. It is for this reason that the play has lived a dual afterlife—infiltrating the imaginations of writers as divergent as Dostoevsky and Charlotte Brontë, both of whom (in very different ways) wrote about split selves, dysfunctional families, and awful pain and suffering.[15]

What pain does *The Robbers* depict and at times euphorically—if temporarily—release through humor?[16] What vision of domestic bliss is being mourned and ironically repulsed?

MY VILLAIN, MY SELF

PERFORMING ABJECTION

Julia Kristeva discusses the problem of the traumatic wound brought on by the loss or unavailability of mother in her challenging study *Powers of Horror*. The result of such a wound is, according to her, a neurotic state of mind that all of us experience to one degree or another insofar as we have all lost the primal unity with our own mothers.[17] Kristeva calls this state *abjection,* which is "the violence of mourning for an 'object' that has always already been lost" (15).[18] Kristeva links abjection with a bewildering array of social phenomena and problems: archaic notions of filth and defilement, the founding of religion, the exclusions and taboos of monotheism (particularly Judaism), and a hypo-critical brand of criminality. At the extreme of this already considerable spectrum, she connects abjection with the psychological foundations of National Socialism's extermination of the Jews.[19] But the actual roots of abjection are infantile and manifest themselves in feelings of powerlessness and repulsion as well as physical sensations of revulsion.[20]

Kristeva's account of the abject connects in significant ways with psychoanalytic readings of sadism such as that performed by Sheldon Bach and Lester Schwartz. In their compelling analysis of a dream recounted by the Marquis de Sade, Bach and Schwartz characterize the Marquis as a sadist, *because* he longs for mother. Sade manifests all the qualities of a "compensatory grandiose self":

> [A] delusional identity—constantly being constructed and reconstructed in an attempt to restitute that grandiose self-representation which had been disrupted in childhood . . . As we know, the integrity of the self in the earliest years is dependent on the support, mirroring, and participation of the mother. . . . under circumstances where the idealized transference is disturbed, the patient may turn to archaic precursors of the idealized parent imago or may regress further. . . . (Bach and Schwartz 459)

In extreme cases of regression, the individual turns on and into what he perceives as the bad mother, "In the end, the fear of the self fragmenting and falling apart has become manifest. . . . He assumes a compensatory delusional identification with the Bad Mother and Destroying Nature; he must 'destroy the universe and dismember the cosmos'; he becomes death in order to avoid death" (467).

These accounts of abjection and aggression in the wake of maternal loss link up in surprising ways with Franz Moor, who, as it turns out, plays a complex role in the drama as both villain and victim. It is notable that Franz is continually presented to us in the play as the abject personified. Always an object of disgust and loathing, he is seen by Amalia as a repulsive monster, by his father as a grotesque wooden doll, and by the robbers as a rat—vermin, an unclean animal that must be exterminated and cleaned away.

Significantly, Franz Moor, the abject humorist, is also the porte-parole of trauma. His speeches are haunted by unspoken agonies; throughout repressed thoughts continually return surreptitiously—displaced but never fully articulated (or understood) into philosophy and metaphor, fantasy and nightmare, dreams of murder and the practice of suicide. His wit proves to be an indicator of his psychic pain.[21] In the same brilliant first soliloquy discussed earlier, Franz also describes his own face as an object of repudiation and revulsion, while hinting in the odd metaphoric leaps, at another, far deeper trouble: "Why was I not the first to creep out of our mother's womb? Why not the only one? Why did nature burden me with this ugliness?" (1.1.33) [Warum bin ich nicht der erste aus Mutterleib gekrochen? Warum nicht der Einzige? Warum mußte sie mir diese Bürde von Häßlichkeit aufladen?] (3:18). Ostensibly, Franz's birth as second son was the cause of his mother's death—hence his odd reference to himself crawling out, reptilelike, from out of the inert shell of his mother's body. An evil Mother Nature becomes consequently conflated with the dead mother; the "sie" in the second part of the quotation connotes both the person who owns the "maternal body" [Mutterleib] as well as (feminine) "Nature" [die Natur] referred to two lines earlier, and it is to this "bad," destructive mother that Franz allies himself in a set of contradictions, in conformance with Bach and Schwartz's reading of the Marquis de Sade, "No, no! I do her an injustice. After all she gave us the gift of ingenuity too when she set us naked and miserable upon the shores of this great ocean of the world" (1.1.33) [Nein! Nein! ich thue ihr Unrecht. Gab sie uns doch Erfindungs-geist, setzte uns nackt und armselig aus Ufer dieser grossen Ozeans Welt] (3:18).

Unable to speak the paradox of the mother who gave him everything— his life and body—and yet who "left" him before he even knew her and had had the chance to know and then separate from her (the shores of the ocean call up the uterine as well as a sense of being shipwrecked on the border of consciousness), Franz's thoughts forcibly retreat from the unbearable direction they are going in: Mother gave birth to me, I killed Mother, Mother made me ugly, Mother has left me. Instead his thoughts veer back—as they will so often—into materialist, proto-Sadeian philosophizing.[22]

Franz juxtaposes his abandoned state with a vision of a compensatory, grandiose self—larger and stronger than others, and determined to demonstrate its superiority in a series of violent, annihilating acts. Deprived of Mother, Franz allies himself with an all-destroying, all powerful, and frightening Mother Nature and fantasizes constantly about mass, destructive acts. These delusions are in full keeping with abjection, "but, devotees of the abject . . . do not cease looking . . . for the desirable and terrifying, nourishing and murderous, fascinating and abject inside of the maternal body . . . How, if not by incorporating a devouring mother, for want of having been able to introject her and joy in what manifests her" (Kristeva, *Powers* 54).

Mother continues to haunt Franz's first speech and is all the more present in the very aggressive ways in which she is dismissed and "devoured"; she is the missing oven in which the two brothers are baked (19), and she is visibly absent in the following truncated rendering of the Freudian primal scene:

> He gave you life, you are his flesh and blood . . . I should like to know *why* he made me? Not out of love for me, surely, since there was no *me* to love? Did he know me before he made me? Or did he think of me while he was making me? Or did he wish for me as he was making me? Did he know what I should be like? (1.1.34)

> Er hat dir das Leben gegeben, du bist sein Fleisch, sein Blut . . . Ich möchte doch fragen *warum* er mich gemacht? doch wol nicht gar aus Liebe zu mir, der erst ein *Ich* werden sollte? Hat er mich gekannt ehe er mich machte? Oder hat er mich gedacht, wie er mich machte? Oder hat er *mich* gewünscht, da er mich machte? Wußte er was ich werden würde. (3:19)

There is a strong sense here of a primal scene memory as well as of Lacanian "pere-version" fantasy. In the former, the child is present in and somehow able to participate in the scene of his own creation (Penley 128) while in the latter the child acts out a transgressive fantasy against the symbolic father who prevents the son from enjoying the mother (Hill 107). Franz's rage against the father suggests that he unconsciously blames him for her death; if Franz killed her by being born, the father killed her too, by having sex with the mother and conceiving Franz in her body.

By fantasizing a memory of what he could not have been a part of but which was the occasion for his being at all, Franz attempts to intervene on the primal scene, but the place he takes—interestingly—is that of the mother rather than that of the much hated and despised father. He sounds, in this portion of the speech, more like a jilted girlfriend than like an Oedipal son. This re-placement points to the severity of Franz's psychic wounding, marking him as what Kristeva calls a phobic narcissist.[23] Such a person, she argues, is wounded so early that they do not seek out an object in the mother—at least not directly, "Since it [the drive] is not sex-oriented, it denies the question of sexual difference, the subject that houses it can produce homosexual symptoms while being strictly speaking indifferent to them; that is not where the subject is" (*Powers* 45). It is to the father, rather than to the mother, that the phobic personality turns for reassurance and identity: "A representative of the paternal function takes the place of the good maternal object that is wanting. There is language instead of the good breast. Discourse is being substituted for maternal care, and with it a fatherhood belonging more to the realm of the ideal than of the superego" (45).

But it is precisely the father in *The Robbers* who does not love him and indeed who does not even "think of him." Franz's desire to be "thought of" returns obsessively and angrily, as the structural repetitions in the speech above—Did he think of me, know me, want me—suggest. In this manner Franz's opening speech displays a tenuous sense of identity, which must shore itself up, desperately, provisionally, through two envisioned homicides: first, the murder of the parent who killed the mother and who refuses to acknowledge him; and second, the death of his double, Karl Moor, who as the acknowledged and beloved son, stands to be both the literal and figurative inheritor of patriarchal power. But even at this point in the play this project is clearly doomed to failure. Franz himself already understands that this gambit will not work, as the final lines of this first speech pathetically suggest, "And master I must be, to force my way to goals that I shall never gain through kindness" (1.1.35) [*Herr* muß ich seyn, daß ich das mit Gewalt ertrotze, wozu mir die Liebenswüridigkeit gebricht] (3:20).

Franz Moor longs for what Jessica Benjamin calls the first and most important bond between mother and child—the experience of *recognition*. "The process or recognition . . . always includes this paradoxical mixture of otherness and togetherness: You belong to me, yet you are not (any longer) part of me. The joy I take in your existence must include both my connection to you and your independent existence—I recognize that you are real" (Benjamin 15). But, deprived of Mother and ignored by Father, Franz is never recognized as a full person in his own right by anyone in the play.

Significantly, the play never contradicts Franz's assessment of his domestic situation. From the outset it is clear to the audience that the Count does not regard his second child as anything other than a surrogate for the son he truly loves; on a certain level Franz does not exist for him as an independent entity. Moreover, the father does not deny the acts of overt favoritism described by the younger son, or deny making any of the terrible judgments about his younger son Franz says he makes:

> And then that everyday dullard, that cold, wooden Franz and all the other
> names that the contrast between the two of us so often prompted, when
> he sat on your lap or pinched your cheek. (1.1.29)

> Und dann der trockne Alltagsmensch, der kalte, hölzerne Franz, und wie
> die Titelgen alle heissen, mögen, die euch der Contrast zwischen ihm und
> mir mocht eingegeben haben, wenn er euch auf dem Schooße saß oder in
> die Backen zwickte.] (3:14–15)

To all of this, the Count apologizes perfunctorily and observes vaguely, "You bear a heavy burden of duty, my son—God bless you for what you have been and for what you shall be to me!" (1.1.29) [Du hast noch grosse Pflichten auf dir mein Sohn—Gott seegne dich für was du mir warst und seyn wirst!] (3:15).

In this manner, Franz Moor finds himself consigned to the prison house of abjection, where the "ego, wounded to the point of annulment, barricaded and untouchable, cowers somewhere, nowhere, at no other place than the one that cannot be found" (Kristeva, *Powers* 47). For such a person, desire itself is a phantom, "Where objects are concerned he delegates phantoms, ghosts, 'false cards'; a stream of spurious egos and for that very reason spurious objects, seeming egos that confront undesirable objects. Separation exists, and so does language, even brilliantly at times, with apparently remarkable intellectual realizations. But no current flows—it is a pure and simple splitting, an abyss" (Kristeva, *Powers* 47).

No wonder that Franz's attempted rape of Amalia falls apart so oddly, or that his dreams of power never get acted upon in any effective manner; these goals are simulacra, stand-ins for a desire that can never be articulated, stunted by traumatic loss to the point of almost silence. Like Kristeva's abject speaker, Franz too is a brilliant rhetorician, but the language has no real connection to his own feelings, and it becomes increasingly hollowed out, and empty.

The Robbers uses Franz Moor to take its audience through an internal, psychological collapse, an increasing hollowing out. Accordingly, Franz's language disconnects progressively from his own specific, lived experience, escaping further and further into abstract metaphor. In the same degree his plans spiral down into inactivity, and then self-destruction. Images of desertion and emptiness proliferate. At one point, Franz projects onto his father his own conflicted, abject suffering:

> Oh then come to my aid, grief, and you repentance, Fury of hell, burrowing serpent that chew again what you have once devoured, and feed again upon your own filth; eternal destroyers and eternal breeders of your poison; and you howling self-reproach, who make desolate your own house, and wound your own mother's heart. . . . Blow upon blow, storm upon storm I will bring down on this fragile life . . . there will be no trace of a wound nor corrosive poison for the anatomist's knife to reveal. (2.1.57–8)

> O so komme du mir zu Hülfe *Jammer*, und du *Reue*, höllische Eumenides, grabende Schlange, die ihren Fraß wiederkäut, und ihren eigenen Koth wiederfrißt; ewige Zerstörerinnen und ewige Schöpferinnen eures Giftes, und du heulende *Selbstverklagung* die du dein eigen Hauß verwüstest, und deine eigene Mutter verwundest. . . . So fall ich Streich auf Streich, Sturm auf Sturm dieses zerbrechliche Leben an . . . des Zergliederes Messer findet ja keine Spuren von Wunde oder korrosivischen Gift. (3:39–40)

Here Franz unwittingly gives the audience a harrowing portrait of a psychologically damaged self rendered as an internalized domestic space haunted by the spectral presence of the lost, wounded mother, longed for but always already gone. At one instead with an archaic maternal destroyer, Franz dreams of falling on the father with repeated strokes of the phallic knife.[24]

Dependent as he is on the detested paternal order—an order he regards with the abject's combination of fear and fascination (Kristeva, *Powers* 45)—Franz cannot bring himself to murder his father. Instead, he reacts as a true devotee of the abject, by throwing away what offends him—by literally ab-jecting. An eternally squeamish proto-Fascist, Franz interprets his own abjection as racial defilement; he is, after all, the "Moor" with the "blackamoors's lips" [Mohrenmaul] and "Hottentot's eyes" [Hottentotten Augen] (1.1.18). He then projects his abjection outward and has his father not killed but "disposed of" in a cowardly, sinister prefiguration of how the Nazis will "clean up" the "Jewish Question." From this point of view, Hermann is engaged as a one-man *Sonderkommando,* to do the "dirty" work of hauling the father away and throwing him in the grave.[25] The father lives on, himself ab-jected—a thing consigned to the unclean space of the cemetery (Kristeva, *Powers* 110), still stubbornly and horrifyingly refusing to die.

Likewise unable to kill Karl directly, Franz resorts to a series of strange displacements: supposed banishment, supposed death on the battlefield. Perpetually disgusted, as abjects always are, Franz repeatedly expresses repulsion at the very nature of human, physical existence:

> Man is born of filth, and wades a little while in filth, and makes filth, and rots down again in filth, till at the last he is no more than the muck that sticks to the soles of his great-grandson's shoes. That's the end of the song—the filthy circle of human destiny. (4.2.116)

> . . . der Mensch entstehet aus Morast, und watet eine Weile im Morast, und macht Morast, und gärt wieder zusammen in Morast, bis er zuletzt an den Schuhsohlen seines Uhrenkels unflätig anklebt. Das ist das Ende vom Lied—der morastige Zirkel der menschlichen Bestimmung. . . . (3:95)

As this observation warns, it is himself whom Franz must ultimately displace and throw away.[26] Acting upon the fear of an ultimate father that cannot be put aside, Franz undertakes the ultimate act of cleansing. He ab-jects himself by literally hanging himself up; he puts his house in order at last, by putting himself away. But even this act contains a germ of rebellion against the Father—this time God, the Father:[27] "No, nor will I pray. Heaven shall not have this victory, hell will not make this mock of me" (5.2. 149) [Nein ich will

auch nicht beten—diesen Sieg soll der Himmel nicht haben, diesen Spott mir
nicht anthun die Hölle] (3:126).

AB-JECTING MELODRAMA

In *The Robbers,* melodramatic virtue never breaks through and never
speaks its name; it cannot, for it is indistinguishable from vice.[28] The character
of Franz Moor undoes the moral polarization that grounds melodramatic char-
acterization—showing such poles to be a lie. Franz actually operates at both
ends of the melodramatic spectrum (and he does so consistently from the outset) as both ultimate villain and ultimate victim, as object of horror and object
of derision (the abject), a person audiences are meant to fear, loathe, and find
amusing. Most important, Schiller's villain is a person whom audiences are
called upon to recognize, however unwillingly, an uncomfortable reminder of
the turbulent feelings that seethe under the surface of family life, an unclean
reminder of the loss we have all incurred and imperfectly recovered from.

In contemplating Franz Moor, viewers come up against the self they are
not, cannot be—the secret, unspoken, traumatized self, the angry, powerless
child who lies behind the supposed "good" one, who dreams, like Gaiman's
Abel, of a restorative family romance, complete, at last with Mother, "Here
you were one day to wander, a great man, dignified and renowned—here to
live your boyhood once more in Amalia's blossoming children—here!"
(4.1.107) [Hier solltest du wandeln dereinst, ein groser, stattlicher, gepriesener
Mann—hier dein Knabenleben in Amalias blueheneden Kindern zum zweyten-
mal leben—hier!] (3:87). The embodiment of abjection, Franz Moor intervenes
on Schiller's fledgling drama as the return of the repressed—that which comes
back to consciousness but which cannot be adequately dealt with by consciousness. Indeed, the abject returns in more spectral form time and again in Schiller's dramas. Most of Schiller's antagonists resemble Franz Moor insofar as they
are angry, ironic, and vengeful characters. Such schemers as Isabeau, Illo,
Terzky and Isolani, Elizabeth I, and the Grand Inquisitor dream up acts of
violence that are ab-jected onto others who must perpetrate their crimes for
them; they are paranoid personalities, filled with self-hatred, feelings of impuis-
sance and a deadly disgust for themselves and for others. But Franz Moor
incarnates the abject in its most unadulterated form in Schiller's oeuvre; the
history of his abjection is clearly situated in the family and grounded in the loss
of Mother and in the cruelty of Father. This honesty—intermittent and partially expressed—makes *The Robbers* at once Schiller's most disturbing play and
also his bravest.[29]

The Robbers

A Traumatizing Play

Schiller seems to have been aware that his first villain would not stay put as a villain, and his writing from the period indicates how much the character of Franz Moor perplexed and troubled him:

> I am much more convinced that the condition of moral evil in the mind of a human being is an incredibly powerful condition which can be reached only when the balance [harmony] of the entire psychic organization . . . is suspended, as is the entire system of animal processes—inflammation, division, pulse and nerves must be completely thrown into disorder, before nature could allow such a fever or convulsion to take place. Our young man, raised in a circle of a happy, guiltless family—how did such a heartbreaking philosophy occur to him? The poet leaves us with this answer completely unresolved; we find no adequate basis for all these horrifying principles and works than the poor necessity of the artist, who, in order to deck out his portrait, publicly exposed all of human nature in the person of a devil.

> Ich denke vielmehr überzeugt zu sein, daß der Zustand der moralischen Übels im Gemüt eines Menschen ein schlechterdings gewaltsamer Zustand sei, welchen zu erreichen zuvörderst das Gleichgewicht der ganzen geistigen Organisation . . . aufgehoben sein muß, so wie das ganze System der tierischen Haushaltung, Kochung und Scheidung, Puls und Nervenkraft durcheinander geworfen sein müssen, eh die Natur einem Gefieber oder Konvulsionen Raum gibt. *Unserm Jüngling, aufgewachsen im Kreis einer friedlichen, schuldlosen Familie—woher kam ihm eine so herzverderbliche Philosophie? Der Dichter läßt uns dies Frage ganz unbeantwortet; wir finden zu all denen abscheulichen Grundsätzen und Werken keinen hinreichenden Grund* als das armselige Bedürfnis des Kuenstlers, der um sein Gemälde auszustaffieren, die ganze menschliche Natur in der Person eines Teufels . . . and den Pranger gestellt hat. (Schiller's self review, 1782, Kraft 2:515, my italics)

In this discussion of Franz Moor, Schiller addresses and debunks the Hobbesian understanding of human beings as innately brutal. He suggests instead that people do not do "evil" things unless their very organism has been profoundly disrupted in some way. He describes this disruption as a simultaneous jamming up of the parts of the nervous system—an account that anticipates twentieth-century diagnostic descriptions of traumatic response to terror, involving *hyper-arousal, intrusion,* and *constriction* (Herman 35–50). But once having made these remarks, he immediately backs away from them. Pointedly citing his character's family upbringing as unimpeachable, Schiller hastens to interject that Franz Moor's behavior cannot be explained at all. The character is, he explains, an aesthetic necessity stemming from the beleaguered play-wright's need for contrast. Given this state of affairs, it is up to the viewer to "dream" up a cause.

> Here we know only facts, our fantasy has room to dream up such main drives to it. . . . Here the poet himself exhibits the limitations in which he exposes the composite of drives to us, our fantasy is chained through historical facts.

> Dort wissen wir nur die Fakta, unsre Phantasie hat Raum solche Triebfe-dern darzu zu träumen. . . . Hier zeichnet uns der Dichter selbst die Schranken vor, indem er uns das Triebwerk enthüllt, unsre Phantasie wird durch historische Fakta gefesselt. (Kraft 2:515)

This act of imagination too, Schiller quickly adds, must be constrained by the facts given to the audience in the play.

In this self-review, Schiller, in his guise as objective critic, raises preco-ciously sophisticated questions pertaining to psychopathology and makes astute connections between the mind and the body. He then retreats before his own commentary in a series of odd, contradictory maneuvers. The self-critique re-peatedly attempts and then abandons an understanding of the villain who, the author admits, "is a universe unto himself" [ist ein eigenes Universum]—a series of masks and identities that he himself is at pains to explain, but with whom he feels sympathy: "The poet himself seems to have felt enthusiasm for him at the end of his role" [Selbst der Dichter scheint sich am Schluss seiner Rolle fur ihn erwaermt zu haben] (Kraft 2:516).

Schiller's self-critique reveals the author's ambivalence toward the play's villain—a character whom he claims not to understand, who is not understand-able, by anyone, and yet with whom he unwillingly sympathizes. At the same time, the halting and almost immediately suppressed attempts of the author to account psychologically for the transgressions of his own creation do indeed hint at a cause, and the cause is the one mentioned and immediately elided—the family and unspoken troubles of a seemingly happy home.[30]

In this manner, Schiller's own writing about his first play corroborates an understanding of it in terms of trauma—of that which cannot be spoken. This trauma circulates around a lost or unavailable mother and an actively abusive or unloving father. In this sense, The Robbers is a valuable and fascinat-ing cultural document that precociously uncovers and bears witness to the ways in which the sacrosanct world of the family is an ideological receptacle of power relations that becomes in turn the site of abuse and of pain.[31] The boundaries of the domestic bleed back into the sphere outside, poisoning the world of the public; private pain inflects "public" "political" questions of race, masculinity, privilege, power, and money.

By linking the perversion of home with the dysfunction of the German *polis,* Schiller anticipates the point made by Frederick Jameson two hundred years later that the unconscious is indeed political and that consequently such distinctions as public/private, social/psychological, political/poetic, and history/society/individual do not really exist (20). This is perhaps why Schiller's first play does not—logically—make sense, nor can it provide a reassuring experience of "cure" to its audience. As a spectacle of private atrocity not quite remembered, *The Robbers* cannot proceed in a linear, sensible sequence, but is instead haunted, fraught, contradictory, split, messy, chaotic, itself a strange flight of abject fancy, a vacillating, nomadic act of resistance without a grounded vantage point. If outside and inside are the same, and if consciousness is always already inflected by ideology, from what place *can* the individual resist and avoid reenacting the same oppressive patriarchal structures of power that oppressed/shaped his consciousness? This is the unspoken, agonized question of Schiller's play.[32]

Last but not least, Schiller's writing about *The Robbers* suggests that Franz Moor and his creator have something unspeakable in common. Schiller was never able to articulate that commonality. But one thing is certain: in a weird replication of the father-son dynamics outlined in the play, the actual production of *The Robbers* itself produced dire and awful consequences for its creator/father, and these events both shaped and scarred his career. Ruling prince Karl Eugen's reaction to the play was so punitive that it precipitated Schiller's flight from his family and his homeland.[33] Schiller's letter to Karl Eugen from Mannheim reads like an excerpt from the play:

> The unhappiness of a subject [underling] and of a son can never be a matter of indifference to a gracious ruler and father. . . . These same authorities have forbidden me in the strictest possible terms to engage in literary writing, or to have dealings with foreigners . . . I hoped to be able to present weighty grounds for the opposite argument to your Highness, to permit myself the liberty of laying before you my humble plea in writing. As my request was rejected with the threat of arrest and while my circumstances urgently necessitated a kind mitigation of the prohibition, so driven by despair, I grasped the present path . . . I know, that I cannot win anything in the great world, that I am falling into the greatest possible misfortune; I have no other prospect, if your Ducal Highness should refuse me clemency with the permission to be a writer. (To Karl Eugen, September 24, 1782)

> Das Unglück eines Unterthanen und eines Sohns kann dem gnädigsten Fürsten und Vater niemals gleichgültig sein . . . Höchstdieselbe haben mir auf das strengste verboten, litterarische Schriften herauszugeben, noch weniger mich mit Ausländern einzulassen. Ich habe gehofft, Eurer

Herzoglichen Durchlaucht Gründe von Gewicht unterthänigst dagegen vorstellen zu können, und mir daher die gnädigste Erlaubniß ausgebeten, Höchstdenenselben meine untertänigste Bitte in einem Schreiben vortragen zu dörfen; da mir diese Bitte mit Androhung des Arrests verwaigert ward, meine Lage aber eine gnädigste Milderung dieses Verbots höchst notwendig machte, so habe ich, von Verzweiflung gedrungen, den itzigen Weeg ergriffen . . . Ich weiß, dass ich in der grossen Welt nichts gewinnen kann, dass ich in mein grösestes Unglück stürze; ich habe keine Aussichten mehr, wenn Eure Herzogliche Durchlaucht mir die Gnade verwaigern solten, mit der Erlaubniß Schrifsteller seyn zu dürfen. (Letter 27 of *Schillers Werke* 23:41–2)

Here both Moor brothers seem to take turns speaking to a remote and angry father figure, eerily named Karl. Accordingly, the letter's rhetoric negotiates between submission and rebellion in the alternatingly guarded, angry, hysterical, self-righteous, and reverential tones of the abject—the wounded son's agonized, resentful quest for a recognition, validation, and salvation that was never to be forthcoming.

Schiller bravely chose rebellion over obedience. Indeed, in a bizarre reversal of *The Robbers*, it is Karl Eugen who makes the highwayman's demand of "your money or your life" to the young would-be playwright. Schiller abandons his money—his meagerly paid position as physician—and chooses artistic *life*. But as Lacan's quip—cited at the beginning of this chapter—makes clear, such a choice is not a simple one. Choosing life over money, ensures existence which is, in Lacan's words, "deprived," and this was, in a very real way, to be Schiller's situation in Mannheim and beyond.

Moreover, Karl Eugen's condemnation implicitly stamped Schiller's writing as an act of transgression against the father and against the fatherland:[34] as defilement from within—as that which is forbidden, suspect, and unauthorized; unprofessional and unclean; a violation of boundaries and identities, of allegiances and kinship ties. The condemnation marked the author not as revolutionary but as traitor, as Franz, rather than as Karl. Long before Neil Gaiman's *The Sandman*, Schiller understood that to write meant to become Cain: to commit unforgivable transgressions, to be banished, to be rendered at once beyond the pale and visibly different, branded by the sign of the abject.

The degree to which this condemnation was traumatic is suggested by the fact that, over and over again, Schiller would wrest treacherous figures from history, and transform these traitors into heroes; it seems as though he were continuously attempting to effect a creative, therapeutic correction of his own positioning as a faithless son/citizen.[35] Moreover, after his flight to Mannheim, writing came to pose an increasingly heavy burden for Schiller, as though he were progressively internalizing and battling from within the silencing, annihilating voice of the father/leader he thought to leave behind.[36] From now on, the playwright would always dream of departures as the solution to problems, and he would quest desperately and unceasingly for legitimacy, recognition, money, and fame.

In an essay for the *Rheinische Thalia* Schiller observed the high price that *The Robbers* had exacted from him, "The [Robbers] cost me family and fatherland. . . . The public is now everything to me, my study, my sovereign, my trusted confidant. To it alone do I now belong" [Die (Räuber) kosteten mir Familie und Vaterland. . . . Das Publikum ist mir jetzt alles, mein Studium, mein Souverain, mein Vertrauter. Ihm allein gehoer ich jetzt an] (October 18, 1784, Kraft 2:522–3). Here Schiller briefly invokes a fiscal image that was to become crucial for him. Writing *costs,* and the losses that writing has incurred for the author will need to be reimbursed by the public, who now owns him. Paradoxically, the public will pay back the dispossessed author by purchasing that which incurred the loss in the first place—namely, his writing, of which the *Rheinische Thalia* is itself an example. But how can the original loss ever be made good? Schiller would repeatedly confront this issue, without ever finding a satisfactory solution.

Schiller would successfully depart from Wuerttemburg, but he would bring with him the wound inflicted by Karl Eugen—which may have triggered earlier, unspoken traumas. Carrying the painful crisis of departure from home, Schiller would shoulder other hurtful burdens: the damaging and humiliating experience of material deprivation and financial want; physical disconnection from those he loved; and last but not least, the contradictory identity of the artist as traitor to the state, and bereft servant to the public.

Schiller never wrote another play like *The Robbers,* but the play left behind a complicated, and as yet not fully traced legacy: the history of Anglo-European literature's absorption in the spectacle of abjection. Taking its cue from the abjection-driven dramaturgy of Lessing (Gustafson, *Absent Mothers and Orphaned Fathers*), Schiller's first drama displays the abject in all its vertiginous, slippery, and horrifying glory. This abject inheritance would trace its way through the plays of Kleist, Buechner, and Strindberg, to the fictions of Dostoevsky, culminating in our century in the grotesque antics of writers like Kafka, Borges, Celine, and Anthony Burgess, in the weird dramas of transgression composed by the young Berthold Brecht, Heiner Müller, Peter Weiss, Peter Handke, and David Mamet, the feverish films of Werner Herzog, and the simultaneously moving and alienating comic book practices of Neil Gaiman. For them, as for many modern writers, words become "a sword that is perhaps not even an instance but a distance—an ideal and a superego, a being-removed, which cause horror to exist and at the same time take us away from it, grip us with fear and by that very fright change language into a quill, a fleeting and piercing one; a work of lace; a show of acrobatics, a burst of laughter and a mark of death" (Kristeva, *Powers* 138).

CHAPTER 2

Piles

Unblocking *Don Carlos*
and Schiller's Passage to Weimar

Displacement from behind forwards; excrement becomes aliment; the shameful substance which has to be concealed turns into a secret which enriches the world.

Freud

Forgive my returning to this lewd orifice. Tis my muse will have it so.

Beckett

It is as if the world were burning up
Behind my back

Schiller, Don Carlos

Mir wird, als rauchte hinter mir die Welt.

Schiller

LAYER 1

Two days after his arrival in Berlin in 1937, quintessential twentieth-century novelist-dramatist Samuel Beckett has this to say about Germany and the state of his own writing: "The trip is being a failure. Germany is horrible. Money is scarce. I am tired all the time . . . And not the ghost of a book beginning. The physical mess is trivial beside the intellectual mess. I do not care and I don't know whether they are connected or not. It has turned out to be a journey *from*, and not to, as I knew it was, before I began it" (Beckett quoted in Knowlson 227). Beckett's letter to Mary Manning presents to our view a familiar, modernist portrait of the artist as both blocked and broke. Beckett conflates physical and mental suffering and piles on top of those two pains the equally unpleasant psychological awareness that his planned journey through Germany has proved to be not an artistic quest *toward* an aesthetic goal but rather an ineffectual, juvenile escape *from* something unnameable that

51

cannot be left behind. A few weeks later, however, during this same ill-fated *deutsche Reise*, Beckett successfully purges his frustration through an aptly chosen set of metaphors:

> My next work shall be on rice paper wound about a spool, with a perforated line every six inches and on sale in Boots. The length of each chapter will be carefully calculated to suit with the average free motion. And with every copy a free sample of some laxative to promote sales, The Beckett Bowel Books, Jesus in farto. Issued in imperishable tissue . . . All edges disinfected. 1000 wipes of clean fun. Also in Braille for anal pruritics. All Sturm and no Drang. (Beckett quoted in Knowlson 231)

Through the enema of humor—the act of "sending in" punning wordplay (Ronell, "Le Sujet Suppositaire" 129)—Beckett is able eventually to flush out the blocks to his creativity. In this manner, Beckett uses his own artistic quirks as the medication that brings on his cure—the renewed ability to write. Beckett is at once analyst and analysand; through the enabling mechanism of his own defecatory imagination, he is able to break through his own blocks, and create an art of unspeakables and unspeakable fun.

James Knowlson, Beckett's biographer, interjects a tantalizing observation, noting that, along the way, the author found time to visit Weimar, where he made careful and detailed notes concerning Goethe's and Schiller's houses. The last piece of information fascinates and frustrates the Weimar scholar with questions that cannot be answered. Did visiting Weimar accelerate or slow Beckett's recovery? And how might the visit to Weimar have contributed to his subversive vision of art as exuberant, plentiful, pre-romantic anal jouissance—"all Sturm and no Drang"?

A very different story of blockage and travel *from* inflects the narrative of the anally obsessed Rat Man, Freud's famous patient. Here compulsion, not creation, is the matter at hand, and the outcome is not art but the fulfillment of one's duty as soldier and citizen. Mistakenly convinced that he owes money to another officer who refuses payment, the young lieutenant gets on a train going in the wrong direction; as a result, he finds himself on an ass-backwards excursion, from which he constantly and vainly strives to eject himself: "In this way he had struggled through from station to station, till he had reached one at which it had seemed to him impossible to get out because he had relatives living there. He then determined to travel through to Vienna, to look up his friend there and lay the whole matter before him . . . when he had arrived in Vienna however, he had failed to find his friend at the restaurant at which he had counted on meeting him" (Freud, "Rat Man" 17). Rat Man frantically attempts to reach the post office to pay off his debt and to make things right, but he is unable to arrive at his destination. He is repeatedly blocked by his own compulsions, till he purges his troubles successfully, not with the missing friend mentioned above—whom he reaches too late, and who gives him an explanation of his actions disappointingly similar to his own—but rather with Dr. Freud himself. The young man is eventually cured; psychoanalysis clears the roadblocks to his mental health, and the rat punishment that triggered the appearance of the illness is explained and also cleared away.

Arguably, Beckett and the distraught lieutenant have little in common other than the obvious—an interest in the anus and what comes out (Beckett) versus what goes in (Rat Man). They are strikingly different in most other respects: the one an author and the other a military man; the one an angry artist and the other a faithful son; the one Irish, the other Austrian; one long lived-lived, the other dead prematurely in battle. But their anally directed circuits through Austro-Germany (in particular, Beckett's passage through Weimar), their internal psychological obstacles, and their concern with cash provoke intriguing questions about Schiller and his crucial, career-making move to Weimar. This chapter uses Beckett—and behind him the furtive but equally important figure of Freud's Rat Man—as a proctological instrument to explore, excavate, and diagnose passages from Schiller's textual body, extracted from the time period that includes the Weimar journey.

Significantly, behinds find a prominent place in the cultural work of the Enlightenment, which was continually obsessed with backsides as political and social metaphors. In Voltaire's *Candide*, the buttocks of the innocent literally furnish the nourishment of the wicked, and in earlier writers like Swift, and in visual artists like Hogarth, the underbelly of the body politic refers always to the anus. Throughout this period, cultural practitioners employed the bottom in an attempt to get to the bottom of social injustice and an untenable state of political affairs. At the same time, essayistic and dialogic investigations of nation, of natural right and natural law went hand in hand with speculations about the physiological and psychological nature of both the child and the (male) citizen, as well as the mechanics of the human body, the categorization of sexual behaviors, and the anatomy of the state. Odd and sometimes monstrous generic innovations characterized eighteenth-century writing, and the bourgeois tragedy, the critique, the travelogue, the pornographic and epistolary novels, the Declaration of Independence, and the proceedings of the sodomy trials in England may be seen as only a few examples of the long and short forms through which such discussions ran their course.

Piled upon the mass of texts, pictures, and scandals that passed through the eighteenth century, Beckett's and Rat Man's concern with the anal looks familiar to us indeed, but it does not, at least at first glance, seem to have anything to do with Schiller. Indeed, as it developed away from the horrific corporeality of *The Robbers*, Schiller's dramas came to lack the visceral attention to the body that marks the more cosmopolitan work of his mentor-rival Goethe and the more overtly queer sensibilities of his almost coeval Kleist. But the fact that the body progressively disappears—both visually and discursively—from Schiller's plays is itself noteworthy. The absence of the physical at the site dedicated to the display of bodies—namely in the theater—indicates the degree to which the body operates increasingly as contested, repressed territory for the dramatist.

Further, while the overly scatological does not taint the pages of Schiller's work, the imperfect repressions of such problematic identities as masculinity, nation, and the child certainly do. Moreover, the notion of the backside in the more general sense of the back (of that which is concealed, of that which is turned around, of that which is hidden and secret) is particularly prominent in the transitional play *Don Carlos*, which Schiller struggled and reworked in four different phases.[1]

LAYER 2

The composition of *Don Carlos* clearly functioned in Schiller's own career as his ticket to Weimar; his reading of the prose version of act 1 for Duke Karl August (December 1784), marks the first, important step toward making a permanent move there (Von Wiese 240).[2] *Don Carlos* was, then, profoundly motivated by a desired transit to Weimar. This utopian space would endow the struggling playwright with all the things he lacked and needed: economic and psychological safety guaranteed by a good, providing father figure (Karl August replacing Karl Eugen's role as bad, withholding surrogate father); artistic freedom and friendship (the venue of the Weimar theater and the active support of Goethe); and intellectual legitimacy (a university post at nearby Jena).

The intention to get to Weimar is evident from the exuberant pronouncement Schiller makes in the *Rheinische Thalia*, shortly after the meeting with Karl August:[3]

> How dear to me is the present moment when I may loudly and openly proclaim that *Karl August*, the noblest of Germany's princes and the sympathetic friend of the muses now wishes to be one of mine, that *he* has permitted me to belong to *him*.

> Wie teur ist mir der jetzige Augenblick, wo ich es laut und oeffentlich sagen darf, dass *Karl August*, der edelste von Deutschlands Fuersten und der gefuehlvolle Freund der Musen, jetzt auch der meinige sein will, dass *Er* mir erlaubt hat, *Ihm* anzugehoeren. (Kraft 2: 539)

The elegant sentimentality of the passage shows us a different Schiller than the one at work on *The Robbers*. In these pages we already see a young author very much on the make, already hard at work creating the persona of flattering protégé. This segment from the *Rheinische Thalia* also indicates how well Schiller understood that the shrewd marketing of *Don Carlos* to Karl August could make his own story as well as that of the Spanish prince into a successful one. At once résumé and passport, the play could ensure Schiller's passage to a new identity and a greatly improved self-narration. No longer the Swabian provincial, Schiller could hope to become a Weimar cosmopolitan: a man who had literally and figuratively arrived.

Significantly, the play bears witness to many other passages in Schiller's career—formally from prose to verse, from the bourgeois to the classically inspired tragedy, from Sturm und Drang to Klassik, from young to mature writer, and from a critique of unbridled individualism to a resigned and selfless nationalism that takes the place of all other love attachments.

But most important, the play was conceived and written during a complicated and tortuous passage from Mannheim to Weimar/Jena. Schiller voyaged jaggedly from Mannheim to Dresden to Leipzig to Hamburg in a set of geographic maneuvers that oddly prefigures those of Beckett and Rat Man. Like the former, he wandered from city to city and was broke most of the time. Like the latter, he vacillated frenetically from place to place, unable to get to the person and destination he desired most. And, just as Beckett's and Rat Man's peregrinations were outward manifestations of inner turmoil, so did Schiller's state of mind exactly match his physical movement and economic circumstances. The troubled transition was not only geographical and artistic but psychological as well, as the aptly named Charles Passage reminds us; he terms this period of Schiller's life a "crisis"—from which Schiller was never to recover altogether (Passage, *Friedrich Schiller* 63–66). The creation of *Don Carlos* seems to have represented yet another traumatic transition for the playwright.

Reading backwards, we can be struck by the adolescent emotionalism of Schiller's letters to his intimate friends. In stark contrast to the courtly language of the *Rheinische Thalia,* these resonate both with the Beckettian obsession with getting away *from* at any cost and with the Rat Man's grammar of discombobulated thoughts and truncated sentences.[4] A hysterical turning-point letter to Körner begins, stops, and recommences after a parenthetical interruption; even his letters cannot proceed straight from beginning to end. The letter invokes a disturbance, framed as at once outside and inside—as phenomenon and as a physical attack, as an onset of symptoms:

> (Here I have been newly interrupted by an unexpected visit, and during these twelve days a revolution has occurred in me and with me that has endowed this present letter with more significance than I had allowed myself to imagine . . .) I cannot stay in Mannheim any longer . . . I cannot stay here any longer. For twelve days I have carried it [the decision]

around in my heart, like the decision to leave this world. (Letter to Körner, February 22, 1785)

(Hier bin ich neulich durch einen unvermuteten Besuch unterbrochen worden, und diese 12 Tage ist eine Revolution mit mir und in mir vorge-gangen, die dem gegenwärtigen Briefe mehr Wichtigkeit gibt, als ich mir habe träumen laßen . . .) Ich kann nicht mehr in Mannheim bleiben. . . . Ich kann nicht mehr hier bleiben. Zwölf Tage habe ichs in meinem Her-zen herumgetragen wie den Entschluß, aus der Welt zu gehn. (*Schillers Werke* 23:176)

Linked to this desperation is still another preoccupation—that of getting to Weimar:

In addition, my present connection with the good Duke of Weimar neces-sitates my going there myself and negotiating for myself, albeit that I conduct myself miserably in such business affairs as a rule.

Außerdem verlangt es meine gegenwärtige Connexion mit dem guten Herzog von Weimar, daß ich selbst dahingehe und persönlich für mich negotiiere, so armselig ich mich auch sonst bei solcherlei Geschäften be-nehme. (176)

Here, abruptly, the language of commerce injects itself.

In a paper for the Second Davidson Symposium on German Studies, *Unwrapping Goethe's Weimar*, Thomas Wirtz argues for the emergence in late-eighteenth- and early-nineteenth-century Germany of a crucial new hermeneu-tic that circulates around the notion of *credit*—an idea that neatly unifies the economic with the transcendent (Wirtz 2–3). Certainly, Schiller seems quite aware of such transactional possibilities vis-à-vis his own art, and his letter is clearly motivated by the desire to use the credit he has already established with the Herzog to—in the discourse of Bank of America—elevate his credit limit and gain more financial power.

But what commodity is being credited and symbolically traded here? It is—at least in this letter—the writer himself who emerges as the goods in question. Small wonder then that the prospect of buying and selling himself arouses disgust in the young writer. Thus, for Schiller, the hermeneutics of credit bears none of the transcendent markings of Adam Muller's theories. Rather, such interactions inaugurate a terrible and traumatic splitting of his own subjectivity, making him at once a thing, a literal object of exchange, and an unwilling salesman, or worse yet, a prostitute, an individual who sells him/herself for the pleasure of others. This conception of the artist as personal prop-erty is hinted at in Schiller's concluding remark in the *Rheinische Thalia* that he now "belongs" to Karl August. Strikingly, Schiller's republican vision of the artist as servant to the public outlined in an earlier *Rheinische Thalia* (see the previous chapter) has melted away. The playwright has seemingly resigned himself to pursuing another master and father.

Clearly, Schiller despises such negotiations; the Frenchified verb "negotiieren" marks his entry into enemy, foreign, feminine, corrupt territory where he must make himself an object of exchange. Yet, his letter indicates his full recognition that such business deals are inevitable if he is to survive; the impersonal "es verlangt" signals his awareness of this necessity. The Latinate "Connexion" and not "Freundschaft" is—regrettably—what counts here. And money matters also, although Schiller clearly resents this fact.

Schiller's subsequent letters to friends during this period all betray such a double, vacillating perspective. Schiller represses questions of money as much as he can; claiming to each correspondent the importance of the particular friend, he continually expresses longing and delight for whichever place he will be going to visit. But behind it all lies the concern with Weimar and with the Herzog, and the not-quite-spoken anxiety of making something concrete happen. Frequently, passionate homosocial attachment on the heroic friendship model—in particular to Körner and Huber—goes hand in hand with questions of artistic inspiration, a stated desire for a *Zuhause*, *and* the unwilling, resentful pursuit of filthy lucre, and of the Herzog himself as the means to that end.

This aggravated sense of the importance of money appears elsewhere in Schiller's early work, as the tortured critiques of capital in *The Robbers* and of both bourgeois and aristocratic *arrivisme* in *Intrigue and Love* [*Kabale und Liebe*] make plain. The letters to friends from this period share the early theatrical view, articulating an ambivalence toward money heavily infiltrated by what Max Weber would call a Puritan stance. Near the end of *The Protestant Ethic and the Spirit of Capitalism* Weber observes that this mode of thinking is particularly problematic vis-à-vis artistic production:

> We should call attention to the fact that the toleration of pleasure in cultural goods, which contributed to purely aesthetic or athletic enjoyment, certainly always ran up against one characteristic limitation: they must not cost anything. Man is only a trustee of the goods which have come to him through God's grace. . . . The idea of a man's duty to his possessions, to which he subordinates himself as an obedient steward, or even as an acquisitive machine, bears with chilling weight on his life. The greater the possessions the heavier, if the ascetic attitude toward life stands the test, the feeling of responsibility for them, for holding them undiminished for the glory of God and increasing them by restless effort. (Weber 170)

Such a view places the artist in a complicated relation to the acquisition of money, as Schiller's attitude painfully exemplifies. The Puritan view of work insists on its nature as "calling" (Weber 181) with the paradoxical result that material acquisition becomes more rather than less important. In this scheme, material and financial success are the physical signature of a rational and virtuous economic life (not wasteful, not profligate). These views produce an irreconcilable ambivalence. Schiller considers himself an artist and wants to make art, but not for money and prestige, both of which he needs in order to make art, although attempting to obtain these goods prostitutes him, taints his German, and blocks his creative output.[5]

Schiller's letter bespeaks a conflicted attitude toward a means of employment in which calling and business are messily intermeshed. The conflict becomes especially clear in such comments as the following, which dates from January 1784: "My climate is the theater in which I live and move, and my passion is happily also my employment" [Mein Clima ist das Theater, in dem ich lebe und webe, und meine Leidenschaft ist glucklicherweise auch mein Amt] (von Wiese 222). In the original German the interplay in the young playwright's mind between the official and the religious is very strong. The turn of phrase "leben und weben" plays on the Christian profession of faith, "in Him we live and move and have our being" [in Ihm leben, weben und sind wir], while "Amt" stresses the official, bureaucratic function of the author's work.

Not surprisingly, the production of the manuscript of *Don Carlos* is at once dirtied and backed up by such contested, unwilling negotiations. Tacked on to Schiller's expression of worldly concern in the letters is the awareness of *Don Carlos* itself as a burden, a chaotic mess, a left-over remnant that will not be cleaned away, and that adheres, piles up on top of the new and improved work that Schiller was trying to create out of the subject matter. "Still I contemplate the chaotic mass of the remaining Karlos with despondency and terror" [Noch sehe ich die chaotische Maße des übrigen Karlos mit Kleinmut und Schrecken an] (Schiller to Huber, October 5, 1785, *Schillers Werke* 24:27).

LAYER 3

Fittingly, the play itself, so labored upon during this period, is also about obstructions and obstacles, about that which can never come to the surface; about secrets and infiltrations, perverse loves and family romances gone awry, about the failure of fatherhood and fatherland—all of which can never be revealed but does painfully leak out nonetheless. Three secrets combine and cohere at the beginning of *Don Carlos*—the secret of rebellion, the secret of the son's forbidden love for his young stepmother, and the deepest secret of all: a traumatic experience involving the father. Although *Don Carlos* is a drama rather than a novel, it is narrative and not exposition that drives the work—making it an internal drama of telling.[6]

Act 1, scene 2 regresses through layers of reminiscence toward the recollection of a traumatic incident from the past. The Infante—an apt title, connoting innocence and a childishness bordering on the babyish—is a manchild who must do without, a deprivation that makes itself felt in a halting set of speeches that outline a baffling array of desires: for a mother who is and is not his mother, for a friend who is and is not really a friend, for a father who is and is not a father. In the space of a few minutes we learn that the present clash of agendas between the two friends—Posa's intention to win Carlos's support for the Flanders campaign, and Carlos's hopes to win Posa's in the amorous pursuit of the queen—replays in more overtly political terms the equally politicized homosocial dynamics of a much earlier relation.

Having referred to himself cryptically as an orphan without a father, Carlos descends through an accumulation of memories and arrives at one horrifying incident—where he took the blame for an offense he did not commit. Even as he invokes these memories, he becomes enthralled by them—becoming in his own mind's eye not the hero that Posa hoped to find in the present but an abject victim of violence:

> In view of all the members of the court,
> Who stood in sympathetic circle round me,
> Revenge was taken on me like a slave . . .
> I did not cry. Although my royal blood
> Flowed basely under unrelenting blows,
> I looked at you and did not cry.
>
> (*Plays* 1.2.112)

> Im Angesicht des ganzen Hofgesindes,
> Das mitleidsvoll im Kreise stand, ward sie
> Auf Sklavenart und deinem Karl vollzogen . . .
> Ich weinte nicht. Mein königliches Blut
> Floß schändlich unter unbarmherz'gen Streichen.
>
> (*Schillers Werke* 7I:373)

The account of Carlos's childhood punishment is shocking—both in its brutality and in the odd lack of emotional affect with which it is delivered, ending, not with agony, but with the disconnected fiscal language of payback; according to Carlos, Posa declares "I will repay you when you are king!" [Ich will bezahlen, wenn du Koenig bist!] (373)—a response that introduces in the play the very same unhappy correlation between bodies and money suggested in Schiller's correspondence. Carlos's disjointed relating of the tale *as though he were still there* placed with the emotional disconnection from the event points to its status as traumatic moment.[7] The narrative also displays a typically disjunct mode of telling wherein pieces of vision and sensation stand in for the lost terror of the entire event.[8] There is in Carlos's narration little sense of the heroic, although he would clearly have it read in those terms; rather, the emphasis is, despite him, on being at once humiliated and annihilated (as Kristeva notes about Celine's writing, "there is no glory in this suffering" [*Powers* 147]). Ironies abound: Carlos's princely identity is reduced to a fluidity that shamefully leaks away into nothing; he claims he could control his tears but not the "tears" in his skin opened by the punitive strokes of the father, who is completely disembodied and invisible.[9]

The unseen and unseeable nature of the king indicates the degree to which repression of feeling vis-à-vis the father is operative in Carlos's traumatized memory.[10] To look the father and the state in the face is also to recognize and to acknowledge; to look is to assume command of the gaze and of one's feelings for the father, in particular feelings of hatred for one who stands between the son and the fulfillment of his sexual desire. This is a key feature of the goal in Freud's treatment of the Rat Man, behind whose adulation of his departed father lies hatred and fear. But it is precisely his hatred for the father that Don Carlos most wants to deny. Posa asks him pointedly if he hates his father, to which the prince responds with a frightened denial that literally foreshadows our current slang expression "Don't take me there!":

> No! Oh no!
> I do not hate my father—but such fear
> And sinner's apprehension seizes me
> At the mere mention of his fearful name.
>   (1.2.114)[11]

> Gott!
> Hier fühl ich, daß ich bitter werde—Weg—
> Weg, weg von dieser Stelle.
>   (71:375)

This uncannily precocious picture of child abuse, which culminates in a nightmare scene of public spectacle, is the most important scene in the play, and it drives everything that happens afterward. Interestingly, a similar traumatic event inaugurates the illness of Rat Man, "When he was very small . . . he had done something naughty, for which his father had given him a beating" (Freud, "Rat Man" 46).

Like Freud's patient, the consistently fearful military man, Carlos behaves ever after in the hold of the trauma—an event that he seems, despite himself, driven to reenact. His last-ditch effort to win his father's approval is a case in point; Carlos behaves with such unbridled emotionalism that the interview backfires drastically, inaugurating a traumatizing repetition of the pain and humiliation that he encountered as a child. Love and hatred and the fierce frustrated desire to be taken notice of permeate this scene, as Carlos compulsively re-creates the behavior necessary to precipitate Phillip's wrath:[12]

> My wish is to destroy this doubt—I want
> To hang upon my father's heart—I want
> To pull upon his heart with such great strength
> That the rock-hard encasement built by doubt
> Will fall away . . .
> If you want love, there here within this bosom
> There is a spring more vigorous and fresh
> Than in those dull and boggy reservoirs
> That Philipp's gold must open first. . . .
> . . . I can
> Not comprehend, cannot endure it, if you
> Deny me *every every every* thing.
>
> (2.1.140–45)

> Ich will ihn tilgen, diesen Zweifel—will
> Mich hängen an das Vaterherz, will reißen,
> Will mächtig reißen an dem Vaterherzen,
> Bis dieses Zweifels felsenfeste Rinde
> Von diesem Herzen niederfällt . . .
> Sie wollen Liebe?—Hier in diesem Busen
> Springt eine Quelle, frischer, feuriger,
> Als in den trueben, sumpfigen Behälten,
> Die Phillipps Gold erst öffnen muß . . .
> . . . ich kanns nicht fassen
> Nicht standhaft ertragen wie ein Mann, dass Sie
> Mir alles, alles alles so verweigern.
>
> (7I:414)

Phillip angrily dismisses the matter out of hand, re-creating, despite/ because of his son's pleas—the terrible shuttlecock terror. Carlos recognizes the connection between the scenes in his frightened use of key imagery:

> Oh, do not *shame* me, Father, do not *wound*
> Me mortally nor sacrifice me to
> The mockery of the whole court that knows
> That strangers revel in your favor when
> Don Carlos' pleas will not prevail.
>
> (2.2.144, my italics)

61

Beschämen Sie mich nicht! So tödlich, Vater,
Verwunden Sie mich nicht, dem frechen Hohn
Das Hofgesindes schimpflich mich zu opfern,
Daß Fremdlinge von Ihrer Gnade schwelgen,
Ihr Karlos nichts erbitten kann.

(7I:418, my italics)

But here again money makes its appearance, for the scene suggests that unrequited love is inevitably confused with the very material acquisition it opposes itself to. Carlos passionately claims that he wants his father to love him, and declares that he can deliver to the king his own, literally "priceless" filial devotion in return. Love, he implies, cannot be bought in contrast to the paid-for affections of his advisors. But the audience knows that Carlos's very appearance in the hall has a considerable price tag attached; he has come because he wants control over Flanders. The awful, hateful interrelation between love and currency emerges again in Carlos's conversation with Eboli (2.8) with similarly dubious results. Like Carlos, Eboli claims that her emotions are above the market, but the play quickly shows us that her sexual services, if not her love, are indeed for sale.

But if the dearth of familial love leads to an obsession with payback, it also leads in a quite surprising direction. The shell-shocked victim of a castrating father figure and an absent mother, Carlos's desires split and go two ways at the same time: toward youthful stand-ins for both male and female members of the family romance (since the queen is in fact his contemporary). An idolater of idealized men and women, Carlos simultaneously quests for Posa's friendship and the queen's love; these relationships alone hold out the hope of sanctuary from the angry kingdom of the fathers.

Thus, if the father cannot love the son or be hated outright by him, then it is the circuitous affections of male love, or the symbolically incestuous promise of mother love toward which Carlos turns.[13] The conflation of man-to-man with man-to-woman love is clear in the first scene, which juxtaposes Carlos's passionate reminiscence of his boyhood relationship with Posa (where boyish competition is transformed into something far more ambiguous) with his present agenda of winning the queen. Is it not both the man and the woman that Carlos has in mind when he declares, with characteristic simplicity and naiveté, "I need love" [Ich brauche Liebe] (1.2)?

Thus, obstructed by the father, the son's emotional capacity to love and the sexual desire that drives love must do their work perversely, through strange directions and maneuvers. Accordingly, the erotic circuits of the play continually go in unauthorized directions, marking Eros *queer* in the double sense of being either unusual and/or displaying homo- or otherized sexuality. Curious charges of desire certainly inform the relations between Carlos and

Posa, but they also are present in the encounters between Posa and the king, Posa and the queen, and Eboli and the queen, between Eboli and Carlos. In these relations Posa repeatedly emerges as a homosocial mastermind, able to seduce men and women alike: the otherwise inaccessible king is mysteriously enthralled by a young man who is his political and moral opposite; the queen passionately vows to value no other man after Posa. But the diverted, displaced nature of desire drives the other characters as well. Eboli betrays the queen as much out of disappointment with the object of her idolatry as out of jealousy of Carlos's love for her; the queen makes her declaration of love for Carlos, not to him personally, but to the Marquis Posa. Even Eboli's and Carlos's seemingly straightforward encounter hints at a sexuality not quite in order:

> When suddenly—were you to blame?—the clothes
> Of certain ladies rustled at your back,
> And then Don Philipp's one courageous son
> Began to tremble like a heretic
> Before the Host, and on his pallid lips
> His spoiled prayer expired—a victim of
> His passion—what a touching game was played
> There, Prince—You seize the fingers of our Lord's
> Own Mother, cold and holy fingers and
> Then shower fiery kisses on the marble.
>
> (2.8.162)

> Als plötzlich—konnten Sie dafür?—die Kleider
> Gewisser Damen hinter Ihnen rauschten.
> Da fing Don Phillips heldenmüth'ger Sohn,
> Gleich einem Ketzer vor dem heil'gen Amte,
> Zu zittern an, auf seinen bleichen Lippen
> Starb das vergiftete Gebet—im Taumel
> Der Leidenschaft—es war ein Possenspiel
> Zum Rühren, Prinz—ergreifen Sie die Hand,
> der Mutter Gottes heil'ge kalte Hand,
> Und Feurküsse regnen auf den Marmor.
>
> (7I:444)

Eboli's fetishization of the rustling clothes, the emphasis on the hidden and the secret, and the elaborate, voyeuristic description of Carlos's passionate kissing of the statue (appropriately of the Holy Mother) is indicative of the degree to which thwarted desires find scandalous expression in the world of the play. Finally, even enmity carries a sexual charge in this play; the perplexed Duke of Alba reports to the king that he was accosted and then "hotly kissed" by the unpredictable Infante. Desire travels desperately in *Don Carlos*, without ever reaching its proper destination.

Thus, desire in *Don Carlos* is literally deviant (Dollimore 104), insofar as it is continually forced into unusual paths, thwarted, blocked, resorting to hidden and forbidden channels of entry and expression, finding a different body other than the one it wants to, in the words of Beckett, "rub up against" (Beckett 56). Yet, even these unorthodox, displaced emotional relationships come to naught. The result of such thwarted love is always betrayal and/or renunciation but never fulfillment.[14] Carlos, flanked by his parental doubles, Posa and Elizabeth, must again do without love, as he did as a child. Like Freud's Rat Man, he travels a psychic route that eternally loops back on itself—ending, not in cure, but in premature obliteration—a debt that is paid off only by death.[15] "The voice of nature has totally departed from my breast" (*Plays* 302) [Ausgestorben ist/In meinem Busen die Natur] (5:11), Carlos tells the queen near the end of the play, and there is, it seems, no other possibility for desire but to die. But he cannot do his duty either, and dies a blocked man of rebellion—a revolution that remains purely internal, and that assures his eventual annihilation by the very father he hoped both to win over and to rebel against.

Layer 4

Like the unauthorized *Eros* that it heartbreakingly displays, Schiller's play demarcates a Spain that is itself a curious place. Rigid and regimented, this Spain that is not Spain lacks anything that could be construed as Mediterranean; this Spain is militaristic and displays a Catholicism that is spare, doctrinaire, and authoritarian, where the French queen feels surprisingly constrained and out of place. In fact, this Spain manifests all the qualities that will contribute to the stereotype of what is Prussian.

Read one way, the world of *Don Carlos* is clearly Schiller's Germany—the Fatherland that does not yet exist but that dreams of itself as a nation of Enlightenment principles even as the fractured remnants of the Reich operate on a ducal system as antiquated as the system that governs that of King Phillip—where provincialism and rigidity prevail, despite the efforts of the most enthusiastic artists and intellectuals. When Posa declares his time has not yet come, is it not place rather than time that is the problem? Finished in 1787, Schiller's play fairly bristles with the frustration of a revolutionary wave that is *now* but is not *here*. In this light, both Posa's and Carlos's inability to get to Flanders marks the larger inability of Schiller's Germans to get to the place where revolution happens.[16]

But, read autobiographically, Schiller's Spain represents not only Germany in general—a national dream space of the future—but also specifically the place that Schiller was trying so desperately to get away from—namely Mannheim, which his letters describe as a prison from which he plans a criminal escape.[17] From this point of view, Flanders is not only the place where revolution happens but the place where Schiller's own private revolution, the "inner Revolution," can find free expression in the realm of economic safety; Flanders becomes, according to this schema, a projection of the hoped-for Weimar.

Such a reading gives us some insight into the strange character of Don Carlos the dreamer, queer mother-lover, and homosocial dropout; the prince who does not speak or act like a prince, the traumatized son who can remember but who cannot get over. In his final meeting with the queen, Posa requests Elizabeth's undying affection for Carlos. But the terms of this request are surprising and would seem to reveal yet another dimension to this play about suppression and repression:

> And does the lovely harmony that sleeps
> Within the lyre [the play of strings] belong to one who buys
> It and who guards it with deaf ears? He has
> Bought up the right to smash it into pieces,
> But not the art to summon silvery tones
> And melt away into the song's delight.
>
> (4.21.262)

> Gehört die süsse Harmonie, die in
> Dem Saitenspiele schlummert, seineim Käufer,
> Der es mit taubem Ohr bewacht? Er hat
> Das Recht erkauft, in Trümmern es zu schlagen,
> Doch nicht die Kunst, dem Silberton zu rufen
> Und in des Liedes Wonne zu zerschmelzen.
>
> (7I:586)

Significantly, the play reports yet another unseen drama of blows meted out on an innocent victim—wherein an all-powerful buyer shatters the orphic stringed instrument, to which he has purchased complete rights. Art survives, just barely and only momentarily, as the sound leaks out of the destroyed body. This artistic utterance complements the traumatized memory of Carlos, and aligns the hero with the production of art in a violent marketplace to which the instrument belongs and by which it is enthralled and shattered. Read as a series of autobiographical displacements, the smashed lute stands in for Carlos standing in for Schiller,[18] who emerges as the traumatized bourgeois producer of German art, a commodified (and therefore reified—thingified) humiliated son of a patriarchal market moving into capitalism. In such a system the art-ist—like Carlos—is always relegated to the status of child—to be tolerated, trained, disciplined, and punished but never to achieve full majority, never to be home, never to be safe.

Such a reading of the play is shored up by Schiller himself, who used a variation on the same metaphor invoked in the play when he assured Körner in February 1785, "In your circle, I will more happily and more ardently touch my lute" [In Ihrem Zirkel, will ich froher und inniger in meiner Laute greifen] (Letter 122 of *Schillers Werke* 23:178). But his comment a few lines earlier is even more to the point: "My heart and my muses must at the same time succumb to [literally: lie under] necessity" [Mein Herz und meine Musen mußten zu gleicher Zeit der Nothwendigkeit unterliegen] (177).

Beckett understood the paradoxical nature of this kind of necessity full well. The 1955 novel *Molloy* opens with the portrait of the artist as a resentful childish invalid which postfigures that of the physically wrecked Schiller trying to eject the rest of *Demetrius*, his last play, from his dying body, "There's this man who comes every week. . . . He gives me money and takes away the pages. So many pages, so much money. . . . What I'd like to do now is to speak of the things that are left, say my goodbyes, finish dying. They don't want that. Yes, there's more than one apparently. . . . Yet I don't work for money. For what then?" (7).

Interestingly, Beckett's hero is also a deviant lover: a confused pursuer of both women and men, Molloy "rubs up against" both female and male objects, confuses the anus with the vagina, and dreams of a return to an original dyad—which always escapes him:

> And of myself, all my life, I think I had been going to my mother. . . .
> And when I was with her, and I often succeeded, I left her without having done anything. And when I was no longer with her I was again on my way to her, hoping to do better the next time. And when I appeared to give up and to busy myself with something else, or with nothing at all any more, in reality I was hatching my plans and seeking my way to her house. This is taking a queer turn. (34)

Like the confused writer-cyclist in Beckett's *Molloy* and like the frustrated traveler, the Rat Man, Schiller's *Don Carlos*, and the texts around it navigate a queer circuit, functioning as a repressed, traumatized autobiography (*Don Carlos* is possibly Schiller's most confessional work) where fundamental anxieties leak out, and as a docudrama and dramatic case study of the author's agonized quest for legitimacy and for solvency.[19] The concern with cash and the resentment against negotiations mark Schiller's unwilling move into the emerging space of commodified literature, what Horkheimer and Adorno have called the "culture industry" (157). Within this framework the writer in Anglo-Europe would have two salient choices—to become a best-selling celebrity, salon guest, and man-about-town who schmoozes with the powerful and the famous (Goethe's choice), or to become an academic, who schmoozes too, but differently, for he must seem not to write *for* money and yet write *to obtain* money all the same.[20] Further, Schiller seems to understand in *Don Carlos* that the artist-qua-intellectual person must always, in such a scheme of market values, be positioned as perverse, as not quite "straight," as having suspect desires and penchants for an economy that is more or at least other than the possession of coin.

Seen in this light, the consistent scholarly preferences for Goethe over Schiller (in Germanistik and elsewhere) points to an intriguing discursive repression—namely the denial of the historical connection between Schiller's cultural positioning and our own. His predicament reveals the fundament of our predicament—that of the academic intellectual who would be, and can never be, free of the concerns of enterprise. Like Schiller, the academic humanist also writes, thinks, and teaches for a market, no matter how displaced, and no matter how small, while s/he survives in such a market precisely by appearing to concentrate purely on the authenticity of his/her "calling."

LAYER 5

Don Carlos never left for Flanders, Rat Man could not reach the post office, and Beckett did not uncover the inspiration he had hoped to find during his trip to Germany. His fictional double Molloy never finds his mother. Like these frustrated travelers, Schiller never quite arrived at Weimar, for the Weimar he discovered proved to be a more intense variation on the Mannheim he had left. Weimar as described in Schiller's letters emerges as something of a company town, and in its constituency, far more like a creative consortium than like a gentlemen's club.[21] The group that Schiller depicts resembles an enterprise not unlike DC Comics, where free-lance creative men (and a few women) all jockey for position in a sometime cooperation, sometime competition with the editors in chief. The editor in chief here is clearly Goethe, whose birthday Schiller and others celebrated in Weimar at Goethe's house in 1787, while the author himself was still in Italy—an odd prefiguration of the ubiquitous second-tier Academy Award parties in Los Angeles, where the famous guests of honor rarely, if ever, show up.[22] Schiller attended the party for Goethe, at once resentful and hopeful—wondering, with some justification, what actual good it would do (Letter to Körner, August 29, 1787, Letter 97 of *Schillers Werke* 24:149–50). And, as he pursued the doubtful fellowship of the Herders and the ever-absent Goethe, he was repeatedly unable to win the

attention of the Duke, and spends a full two months trying to gain an audience
with him.

Against this personal history, Weimar already looks a bit like Klassik,
Inc.—as Schiller's descriptions of it make clear. His first letter to Körner from
Weimar specifically describes an arrival that contains all manner of frustrations,
a journey fraught with obstacles and the more painful problem of self-mar-
keting:

> I arrived here last night. . . . In Naumburg I had the misfortune to miss
> the Herzog of Weimar by an hour at the post house, where he well nigh
> took the horses away from me. What I wouldn't have given for such a
> fortuitous chance! Now he is in Potsdam, and as of yet, no one knows
> how soon he will return. . . . The expectation of the many things which
> will throw themselves in my way has captured my consciousness. As
> things stand, you know that I soon become stupefied by the things which
> surround and nearly concern me. The many sorts of relationships into
> which I must apportion myself, in each one of which, however, I must be
> fully present terrifies my spirit and causes me to feel the limitation of my
> being. (Letter to Körner, July 23, 1787)

> Vorgestern Abend kam ich hier an . . . In Naumburg, hatte ich das Un-
> glück, den Herzog von Weimar um eine Stunde im Posthauße zu verfeh-
> len, wo er mir beinah die Pferde weggenommen hat. Was hätte ich nicht
> um diesen gluecklichen Zufall gegeben! Jezt ist er in Potsdam und man
> weiß noch nicht wie bald er zurückkommen wird. . . . Die Erwartung,
> der mancherley Dinge, die sich mir hier in den Weg werfen werden, hat
> meine ganze Besinnungskraft eingenommen . . . Überhaupt wißt ihr, daß
> ich bald von den Dingen, die mich umgeben und nahe angehen, betäubt
> werde. . . . die vierlerlei Verhältnisse in die ich mich hier zerteilen muß,
> in deren jedem ich doch ganz gegenwärtig seyn muß, erschröckt meiner
> Mut und läßt mich die Einschränkung meines Wesens fühlen. (*Schillers
> Werke* 24:105–6)

Like the Rat Man in the restaurant, Schiller literally arrived in Weimar too
late—narrowly missing his hoped-for patron along the way. He now found
himself stuck in an uncertain position waiting for Karl August to return while
having to struggle to make ends meet in the meantime. Moreover, from the
moment he arrives in Weimar, he understood that the dirty business of "negotiieren" for money and position, for legitimacy, for "Connexion" as opposed
to "Freundschaft" had not ceased. Rather, these transactional processes had
redoubled, and the stakes are higher. Significantly, the opportunities for ad-
vancement struck Schiller not as positive but as negative; these possibilities
resembled literal obstacles thrown in his artistic path. These "things" threw

68

him psychologically off course by triggering unwelcome thoughts and feelings—the painful awareness of inner obstacles, unspoken but powerful constrictions that blocked him even more.

The confession to Körner eerily predicts Schiller's future in Weimar. The obstacles would only accrue as time passes, and almost two years later Schiller would write in similar fashion about yet another thing lying in the way—Goethe himself:

> This person, this Goethe is just in my way; and he so often reminds me that fate has treated me harshly. How easily was *his* genius carried by fate and how, until this very minute, must *I* still fight! (Schiller to Körner in Ronell, *Dictations* 56)

> Dieser Mensch, dieser Göthe ist mir einmal im Wege, und er erinnert mich so oft, daß das Schicksal mich hart behandelt hat. Wie leicht ward *sein* Geist von seinem Schicksal getragen, und wie muß *ich* bis' auf diese Minute kämpfen! (Letter to Körner, March 9, 1789, *Schillers Werke* 25:222)

Throughout Schiller's career in Weimar, outside "things" (including his famous friendship) would remind the author of increasingly heavy interior burdens, as an accumulating mass of psychological and socioeconomic pressures would mold Schiller's art into an ever more static classicism.

Thus, *Don Carlos* is a testament to both horror and finance—family trauma and the traumatic experience of creating art for a marketplace that consumes and destroys the artist, even as it makes his career. From this point of view, Weimar's Schiller emerges, not as the ethereal idealist partner to Goethe's virile realist but as a powerful and powerfully repressed prototype of one sort of modern artist, upon whom layers of resentful and withdrawn male visionaries load up a melancholy legacy. Blocked intellectuals who are aggravated priests of an increasingly hard-to-market high culture, they are frustrated men of feeling who vacillate between hating to sell and feeling utterly compelled to market themselves—from Victor Hugo to Dostoevsky and Kafka, to Thomas Wolfe and J. D. Salinger, to Peter Handke, Heiner Müller, and beyond. Neither altogether obedient sons of the state nor rebellious producers of scatological jouissance, these authors circulate within the stopped-up interstices between the Rat Man's therapy and Beckett's curative theatrics.

And Schiller's Weimar? Against this reading of Schiller, the murky outlines of a different city appear—an urban space, not of classical statuary, but of crooked, narrow streets where struggling cultural practitioners hide out in the studies of their constricted houses, barricaded against the realities of a cultural dumping ground whose slimy detritus we are only now sifting through, "So many families, ever so many isolated snail shells, from which the inhabitant barely comes out to sun himself . . . I go out very seldom now" (Letter to Körner, September 10, 1787) [Soviele Familien, eben so viele abgesondere Schneckenhäuser, aus denen der Eigentümer kaum herausgeht, um sich zu sonnen . . . Jezt gehe ich sehr wenig aus] (*Schillers Werke* 24:152). Schiller fleetingly makes a connection that psychoanalysis would have leapt upon: the Weimar citizen as snail, a shelled worm. Worms, Freud tells us, resemble rats, turds, phallic remnants, bills of money, or chthonic children (Freud, "Rat Man" 52–53). *Don Carlos* and Schiller's uncertain passage to Weimar pile up these concerns in which we are still enmeshed as critics and as writers, which block us, which pile up within our own discourse about the Weimar greats, and which implicate us in the perpetuation of their myth.

CHAPTER 3

War Photo/graphs

Pictures, Time, and the Aesthetics of Trauma in *WALLENSTEIN*

Have you seen anything of the mechanical imitation of paintings?

Haben Sie schon von einer mechanischen Nachbildung von Mahlereyen etwas gesehen?

Schiller to Goethe, April 14, 1797

Since it was civilization itself which "dealt modern man this wound," only a new mode of civilization can heal it.

Herbert Marcuse

Culture = Battalions

Klaus Theweleit

In the controversial and critically acclaimed film *The Thin Red Line* a network of disembodied male voices roam over the images of American soldiers dying during the battle to take Guadalcanal. There is no one narrative voice and consequently no master narrative prevails. Instead of epic, the three-hour-long war film submerges the viewer in a seemingly endless stream of surprising pictures juxtaposed against each other. Jungles give way to bedrooms, and Japanese enemy soldiers blend in with Melanesian natives; terrified enlisted men hiding in a river look up to see bats, hanging upside down from the trees curiously watching the creatures with guns; owls hoot, a dead bird flutters on the ground, and the sun glints through the leaf fronds in an impossibly beautiful landscape littered with the screaming bodies of the almost dead. Water pools in lakes as buildings and wooden statues of the Buddha burn.

More perhaps than any other war film, *The Thin Red Line* attempts to speak and show the collective voice of war; the shards of "one large mind" splintered off into individuals themselves terribly fragile and incomplete.[1] These persons are not heroes, although they are brave remnants of the blasted

71

dream of military heroism. This dream—which has consistently haunted Western culture as early as the breached walls of Jericho and the treacherous horse of Troy—fragments during the course of the film into the poignant shards of almost stories. These frames precede before our eyes like an odd slide show, a home movie gone haywire. Scraps of lives, the pictures intervene and fade out, unfinished and unresolved. One young man thinks only of his beautiful wife, and he crawls through the jungle dreaming of their bedroom, her body in a silk dress, the lace curtain on the window, her hair floating in the water as the two of them take a bath. He believes passionately in the sanctity of love that cannot be killed, although indeed it is, for his lengthy absence causes his wife to leave him for someone else. A captain, who is a highly intelligent attorney, finds himself placed in the impossible position of having to lead his men on a frontal assault that will mean certain death for all of them. He refuses to lead a charge, and perhaps saves his men, but he is stripped of command and returns home uncertain that he has made the right choice. A surly, self-assured veteran blows himself up by accident. A potato-faced red-haired kid is terrified but discovers he is a wonderful fighter. A new recruit becomes old in the process of fighting.

And yet, amidst this blasted narrative landscape—at once ruined and lush—and amidst the panoply of almost identical men in fatigues, three characters emerge as particularly important.

The first is the colonel in charge—older, resigned, angry, resilient—a politician, who has waited for his chance to play at a real war. Colonel Tall is ruthless, has useless bombs dropped to "buck up the men," and is unwilling to give the soldiers water. He wants to win at all costs and does achieve his aim, scattering the dead young men about him.

The second is a visionary. A young country boy from the south, Private Witt is the character whose memories and actual figure ground the film's beginning; the first frames of the film flash back to his mother's death—which becomes for him a guiding thought and principle. Gone AWOL many times in order to live among the Melanesians, Witt is part Rousseauist, part good Samaritan. Drawn to the simplicity and beauty of native life, Witt becomes the film's passive resistor to the violence that goes on around him. Imprisoned and then sent to nurse the wounded and dying, he eventually sacrifices himself to save his squad. Miraculously gifted with the power of empathy—the true ability to bear witness to the sufferings and death of the others—he claims to his sergeant that he can see something beyond the world of war, another world, a beautiful world, one filled with glory. When he dies he sees himself returning to the Solomon Islands, to the ocean, to swim playfully with the native children.

The third person is Witt's antagonist, Sergeant Welsh. Younger than the older man and older than the younger man, Welsh looks at first glance like the coldhearted son of a bitch who tends to populate war movies: a man who shaves calmly before combat, unimpressed by the fears of those around him. A seemingly professional army man concerned above all with the organization of the outfit, Welsh is tough talking, and chain smoking. The sergeant claims not to care about anything but surviving, but the film shows us repeatedly that he is lying, and it is the dynamic of this lie that makes him arguably the most compelling character of the film. Unable to enter into the illusions of military heroism—which he regards as hypocrisy (he threatens to kill the colonel who promises him a medal for his courage on the battlefield)—Welsh is equally incapable of sharing Witt's mysticism, his serenity. A man who is, by his own admission, "frozen up a long time ago," Sergeant Welsh observes Witt with a mixture of contempt and envy—admiration and resentment for the latter's "magician's talent" to see the "spark" where indeed no spark is.

Torn between opposing views of what reality is and what human existence means, Welsh lives in disconnected agony, a man unable—despite his best efforts—not to care. A man without desire, perpetually irritated, easily angered, and a man of a few, tersely spoken words, Welsh is the quintessence of battle fatigue; he wears the face of combat trauma—a young face, prematurely old, seemingly affectless, deeply sad.

One the last shots of the film shows Welsh's face sheathed in his helmet as he sits on the boat, heading out for yet another battle: a haunted and haunting face, a living portrait on film, a moving snapshot in both senses. As I write these words, I think about that face. Then I realize that I am moved by a visage I have never actually seen; I am touched by a projection of light through celluloid onto a screen, by a photographic trace of what was once a physical presence. I am haunted by a specter, which is in fact an imprint of light on darkness.

"CAN YOU SEE IT?"[2]

In his book on photography, Roland Barthes links the photographic image with mourning, with death, and with the loss of history (Barthes 92) "It was there and is there no longer," the photograph tells us, and the picture stands in for the loss of the whole event—an event not containable by the frames of the picture, and yet for which the picture stands in as testimony and testament. "I was real," the photograph says. "I lived."

Small wonder that since the Civil War, most wars live in our memories and impact upon us as true and as real through photography (Rosenblum 180), and now through photography's descendant—the movies. The lens of the camera seems particularly suited to the representation of war, for as Oliver Wendell Holmes observed, the photograph may contain particulars that the participants do not see (Rosenblum 155). Placed in a privileged position vis-à-vis the event depicted in the photograph, the observer sees and understands what the people in the frame do not, and thus s/he possesses knowledge in a curious isolation. Seer of the past, the observer in the future cannot share what s/he knows and cannot save or assist those represented. S/he sees but cannot enter the frame of the picture (Barthes 106).

Significantly, Barthes's work also declares the photograph is deeply personal; when we mourn history, we are mourning *our* history; we mourn *our* own dead, we mourn what *we* have lost personally and irretrievably. The photograph is always about in some ways our own death, the irretrievable loss of a part of ourselves, "It is because each photograph always contains this imperious sign of my future death that each one, however attached it seems to be to the excited world of the living, challenges each of us, one by one, outside of any generality (but not outside any transcendence)" (97).

The first *Terminator* film understands the complex relationship between war and the photograph and progressively tightens the connection between military Armageddon, the redemptive possibilities of love between a man and a woman, and the inevitability of death. A much valued Polaroid snapshot appears, disappears, is rhetorically invoked, and then reappears at the end of the film. The picture—paradoxically fading into rather than out of view (in that curious way that Polaroids do)—dramatizes what modernist photographer Cartier-Bresson has called "the decisive moment" (Rosenblum 485); in the closing frames of the film Sarah Connor contemplates her own face in a snapshot that captures the instant in which she both mourns Kyle Reese and leaves him and a part of herself behind forever. This same image will seduce Kyle Reese in the future through the mediation of his unborn son; it is the photograph that compels him to return to the past in order to become precisely the object of mourning—the *punktum*—the invisible referent of the picture we see before us.

Screen image, photographic print, stage spectacle: there are clearly differences between these aesthetic technologies. Two of them move while one is still; two display mere visual traces of things and people, while the other displays real bodies of the persons, and sometimes objects as well, as immediately actual and tangible. Depending on where one is seated in the theater, these persons and things may be proximate to the point of discomfort—all this in stark contrast to the absences displayed by photos and films.

Yet, in his playful essay "What Is a Picture?" Lacan provocatively argues for the essential congruity between all these representational modes. Citing paintings, animal mimicry, and the Chinese National Opera, Lacan implies that they are all "pictures" and we ourselves become pictures for others as soon as they look at us. In this sense to be seen is always to be "photo-graphed" (Lacan, *Four Fundamental Concepts* 106). Thus we are all actors for the camera lucida of the person who watches us. By implication then, the theater, as the originary

74

site of moving artistic visual representation, becomes linked inextricably to the arts of photography and filmmaking.[3]

Obviously, Schiller lived and wrote long before the advent of either of these technologies. Yet, he was fascinated by the mechanical reproduction of images that was occurring during his own time. Moreover, he seems to have understood that pictures—both moving and still, representing objects physically present and physically absent—offered the perfect means to know war. He seems to have been equally cognizant of the connections between the visual representation of war and the performance of mourning related to the self's terrible loss.

"LOOK AT ALL YOU HAVE MADE"

The justification for interpreting the *WALLENSTEIN* trilogy in photographic terms does not seem immediately apparent. Indeed, *WALLENSTEIN* overwhelms by its sheer magnitude. It is Schiller's most ambitious project—the play most overtly tied to German history, the play most overtly connected to the author's own wishes to create a poetic work of literal epic proportions. As early as 1790, Schiller and Körner began discussing a proposed epic poem related to the Thirty Years War, and in certain respects *WALLENSTEIN* is that poem.[4] If *Don Carlos* is Schiller's masked autobiography, then *WALLENSTEIN* seems in comparison his most public, least private dramatic offering. Its command of poetic high diction further contributes to the sense that the work is profoundly removed from Schiller's own lived experience during the lengthy period of composition (1791–99).[5]

That lived experience is itself bewilderingly complex, because the decade of the 1790s represents the busiest period in Schiller's literary career and personal life. During this time, he became a professor, a husband, and a father. Harried by so many urgent demands, Schiller became deathly ill; he began his close association with Goethe, and he emerged during the 1790s as a professional intellectual. Close to penniless, he was rescued temporarily from the financial problems that beset him by Prince Friedrich Christian of Holstein-Augustenburg and Count Schimmelman of Denmark (Sharpe 119). Given this freedom, and as though building an academic resume that would qualify him as the ultimate Renaissance Man, Schiller worked nonstop, sometimes all night; he translated Virgil and Racine, wrote philosophical treatises on aesthetics, edited a literary magazine, engaged with the most famous literary man of the age, wrote poetry, and even tried his hand at fiction.

Yet, while not originating in the desperate need for money, *WALLENSTEIN* displays and gives voice to desperation on a whole new level. More than any of his dramas, the *WALLENSTEIN* trilogy is overtly and covertly obsessed with the past and with the personal memories of lived experience by which individuals claim the past as their own. The outcome is a drama that attempts to lay out a landscape of trauma at its most vast—a veritable wasteland of memories split off from the lives of the rememberers—through a correlative more objective than any Schiller had used before. The theater of war provides an event and experience of psychological and physical wounding on a grand scale, which most audiences can understand and identify with, even today. Appropriately, Schiller chose the most terrible of all German wars, for the Thirty Years War destroyed whole towns and villages; it is the degree zero for many Germans of historical consciousness and collective memory.[6] A cemetery of pictures, *WALLENSTEIN* explicitly details the effects of war on the men and, to a lesser extent, the women, who live it. It speaks consistently in terms of dehumanization, fear, unremitting violence, as well as separation and disconnection from family. Accordingly Schiller's soldiers exhibit attitudes that will later become casebook symptoms of the trauma survivor, whose inner life is made up not of drama but of "what is missing" (Herman 49).

Thus, as in the case of *Line*, *WALLENSTEIN* slows down dramatic time in order to convey—on a visceral level—how much time has come out of joint in the world of war. This resetting of the clocks to the time of military service is meant to give audiences a feeling—through distorted duration—of war time and of its numbing effects, its weird psychological reversals, and all the curious places that the mind goes under the direst of circumstances. And the pictures— the memories shuffled like cards in the deck of a collective unconscious—focus the audience not on presence but on the absence of what is lost irretrievably and what must be mourned.

More than any of his other plays, *WALLENSTEIN* attempts theatrically to reproduce the numbness, the disconnection, the fragmentation of the posttraumatic sensibility. In so doing, the plays accomplish a task more radical still. Through this photography that stretches time, freezes the characters into a psychic dead zone, and invokes originals forever lost, the trilogy enacts a critique of war at the same time as it absolutely refuses the simplicities of military heroism.[7] There are no heroes in *WALLENSTEIN*. These complex theatrical gestures, undertaken in the 1790s during the French Revolution and the Napoleonic Wars, make the *WALLENSTEIN* trilogy at once visionary and disturbingly contemporary. As such, the trilogy also represents the author's most coherent statement about how trauma feels and how it is used by governments and ruling bodies to assert a deadly power over individuals.

Appropriately, the strange prologue to this very strange series of plays repeatedly announces not the persistence of memory but rather its disruption by almost nonstop references to absence—on what and who are not there.[8] An opening invocation that the newly restored Weimar theater may "refresh and regain [its] former fame" gives way to an odd description of the art being practiced here—an art indeed of the evanescent:

> For swiftly over our awareness passes
> The wondrous art of mimes without a trace,
> Whereas the sculptor's statue and the song
> Of poets live beyond the centuries.
> Here when the artist ends, his magic ends,
> And as the sound recedes upon our ears
> The moment's quick creation dies in echoes,
> Its fame preserved by no enduring work.
>
> (*WC* in Passage, ll.32–40)⁹

> Denn schnell und spurlos geht des Mimen Kunst,
> Die wunderbare, an dem Sinn vorüber,
> Wenn das Gebild des Meißels, der Gesang
> Des Dichters nach Jahrtausenden noch leben.
> Hier stirbt der Zauber mit dem Künstler ab,
> Und wie der Klang verhallet in dem Ohr,
> Verrauscht des Augenblicks geschwinde Schöpfung,
> Und ihren Ruhm bewahrt kein daurend Werk.
>
> (*Schillers Werke* 8:4)

Performance, Schiller's prologue suggests, is a practice of self-disappearance, a display of self-absenting that impresses and then fades without a trace. The best that the actor can hope for, Schiller continues, is to possess his moment completely, to affect his audience emotionally and thereby "In the feelings of the best and noblest / Build living monuments" (ll.46–47) [Im Gefühl der Würdigsten und Besten / Ein lebend Denkmal sich erbaun] (8:4). The actor's art lives on—if it survives at all—*spectrally* by making an imprint of the performance on the psyche of the viewer, who carries within him/her the sense-memory of the event. And twenty lines later, theatrical art itself emerges as a "shadow-stage"—an ephemeral play of light on dark, a photographic performance that may or may not leave anything behind.

The shadow-stage is an appropriate metaphor because the historical past itself proves to be a problem—at once lost forever and back here again, at once remote and omnipresent:

> Amid these days we see the old fixed form
> Disintegrate, which in its time a hundred
> And fifty years ago a welcome peace
> Imposed on Europe's realms, the precious fruit
> Acquired by thirty dismal years of war.
> Now once again permit the poet's fancy

To bring before your eyes that somber age,
While more content you gaze about the present
And toward the hopeful distance of the future.

(WC, ll.70–79)

Zerfallen sehen wir in diesen Tagen
Die alte feste Form, die einst vor hundert
Und fünfzig Jahren ein willkommner Friede
Europens Reichen gab, die teure Frucht
Von dreißig jammervollen Kriegesjahren.
Noch einmal laßt des Dichters Phantasie
Die düstre Zeit an euch vorüberführen,
Und blicket froher in die Gegenwart
Und in der Zukunft hoffnungsreiche Ferne.

(8:5)

Referring obliquely to the French Revolution and the subsequent Napoleonic wars, Schiller explains that the past is not past and that the present is at
once a return to the past and a departure from it. Time itself seems to be
collapsing, according to the prologue, but not in any way that will facilitate an
understanding of the past, present, or the unreachable hope extended by a
faraway future. Given this state of affairs, it is the drama—the art of the
ephemeral—which must intervene to reorganize time through the present, actual, and visual performance of the past. This time gone by is emphatically
meant to be *seen*, and, more important, this presentation must proceed not
in the manner of straightforward drama but indeed as a series of progressive
pictures:

Forgive the poet therefore if he does not
Sweep you with rapid step and all at once
Straight to his story's goal, but only ventures
To set his might subject forth before you
In series, one by one, of pictures merely.

(WC, ll.119–23)

Darum verzeiht dem Dichter, wenn er euch
Nicht raschen Schritts mit *einem* mal ans Ziel
Der Handlung reißt, den grossen Gegenstand
In einer Reihe von Gemälden nur
Vor euren Augen abzurollen wagt.

(8:6)

In this manner, Schiller devises WALLENSTEIN as a photo album *avant la lettre,*
a retrospective war journal newsreel that will present us (literally, "unroll")

with a set of flashbacks, a set of "decisive moments" taken from the Thirty Years War's connections to Wallenstein. And yet even in this limited presentation, there are significant lacunae. Notably, the main character himself seems completely irrecuperable:

> Blurred by the favor and the hate of parties,
> His image wavers in our history.
>
> (*WC*, ll.101–2)

> Von der Parteien Gunst und Haß verwirrt
> Schwankt sein Charakterbild in der Geschichte.
>
> (8:5)

Despite the fact that the author promises to bring Wallenstein "more humanly / And closer to your eyes and to your hearts" (ll.103–4), the figure of the main character cannot be immediately actualized for the present enterprise. Instead, the scenes from the military camp will have to stand in emblematically for the person who is not there, becoming the light backdrop, against which Wallenstein's unseeable "shadow self" (l.114) may gradually emerge.

Significantly pictures of all kinds—literal and evocative—proliferate: portraits, panels, astrological charts, flags, chalices, emblems, and highly visual flashbacks rendered self-consciously as pictures constitute the most dramatic parts of the play. Indeed remembered pictures and pictures that invoke remembrance play an inordinately important role in the trilogy, and the most crucial events are at once represented and shown as irrecoverable by their being invoked rhetorically rather than actively staged.

Schiller makes rhetorical and structural choices quite similar to that of *The Thin Red Line,* and the similarity is particularly evident in the first play, *Wallenstein's Camp.* Here no one voice dominates, and the prologue and play indeed read and play like the fragments of one large soul speaking in turn. At one point a soldier says that the army is a Gargantua with a life of his own, and in the *Camp* there is the sense that the soldiers are spare parts of a giant self speaking:

> Don't we all look hewn from a single block?
> Don't we stand united against the foe
> As if we were molded and glued in a row?
> Don't we mesh like cogwheels as near as you please?
>
> (*WC* 32)

> Sehn wir nicht aus, wie aus einem Span?
> Stehn wir nicht gegen den Feind geschlossen,
> Recht wie zusammen geleimt und gegossen?

Greifen wir nicht wie ein Mühlwerk flink
In einander, auf Wort und Wink?

(8:42)

The panoply of soldiers go through the motions of drinking, joking, wrangling about goods, and arguing about politics, but, preponderantly, they describe an empty and devastated present torn loose from any shared sense of past, and seemingly devoid of personal memory other than the last skirmish. The first Hunter tersely reminiscences:

You have it snug here. Our life of late
In enemy lands was mighty grim fare.

(*WC* 14)

Ihr sitzt hier warm. Wir, in Feindes Land,
Mußten derweil uns schlecht bequemen.

(8:17)

Collective memory seems to have been boiled down to the following formulation, as the Dragoner notes:

Freedom has vanished from out of the land,
Only masters and slaves will you find;
Deceit and treachery now command
Among craven human kind

(*WC* 40)

Aus der Welt die Freiheit verschwunden ist,
Man sieht nur Herren und Knechte;
Die Falschheit herrschet, die Hinterlist
Bei dem feigen Menschengeschlechte.

(8:52)

Schiller's point throughout *Camp* is a simple but devastating one, relent-lessly repeated and varied: the victims of the Thirty Years War—and all are victims—*have* no collective memory. Their sense of the past has been reduced to what happened yesterday. They have no real, lived recollection of a time of peace, and as a result the past is a cipher—an empty and dead letter, a land-scape of absences. The soldiers' present identity consists only in their shared participation in a greater, military, and overtly phallic power. Speaking for all in one collective male voice, the Sergeant affirms the masculine, phallic power of the army through the emblem of the stick:[10]

80

This coat that I have on
Has the force of the Emperor's own baton.
From that baton all government
On earth, you know, takes its descent;
And the scepter in the royal hand
Is just a baton you understand.
Once a man gets Corporal in front of his name
He has started the ladder to supreme fame
And power. You too can reach that height.

(*WC* 21)

In diesem Rock
Führ' ich, sieht Er, des Kaisers Stock.
Alles Weltregiment, muss Er wissen,
Von dem Stock hat ausgehen muessen;
Und das Zepter in Königs Hand
Ist ein Stock nur, das ist bekannt.
Und wers zum Korporal erst hat gebracht,
Der steht auf der Leister zur höchsten Macht,
Und so weit kann Ers auch noch treiben.

(8:27)

"I HAVE SEEN ANOTHER WORLD"

From this sea of voices—undifferentiated in their imprisonment in a horrible present—voices of memory do emerge and speak with particular force in the second play, *The Piccolomini*. Here the past as officially understood by the government—history as ideology—and history as understood by the army clash with yet another, altogether different notion of what history is and what it in fact signifies.

The Imperial Ambassador Questenberg, for whom the past is reduced to its positive or negative impact on the throne, represents official history in its clearest form:

The sword has made the Emperor poor; it is
The plow that must restore him to his strength.

(*TP* 1.2.49–50)

Der Degen hat den Kaiser arm gemacht;
Der Pflug ists, der ihn wieder stärken muß.

(8:65)

Butler, the eventual murderer, affirms a counterclaim—namely that history
was made by Wallenstein, and that before him was nothing:

> —The army did not yet exist. And Friedland
> Created it. No question of receiving.
> He *gave* it to the Emperor! We did not get
> Our Wallenstein as leader from the Emperor.
> Not so, not so at all.
>
> (*TP* 1.2.53)

> —Noch gar nicht war das Heer. Erschaffen erst
> Mußt es der Friedland, er *empfing* es nicht,
> Er *gabs* dem Kaiser! Von dem Kaiser nicht
> Erhielten wir den Wallenstein zum Feldherrn.
> So ist es nicht, so nicht!
>
> (8:69)

Butler and Questenberg dispute the origin, but both articulate a similar view
of the past. The present is shaped by great men who—God-like—create situations, mold lesser men, and require loyalty, service, and sacrifice. Both articulate values of the heroic and the grand, of patriarchal power and of
unquestioning obedience to the supreme leader.

It is—ironically—Octavio Piccolomini, the weathered, pragmatic, and
Machiavellian general, who briefly indicates that the past may be informed by
more complicated forces than that of single individuals. He shares his surprise
at being one of Wallenstein's intimates and launches briefly into a very different
vision of the past:

> I don't know what it is—that draws and binds him
> So mightily to me and to my son.
> We always had been friends, brothers in arms:
> Long habit and adventures shared brought us
> Together early,—yet I can single out
> The day when all at once his heart to me
> Was opened and his trust in me grew strong.
> It was the morning of the Luetzen battle—
> Some evil dream drove me to seek him out
> And offer him a different horse to ride
> That day. Far from the tents, beneath a tree,
> I found him fast asleep.
>
> (*TP* 1.3.56)

> Ich weiß nicht, was es ist—was ihn an mich
> Und meinen Sohn so mächtig zieht und kettet.

82

Wir waren immer Freunde, Waffenbrüder;
Gewohnheit, gleichgeteilte Abenteuer
Verbanden uns schon frühe—doch ich weiß
Den Tag zu nennen, wo mit einemmal
Sein Herz mir aufging, sein Vertrauen wuchs.
Es war der Morgen vor der Lützner Schlacht—
Mich trieb ein böser Traum, ihn aufzusuchen,
Ein ander Pferd zur Schlacht ihm anzubieten.
Fern von den Zelten, unter einem Baum
Fand ich ihn eingeschlafen.

    (8:73)

Octavio's memory proceeds through layers of reminiscence, becoming increasingly time-specific and personal. As his memory focuses on a particular day and moment, Octavio's past surfaces as image, the picture of Wallenstein asleep beneath a tree, which pictorially encapsulates his own individual lived experience. This treatment of the past is at odds with generalities of both Butler and Questenberg. It is a past that lives on in the psyche of the rememberer and whose persisting emotional impact guides the present. Octavio tells us that this was the moment in which his own trust in Wallenstein faded, even as the other man made a very different decision:

And when I woke him
Recounting dubious fears, he gazed
At me in long astonishment, then fell
Upon my neck displaying such emotion
As that small service could not have deserved.
And since that day his confidence pursues me
In equal measure as mine flees from him.

    (*TP* 1.1.56)

Als ich ihn
Erweckte, mein Bedenken ihm erzählte,
Sah er mich lange staunend an; drauf fiel er
Mir um den Hals, und zeigte eine Rührung,
Wie jener kleine Dienst sie gar nicht wert war.
Seit jenem Tag verfolgt mich sein Vertrauen
In gleichem Maß, als ihn das meine flieht.

    (8:73)

We come upon yet another instance of a strong homoerotic moment emerging in Schiller's work—as it does between Posa and Don Carlos—which is then both violently denied and corrected by behavior going in the opposite direction. Paradoxes abound: Octavio forcefully declares that he does not understand why Wallenstein so favors him and his son, only to completely change his mind a few lines later—delivering a memory so vivid that it seems doubtful it has ever been forgotten; he subsequently tells us he fears and distrusts the extravagant emotionalism of the awakened Wallenstein. Yet, it is he, Octavio, who is troubled by "evil dreams" about the commander. The dream—which is never described—propels him out of doors avidly seeking the commander whose sleeping image he contemplates in a secluded spot. And Wallenstein's gaze—what does it reveal? And how does Octavio return that gaze? We do not know.

In this manner Octavio's narrative points to the odd conflicting boundaries on male-male relations that occur between men at war as Klaus Theweleit describes them (2:164ff.). Since these relations are based on strict hierarchy and discipline, rather than on pleasure, Wallenstein's embrace is transgressive in at least two ways: it violates hierarchy, and it derives from emotion and may provide pleasure—for one, if not for both, of them. That Octavio has mixed feelings about this may be ascertained from his sudden about-face—from absolute, blind devotion and adulation to repulsion, mistrust, and eventual betrayal.

This is a particularly interesting moment in the play cycle since it is Octavio who, of all the main characters of the play, behaves with consistent appeals to rationalism, moderation, good sense, and strict adherence to social codes and rules. But through Octavio, *The Piccolomini* suggests to its audience early on that odd unspoken desires and feelings seem to circulate among the soldiers. If a model officer is driven to act in the present by an intimate moment that obsesses him but whose ramifications he cannot fully admit to, or even (appropriately) fully remember, then military men are *not*—for all their rhetoric—simple war machines. Rather, Schiller suggests that soldiers are pathological creatures, operating on the basis of motives they do not understand. And he also, subversively, points to the submerged homoeroticism that may circulate between these apparent paragons of unproblematic masculinity.

This sense that the past may not be what we think it is and may not work the way we supposed it would intensifies in the following scene, in which Octavio and Questenberg are joined by Max. In this arresting conversation, conflicting references to and understandings of the past abound. Questenberg argues that Wallenstein's fault lies in his "forgetting" his own past, as servant to the emperor (Passage 234), while Octavio stresses the importance of "ancient ordinances" (235)—laws and regulations from the past that are necessary to govern the wayward travelers of the present. But Max Piccolomini immediately reveals himself to be at odds with both these formulations, stressing at once the complexity of the present—its fullness, its ability to challenge individuals in new and unprecedented ways—and a passionately felt, deeply personal sense of the past:

84

In
The field, the present moment presses,—here
One will must give command, one eye must see.
The General uses Nature's every greatness:
Allow him then to live amid her great
Conditions. He must ask the oracle,
The vital oracle within his heart,
He must not ask dead books and moldy papers
And ancient ordinances for his guidance.

(*TP* 1.4.59)

Im Felde
Da dringt die Gegenwart—Persönliches
Muß herrschen, eignes Auge sehn. Es braucht
Der Feldherr jedes Große der Natur,
So gönne man ihm auch, in ihren großen
Verhältnissen zu leben. Das Orakel
In seinem Innern, das lebendige,
Nicht tote Bücher, alte Ordnungen,
Nicht modrighte Papiere soll er fragen.

(8:77)

Max affirms and poetically expresses the heat of the moment, the vi-
brancy of experience that is sensual and immediate, at once a pulse one feels
within oneself and a vivid image that one has to see for oneself truly to feel
and, through feeling, know.

Both Octavio and Questenberg dismiss this understanding of the present, again rooting their disapproval in yet another interpretation of the past.
Octavio claims that Max's limited personal history determines his understanding of the present—invalidating it:

The child of the camps speaks with your voice, my son.
You have been formed by fifteen years of war.
You never knew a time of peace.

(*TP* 1.4.60)

Das Kind des Lagers spricht aus dir, mein Sohn.
Ein fünfzehnjähriger Krieg hat dich erzogen,
Du hast den Frieden nie gesehn!

(8:78)

According to his father, Max cannot speak with any authority about the
present, because his understanding is contextualized and limited by the past;
Max's adulation of Wallenstein is seen as overdetermined by his "schooling" in

85

the theater of war. Knowing nothing else, Max cannot fully appreciate how terrible war is, according to Octavio:

> In war itself the final goal is still not war.
> The swift and might deeds of violence
> And the astounding marvels of an instant,
> It is not these that make our happiness,
> That found serene and massive permanencies.
> In haste and flurry will a solider build
> His flimsy canvas city; in a twinkling
> There is a noise and movement to and fro,
> The market bustles, roads and rivers are
> Bedecked with cargoes, business is astir.
> And then one morning suddenly the tents
> Are struck, and onward moves the horde to leave
> The field deserted like a death-still graveyard,
> With seeded grain all trampled and no hope
> Remaining for the harvest of the year.

> (*TP* 1.4.60)

> Im Kriege selber ist das Letzte nicht der Krieg.
> Die großen, schnellen Taten der Gewalt,
> Des Augenblicks erstaunenswerte Wunder,
> Die sind es nicht, die das Beglückende,
> Das ruhig, mächtig Daurende erzeugen.
> In Hast und Eile bauet der Soldat,
> Von Leinwand seine leichte Stadt, da wird
> Ein augenblicklich Brausen und Bewegen,
> Der Markt belebt sich, Straßen, Flüsse sind
> Bedeckt mit Fracht, es rührt sich das Gewerbe.
> Doch eines Morgens plötzlich siehet man
> Die Zelte fallen, weiter rueckt die Horde,
> Und ausgestorben, wie ein Kirchhof, bleibt
> Der Acker, der zerstampfte Saatfeld liegen,
> Und um des Jahres Ernte ists getan.

> (8:78)

And yet what is being described here? Then or now? Octavio's own description confuses temporal distinctions through its use of the epic present—a rhetorical gesture that displays Octavio's own ambivalence toward the war machine. He claims on one hand that war is a necessary evil and yet, as the speech progresses, Piccolomini Sr. becomes lost in and fascinated by his own description of the hustle and bustle of army life; the army camp becomes for him a moveable city that brings vitality and commerce to the locale it inhabits. The disappearance of that city (again the dramatic stress is on absenting) drains the area of its vitality—leaving behind a wasteland that resembles a graveyard. Thus, despite his insistence that there is more to life than war, Octavio himself can neither remember nor indeed imagine anything else. Despite himself, he becomes enthralled by the very image he wants to dismiss.

In contrast to his seemingly mature and wise father, Max can indeed counter that image of war with the image of peace. At once personal and general, Max's response links the individual with the universal, for his memory is grounded in a set of recent observations and encounters:

> You say I never knew a time of peace?
> O father, but I have, I have! Just now—
> I have just come from it.—My way took me
> Through countries where the war has never been.—
> O life has lovely aspects, father
> That we have never known.—We have but edged
> Around the dreary coasts of lovely life
> Like vagrant predatory pirate folk.
>
> (*TP* 1.4.60)

> Ich hab den Frieden nie gesehn?—Ich hab ihn
> Gesehen, alter Vater, eben komm ich—
> Jetzt eben davon her—es führte mich
> Der Weg durch Länder, wo der Krieg nicht hin
> Gekommen—o! das Leben, Vater
> Hat Reize, die wir nie gekannt.—Wir haben
> Des schönen Lebens öde Küste nur
> Wie umirrend Räubervolk befahren. . . .
>
> (8:78–79)

Max affirms the power of recent memory and dismisses the warrior as a predator, a seafaring criminal who lurks on the margins of real and beautiful life. As his speech progresses it emphasizes—in specific, personal, and autobiographical terms—the effect of war and the individual psyches of the men who live it:

> This was the first real leisure of my life.
> Tell me, what is the goal and prize of this
> Ungrateful work that has robbed me of my youth
> And left my heart all bleak and left my mind
> Unstirred and unadorned with any training?
> The thronging hurly burly of this camp,
> The neighing horses and the trumpets' clangor,
> The clocks monotonously set for service,

87

WAR PHOTO/GRAPHS

The weapon drills, the shouting of commands—
The parched heart profits nothing from all these,
This wretched business has no soul . . .

(TP 1.4.61)

Es war die erste Muße meines Lebens.
Sag mir, was ist der Arbeit Ziel und Preis,
Der peinlichen, die mir die Jugend stahl,
Das Herz mir öde ließ und unerquickt
Den Geist, den keine Bilding noch geschmücket?
Denn dieses Lagers lärmendes Gewühl,
Der Pferde Wiehern, der Trompete Schmettern,
Des Dienstes immer gleichgestellte Uhr,
Die Waffenübung, das Kommandowort,—
Dem Herzen gibt es nichts, dem lechzenden.
Die Seele fehlt dem nichtigen Geschaeft . . .

(8:79)

Max clearly and forcefully elucidates the experience of war in terms of *time*; linear time malfunctions in war, and this time warp further warps the solider psychically through a series of telling contradictions. War, Max tells the older men, has made him prematurely old, and yet both his intellect and emotions have been retarded, leaving him immature and stunted. Time stops in the camp, and the activities repeat in a never-ending infernal circle—starving him emotionally and eventually killing off his very soul. If noise and action represent meaningful activity and progress for Octavio, these same phenomena incarnate antimeaning for Max. He argues that the soldier is at once infantilized and withered by the war experience. The clocks of the military exhaust, deaden, and paralyze.

Max's description exactly matches Judith Herman's analysis of the "chronic trauma" experienced by prisoners of all kinds. Facing the extreme on a day-to-day basis, prisoners develop strangely constricted psychological non-relationships with both the past and future:

> Thinking of the future stirs up such intense yearning and hope that prisoners find unbearable; they quickly learn that these emotions make them vulnerable to disappointment and that disappointments will make them desperate . . . The future is reduced to a matter of hours or days. Alternations in time sense begin with the obliteration of the future but eventually progress to the obliteration of the past . . . Thus prisoners are eventually reduced to living in an endless present. Primo Levi . . . describes "for living men, the units of time always have a value. For us, history has stopped." (Herman 89)

Max's speech makes the astonishing suggestion that the solider is himself a captive of the military camp rather than its thriving warrior-agent. The inhabitants of the *Lager* have no sense of time because they suffer from the chronic trauma, which will also plague concentration camp inmates, POWs, and all political prisoners. Thus, time is meaningless for the soldiers because the business of war and the military experience have blotted out all sense of temporality other than repetition, as the image of the clocks makes plain. Unrooted from the past, unable to remember, and blocked from the future, unable to hope, the soldier's psyche is squeezed shut, like the prisoners in Herman's description. In this way, Max—and Schiller with him—suggests that every solider is a trauma victim: locked into a state of warped temporal constriction, constant hyper-arousal, exhaustion, and distress.

Max understands the deadly mechanisms of military life because he has seen the alternative—the place where war has not been—and more significantly, because he has made a deep personal connection with someone he met in his travels. Through meaningful emotional interaction with another, Max is able to move out of trauma and regain a sense of timefulness. Consequently, against Octavio's picture of the war camp city, Max pits his vision of a city at peace—a vision of the future, which recuperates, as the final lines suggest, his recent encounter with Thekla, with whom he has fallen in love:

> O happy day when finally the soldier
> Comes home to life and to humanity,
> When in the glad procession flags unfurl
> And homewards plays the gentle march of peace . . .
> The walls around are crowded full of people,
> With peaceful people who shout up to the sky,
> Clear ring the bells from all the towers sounding
> Happy Vesper to the bloody day . . .
> Then, glad that he has lived to see the day,
> The old man shakes his son's hand coming home;
> He comes a stranger to his native place
> That he left long ago; and his return
> Is shaded by the tree with boughs grown broad
> That once bent down for sticks when he departed;
> And modestly the maiden comes to meet him
> Whom last he saw upon her nurse's arm.
> O happy he for whom a door is opened,
> For whom arms open in a sweet embrace.
>
> (*TP* 1.4.61–62)

> O schöner Tag! wenn endlich der Soldat
> Ins Leben heimkehrt, in die Menschlichkeit,

Zum frohen Zug die Fahnen sich entfalten,
Und heimwärts schlägt der sanfte Friedenmarsch. . . .
Von Menschen sind die Wälle rings erfüllt,
Von friedlichen, die in die Lüfte grueßen—
Hell klingt von allen Türmen das Geläut,
Des blutgen Tages frohe Vesper schlagend.
Aus Dörfern und aus Städten wimmelnd strömt
Ein jauchzend Volk, mit liebend emsiger
Zudringlichkeit des Heeres Fortzug hindernd—
Da schüttelt, froh des noch erlebten Tags,
Dem heimgekehrten Sohn der Greis die Hände.
Ein Fremdling tritt er in sein Eigentum,
Das längstverlaßne, ein, mit breiten Ästen
Deckt ihn der Baum bei seiner Wiederkehr,
Der sich zur Gerte bog, als er gegangen,
Und schamhaft tritt als Jungfrau ihm entgegen,
Die er einst an der Amme Brust verließ.
O! glücklich, wem dann auch sich eine Tür,
Sich zarte Arme sanft umschlingend öffnen.

(8:79–80)

While Octavio confuses past and present, Max uses the epic present tense with full awareness of its rhetorical significance. Rerooted in memory, Max uses his personal past—namely his encounter with Thekla—to build outward toward a grand future vision so possible, so necessary, and so passionately wished for that he articulates it as if he could see it in front of his eyes. In Max's view of futurity—which skillfully reiterates Homer's description of the city at peace in the shield of Achilles in Homer's *The Iliad*—time returns to its proper functioning. The father has grown old, the sapling has become a tree, and the young girl has become a woman. The ripeness of nature paves the way for the sexual maturation of the beloved, whose arms open like the door of the domicile that the returning solider will share with his presumed wife-to-be.

The soldier embracing the maiden complements and corrects the earlier tainted embrace of Octavio and Wallenstein. For Max, and for Schiller as well, the return from the army represents also a return to an unproblematic, self-evident heterosexuality—man returning from the public sphere to greet woman on the threshold of the private. The father is repositioned not as companion at arms but as gatekeeper; he is the welcoming and aging patriarch, who paves the way for the young man's union with woman.

Love, the play seems to suggest—in particular, romantic heterosexual love—frees the prisoner of trauma and enables the soldier once again to become a full human being, to return to the state of complete "humanity." In this series of speeches Max envisions the two crucial steps of trauma recovery: first, remembrance and mourning of the traumatic experience(s), and second, the reconnection with ordinary life (Herman 155). Of all Schiller's traumatized protagonists, it is Max who understands most clearly what has happened to him, and because he is able to remember, he can move on and "see differently."

In this way Max enthusiastically envisions a society at peace, where families are reunited, and where love prospers and grows. Remarkably his, and later, Thekla's, are the only voices in the entire trilogy that affirm possibility, emotionality, freedom, sexuality, and futurity. Momentarily swept away by the power of Max's rhetoric, even Questenberg murmurs dreamily: "O why must it be of a far, far time / You speak, not of today, not of tomorrow!" (62) [O! daß Sie von so ferner, ferner Zeit, / Und nicht von morgen, nicht von heute sprechen!] (80).

"I WAS A PRISONER. YOU SET ME FREE."

Profoundly attached to another human being through love, Max divorces himself from the life of the army, from his faith in the project of war:

> . . . have all things here changed,
> Or is it only I? . . .
> I seem to find myself
> As if among mere strangers. Not a trace
> Of all my former wishes and my joys.
> Where have these things all vanished?
>
> (*TP* 3.3.91)

> Ist denn alles hier
> Verändert, oder bin nur ichs? Ich sehe mich
> Wie unter fremden Menschen. Keine Spur
> Von meinen vorgen Wünschen mehr und Freuden.
>
> (8:117)

Since to feel differently is to see differently, Max now seeks out new images, different pictures, and finds, appropriately, not the masculine image of war but the feminine portrait of peace:

> There is a cloister there, The Heaven's Gate,
> And there I went, and there I was alone.
> Above the altar hung a Blessed Virgin,
> A wretched painting, but it was the friend
> Whom I was searching for just at that moment.
> How often I have seen the Glorious One

In all her splendor, ardor of adorers—
Yet went myself untouched; now suddenly
I sensed their piety, as I sensed love.

(*TP* 3.4.92)

Es ist ein Kloster hier, zur Himmelspforte,
Da ging ich hin, da fand ich mich allein.
Ob dem Altar hing eine Mutter Gottes,
Ein schlecht Gemälde wars, doch wars der Freund,
Den ich in diesem Augenblicke suchte.
Wie oft hab ich die Herrliche gesehn
In ihrem Glanz, die Inbrunst der Verehrer—
Es hat mich nicht gerührt, und jetzt auf einmal
Ward mir die Andacht klar, so wie die Liebe.

(8:118)

Despite the inferiority of the likeness, Max is able to understand the picture of the Virgin Mary, for he brings to it his own appreciation for peace and his own love of an individual woman.

When Thekla, Wallenstein's daughter, enters into private conversation with Max (her first scene without her father) it is clear that she shares Max's interests in the image. Her speech reiterates Max's and more explicitly juxtaposes war with love. Like Max, Thekla recounts what she has just seen:

Half-circle wise were ranged around me six
Of seven mighty effigies of Kings . . .
The furthest one, a peevish, grim old man
With a star of murky yellow, that was Saturn;
He of the ruddy glow just opposite
And clad in warlike armor, that was Mars,
And both bring little happiness to men.
But at his side a lovely lady stood,
A softly shimmering star upon her head,
And that was Venus, the star-form of joy.

(*TP* 3.4.97)

In einem Halbkreis standen um mich her
Sechs oder sieben grosse Koenigsbilder . . .
Der aeusserste, ein graemlich finstrer Greis,
Mit dem truebgelben Stern, sei der *Saturnus,*
Der mit dem roten Schein, grad von ihm ueber,
In kriegerischer Ruestung, sei der *Mars,*
Und beide bringen wenig Glueck den Menschen.
Doch eine schoene Frau stand ihm zur Seite,

Sanft schimmerte der Stern auf ihrem Haupt,
Das sei die *Venus,* das Gestirn der Freude.

    (8:123)

Joining Christian and pagan imagery, Thekla's memory compliments that of her lover, and the discussion that ensues suggestively posits the connection between erotic love and the original emotions of childhood—thereby establishing a link between the love of the beloved and the love of one's mother:

> . . . Deeper meaning
> Lies in the fairy tales of childhood years
> Than in the truth which later life imparts.
> The happy world of miracles alone
> Provides an answer to the heart's delight
> And opens its eternal realms to me,
> Extending toward me all its thousand branches
> Wherein the rapt soul blissfully is cradled . . .
> The ancient fable creatures are no more,
> The lovely race has emigrated; yet
> The heart requires some form of speech; the ancient
> Impulse brings us back the ancient names.

    (*TP* 3.4.97)

> . . . und tiefere Bedeutung
> Liegt in dem Märchen meiner Kinderjahre,
> Als in der Wahrheit, die das Leben lehrt.
> Die heitre Welt der Wunder ists allein,
> Die dem entzückten Herzen Antwort gibt,
> Die ihre ewgen Räume mir eröffnet,
> Mir tausend Zweige reich entgegen streckt,
> Worauf der trunkne Geist sich selig wiegt. . . .
> Die alten Fabelwesen sind nicht mehr,
> Das reizende Geschlecht ist ausgewandert;
> Doch eine Sprache braucht das Herz, es bringt
> Der alte Trieb den alten Namen wieder . . .

    (8:124)

In terms that are highly reminiscent of Schiller's valorization of the child in *On Naïve and Sentimental Poetry,* Max declares the love between man and woman returns the individual to a more original love—coded as maternal through the image of rocking. This love in turn places him in communication with the primordial cultural forces that first united human beings in language and in civilization.

This primordial language—the literal mother tongue—is also the language of the heart, and it is this language that Max and Thekla proclaim in this scene. As they converse, each redefines and enriches his and her notions of sexuality and identity. If Max is to turn from war, to become more interested in the world of the child, Thekla asserts herself openly as the lover as well as the beloved, expressing a vision of active reciprocity, feminine courage, and passionate sensuality:

> Are we not happy now? Are you not mine?
> Am I not yours? There lives within my soul
> A lofty courage given me by love.
> I ought to be less open and conceal
> My heart more from you; custom so requires.
> But where would any truth be for you here
> If you were not to find it on my lips?
> We have now found each other, hold each other
> In close embrace forever.
>   (*TP* 3.6.100)

> Sind wirs denn nicht? Bist du nicht mein? Bin ich
> Nicht dein?—In meiner Seele lebt
> Ein hoher Mut, die Liebe gibt ihn mir—
> Ich sollte minder offen sein, mein Herz
> Dir mehr verbergen, also wills die Sitte.
> Wo aber wäre Wahrheit hier für dich,
> Wenn du sie nicht auf meinem Munde findest?
> Wir haben uns gefunden, halten uns
> Umschlungen, fest und ewig, Glaube mir!
>   (8:128)

But as in *Line* and *The Terminator,* love is defeated by war in the WALLENSTEIN trilogy. Both Max and Thekla's passion for each other and their passionate shared vision of what human life can be are doomed. Other pictures proliferate and prevail, burying their images with other icons: Thekla knows this, and concludes at the end of act 3 that "This is no theatre where hope may dwell / Here rattles only muffled noise of war."(*TP* 3.7.106). [Das ist Kein Schauplatz, wo die Hoffnung wohnt, / Nur dumpfes Kriegsgetöse rasselt hier.] (8:135; *DP* 3.9) For all her youth, Thekla has no illusions about her father, or about the circle she travels in; she is, interestingly, more realistic than Max in this regard. Disenchanted with his own father, Max still adulates Wallenstein and believes that he may withdraw into private life, as he himself fervently wishes to. Repeatedly, he sees Wallenstein as a version of himself—as Thekla notices when he launches into a fervent admiring description of his prospective father-in-law:

> Max: He knows no guile, he hates a crooked path,
> He is so good, so noble—
> Thekla: Such are *you*!
>
> (TP 3.6.99)

> Max: Er soll mein Glück entscheiden, er ist wahrhaft,
> Ist unverstellt und haßt die krummen Wege,
> Er ist so gut, so edel—
> Thekla: Das bist du!
>
> (8:127)

Eventually, Max is disillusioned with both of his "fathers" and chooses duty over all other considerations. However, it is important to remember that Max's decision to remain true to his original oath of allegiance to the Emperor is taken under the guidance of Thekla. Realizing that the couple can never be married, Thekla chooses death over the sacrifice of their common vision. Both make a desperate choice, and immolate themselves as the only means to affirm their regard for each other as well their desire to be true to themselves in the deepest possible emotional sense, as Thekla aptly states: "As you are faithful to yourself, so will / You be to me" (DW 3.2.218) [Wie du dir selbst getreu bleibst, bist dus mir] (8:280).

Max's personal gesture of integrity actually results in a death, which is a direct rebuttal of the military ideal, as the captain's report of Max's end on the battlefield makes clear:

> We knew him
> By token of his helmet-plume and his
> Long hair—it had come down from rapid riding—
> He beckons toward the ditch. Himself the foremost,
> He spurs his noble steed to leap across it.
> The regiment comes rushing in its wake—
> But—then it happened. Pierced upon a pike
> His horse rears back in frenzy, hurls its rider
> Afar, and over him the violence
> Of steeds rides on, rebellious to the reins.
>
> (DW 4.10.243)

> Ihn machte
> Der Helmbusch kenntlich und das lange Haar,
> Vom raschen Ritte wars ihm losgegangen—

Zum Graben winkt er, sprengt, der erste, selbst
Sein edles Roß darüber weg, ihm stürzt
Das Regiment nach—doch—schon wars geschehn!
Sein Pferd, von einer Partisan durchstoßen, bäumt
Sich wütened, schleudert weit den Reiter ab,
Und hoch weg über ihn geht die Gewalt
Der Rosse, keinem Zügel mehr gehorchend.

(8:311)

Max's demise contradicts the warrior's mandate not to allow himself to be "laid low." "If the individual German is to remain upstanding, he must not be laid low [*sich niederlegen*]. Defeat (*Niederlage*, literally "being laid low") is out of the question . . . Being laid low in warfare was considered tantamount to the most monstrous of crimes; for if he allowed the dam to rupture, the man was ultimately forced to prostrate himself to Woman. Once soft, never hard again" (Theweleit 1:70). The description of Max's death reinforces precisely the qualities that Theweleit describes as unthinkable in a German soldier. Max's flowing hair, the plumed helmet, and his quick succumbing to the trampling horses suggest that Max has indeed offered himself to Woman in a poignant but nonheroic act of self sacrifice.

In his refusal to fight and his acceptance of a nonheroic death, Max completes his mission as a nonmilitary man—a man who concedes the victory to feminine earth. Thekla's reaction reinforces this. Rather than averting her eyes from the image of Max's fall on the battlefield, Thekla embraces the narrated picture of his obliteration, and codes it in aesthetic rather than in martial or heroic terms:

What is life led
Without love's radiance? . . .
In splendor lay
Before me a new and golden day,
I dreamed two hours of beauty heaven-shed . . .
Such is the lot of Beauty in the world.

(*DW* 4.13.247)

Was ist das Leben ohne Liebesglanz? . . .
Glänzend lag
Vor mir der neue goldne Tag!
Mir träumte von zwei himmelschönen Stunden . . .
Das ist das Los des Schönen auf der Erde!

(8:317–18)

Appropriately, Thekla's words trace Max's life as a photographic radiance—as light projected onto darkness.

"Where's your spark now?"

Max's death is a significant moment in *WALLENSTEIN* and in Schiller's theater of trauma. Surely the most realized of Schiller's young protagonists, Max is freed of the emotional excesses of Karl Moor, Fiesko, and Ferdinand von Walter, and is devoid of the paralyzing resentment of Franz Moor. He is also able truly to love and accept love—unlike the stunted Don Carlos—from both women and men, and is able to put them in their "proper" places. He lacks either the deranged fear of the father or insane adulation of the same that govern the others, and as a result he is able to resist the manipulative homosocial strategies of Wallenstein to force his loyalty.[11]

As we have seen, Max is able to remember and to name traumatic experience as that which it is—deadening, awful, and without redeeming feature. Thus, of all of Schiller's young male protagonists, it is Max who has the courage of his convictions—a conviction based on the heartfelt self-understanding of what is true for him, and this self-understanding inaugurates a very different perspective on what it means to be a both a man and a *good* man.

Yet, Max too is destroyed. Through Max's fate, Schiller makes the devastating suggestion that the road to personal recovery from trauma is always blocked by a society that conspires against the man who would fully be himself.[12] The culture of Wallenstein's world is always and only the culture of battalions, and this culture destroys all who see it differently, all who would make the world a different place. Like the visionary male nurse of *The Thin Red Line,* Max too dreams of "the glory"—the pulsating vitality and essential goodness of life. But that alternate view is snuffed out, and war continues.

Thus, the fictional introduction of Max and Thekla to the Wallenstein historical material skews the play's meaning in subversive directions. The placement of these characters so early in the drama, their prominence rhetorically, and the highlighted tragedy of Max's death suggest that, far from believing in the war it portrays, *WALLENSTEIN* not only questions the "rightness' of that war but indeed questions the value of any and all wars. Through Max's transformation from soldier to man of feeling, Schiller's trilogy repeatedly implies that violence does not and cannot ultimately resolve political conflict. Moreover, the cycle as a whole unrolls before our eyes a damning set of pictures of war experience and the military institution itself as purveyors of deep trauma. Seen from this point of view, the military camp as extension of the ideology of war becomes an atrocious machine not unlike the terrifying computer-guided robots of the *Terminator* films. As in the science fiction film, war becomes a systems-driven monster that kills off civilians and soldiers alike, that kills off personal history and will eradicate humanity if it gets the chance.

In this sense, *WALLENSTEIN* emerges clearly as a precociously anti-military, anti-authoritarian, anti-war drama. Accordingly, the mature soldiers of

WALLENSTEIN all betray the rigidity of post-traumatic stress, rather than any kind of productive wisdom gained from age and experience. The progressive deadening of the soul—to which Max referred at the beginning of *The Piccolomini*—has already taken place in Octavio, Isolani, and particularly in Butler, so obsessed with the honors that he has not received (which he tellingly feels as wounds to his ego) that he can no longer tell the difference between duty and atrocity.

> Contempt was something I could never bear
> It wounded me to see that birth and titles
> Had more weight in the army than true merit.
>
> (*DW* 2.2.173)

> Verachtung hab ich nie ertragen können.
> Es tat mir wehe, daß Geburt und Titel
> Bei der Armee mehr galten, als Verdienst.
>
> (8:222; *WT* 2.6)

All of the older characters—including the two women—exhibit the battle fatigue of the veteran: exhausted, prematurely aged, angry, paranoid.

But the most extreme example of the chronic trauma of the solider is clearly the title character himself, which is why he is elided so much from the center of the proceedings. As the person most in the hold of trauma, Wallenstein is also the most paralyzed, and the drama cannot move forward with him as the central character for the simple reason that he himself cannot take action.[13]

Shell-shocked rather than toughened, Wallenstein is withdrawn, melancholic, and obsessed with temporal circularity.[14] Insisting that history is really only a reflection of the predictable circular movement of the stars (*TP* 2.6), Wallenstein is neurotically stuck in the past—a past that alternates between glory days and days of shame and humiliation that repeat in the present:

> That was a time worth living in! Throughout the Empire
> No name was honored and exalted more
> Than mine.
>
> (*TP* 2.7.82)

> Das war noch eine Zeit! Im ganzen Kaiserstaate
> Kein Nam geehrt, gefeiert wie der meine.
>
> (8:105)

As opposed to:

Here
I stand once more abandoned, almost as
When I walked from the Diet of the Princes
At Regenspurg.
(*DW* 3.2.199–200)

Jetzt so verlassen wieder, als ich einst
Vom Regenspurger Fuerstentage ging.
(8:257; *WT* 3.3)

At his most honest, Wallenstein sees time in much the same way Max does—as deadening and horrifying repetition:

It is
The humdrum and the eternal yesterday,
What always was and always comes anew
What holds good for tomorrow just because
It held good for today.
(*DW* 1.4.143)

Das ganz
Gemeine ists, das ewig Gestrige,
Was immer war und immer wiederkehrt,
Und morgen gilt weils heute hat gegolten!
(8:185)

War too is a monstrous machine that has no need of him to grind onwards:

That it will, my loyal Isolan.
To ruin, everything we've built with care.
For all that, a General will be found
However, and an army will assemble
Around the Emperor when the drum roll sounds.
(*TP* 2.4.85–86)

Das wird es, treuer Isolan. Zu Truemmern
Wird alles gehn, was wir bedaechtig bauten.
Deswegen aber find't sich doch ein Feldherr,
Und auch ein Kriegsheer lauft noch wohl dem Kaiser
Zusammen, wenn die Trommel wird geschlagen.
(8:110)

Wallenstein's drum corresponds to Max's monotonous clocks: the continuous metronomes marking the temporal rhythms of war. Seen from this point of view, Wallenstein's Hamlet-esque inability to make a decision and act upon it paired with his fanatical belief in astrology represent yet other examples of the prisoner's weird relation with time—all symptoms of combat trauma.[15] "Constrictive symptoms also interfere with anticipation and planning for the future. Grinkder and Spiegel observed that soldiers in wartime responded to the losses and injuries within their group with diminished confidence in their own ability to make plans and take initiative, with increased superstitious and magical thinking, and with greater reliance on lucky charms and omens" (Herman 46).

Wallenstein's inability to deal with futurity and his belief that a part of him has died come across clearly in his reaction to Max's death:

> He is the happy one. He has concluded.
> For him there is no future any more . . .
> And yet I sense what I have lost in him,
> The flower has now vanished from my life,
> And cold and drab I see it lie before me.
> For he stood next to me like my own youth . . .
>
> (DW 5.3.258)

> Er ist der glückliche. Er hat vollendet.
> Für ihn ist keine Zukunft mehr . . .
> Doch fühl ichs wohl, was ich in ihm verlor.
> Die Blume ist hinweg aus meinem Leben,
> Und kalt und farblos seh ichs vor mir liegen.
> Denn er stand neben mir, wie meine Jugend . . .
>
> (8:333)

Small wonder that Wallenstein resigns himself easily and fatalistically to defeat and to dying. For such persons any respite from a simultaneously unbearable and inexpressible pain is devoutly to be wished:

> I wish to go and sleep a long, long sleep.
> The strain of these last days has been extreme.
>
> (DW 5.2.266)

> Ich denke einen langen Schlaf zu tun,
> Denn dieser letzten Tage Qual war groß.
>
> (8:343)

Wallenstein, like his descendent Sergeant Welsh, dreams of a state of not caring, of an indifference that would be "bliss."

In a manner that seems to recapitulate both William Blake and Jean Jacques Rousseau, Schiller uses the mature characters in WALLENSTEIN to drive home the notion that Experience does not understand what is at stake in the Thirty Years War or, for that matter, in human existence itself. But Innocence does understand. Throughout the play cycle Schiller repeatedly suggests that maturity is an illusion; age removes us from the most valuable and the most vital parts of ourselves. Moreover, as we age, our ethical sense weakens. We eventually collaborate with the social order that oppresses us, for we are no longer able to perceive the difference between what is and what could and should be. "They are what we once were" [Sie sind was wir waren] (*Schillers Werke* 20:414), observed Schiller in a discussion of children versus adults, composed during the same period, and it seems no coincidence that *On Naïve and Sentimental Poetry* prizes youth over age, direct experience over the repression and distortion of memory that maturity incurs. We die inside, Schiller suggests in the *Wallenstein* plays, because we live in a culture that *is structurally* traumatizing—which removes us from ourselves forcibly by inflicting inner wounds that we are then prevented from healing. What modern adult does not feel "that a part of himself/herself has died"? This fractured sense of self in which a crucial, living aspect feels to have been lost and killed, Herman tells us, is a common crucial feature of the trauma survivor's inner life (49).[16]

"What difference do you think you can make—just one man—in all this madness?"

There is no question that in many ways, WALLENSTEIN indirectly mirrors Schiller himself: the work's emphasis on death and destruction reflects the terrible destruction and decay of the author's own body, the definitive loss of his youth; it is also, one suspects, in no small measure a powerful rendering of his early miserable experiences at the militaristic Karlschule. Elsewhere I have observed that the process of writing the play series haunted Schiller, and it is not hard to see why ("Schiller, Time and Again"); he was writing about woundedness in the most explicit, clear terms of his career, and this must have been terrifying in and of itself.[17] Such comments as the following seem perfectly understandable in that context: "The material . . . is actually horrifying, and I must, with bitter labor, atone for the giddiness which led me to this choice" (Schiller to Körner, July 10, 1797) [Aber der Stoff . . . ist in der That abschreckend, und mit einer sauren Arbeit muss ich den Leichtsinn büßen, der mich bei der Wahl geleitet hat] (*Schillers Werke* 29:99). Remarkably however, much of the time Schiller *also* repeatedly expressed enormous emotional enthusiasm for what proved to be his longest and most difficult-to-realize theatrical project. Aware of the contradictions at play in his veritable obsession with the work, he

101

observed and marveled at the gap between his negative feelings for the subject matter and characters (except for Max) and his passion for the process of making the drama itself:

> I might almost say that the subject does not interest me. I have never united in my mind such coldness for my subject with such warmth for my work. Up to now I have treated the main character as well as the secondary characters with the pure love of the artist. But it is only for the character next to the main character, the young Piccolomini, that I have any personal sympathy. (Schiller to Goethe, November 28, 1796, Dieckmann 159)

> Beynahe möchte ich sagen, das Sujet interessiert mich gar nicht, und ich habe nie eine solche Kälte für meinen Gegenstand mit einer solchen Wärme für die Arbeit in mir vereinigt. Den Hauptcharacter so wie die meisten Nebencharactere tractiere ich wirklich biß jetzt mit der reinen Liebe des Künstlers; bloß für den nächsten nach dem Hauptcharakter, den jungen Piccolomini bin ich durch meine eisene Zuneigung interessiert. (*Schillers Werke* 29:15)

At the same time, Schiller seems to have recognized that *WALLENSTEIN* was connected to him personally in important, unprecedented ways, as he expressed to Charlote von Kalb, upon receipt of her letter admiring the Weimar production of *The Piccolomini*: "You have found me, and this makes me happy, for I have expressed my very essence in the entirety of this play" (January 31, 1799) [Sie haben mich gefunden, das freut mich, denn im *Ganzen* dieses Stücks habe ich mein Wesen ausgesprochen] (*Schillers Werke* 30:27). Even more intriguing is Schiller's complicated reaction to finishing the project. On one hand, the author seems to have felt a palpable sense of relief at finishing mingled with the desire to move on swiftly to a more cheerful topic, "I shall not feel tranquil until I see my thoughts turned once again with hope and inclination to a particular subject matter" (Schiller to Goethe, March 19, 1799) [. . . Ich werde nicht eher ruhig seyn, bis ich meine Gedanken wieder auf einen bestimmten Stoff mit Hofnung und Neigung gerichtet sehe] (*Schillers Werke* 30:39). But at the same time (and in the same sentence), Schiller expresses an agonized sense of loss—as though he were mourning the very process of creation that—now completed—would be lost to him forever:

> For a long time I dreaded the moment whose arrival I had wished for so much, namely to be rid of my work. And I do in fact find myself worse in my present freedom than in the previous slavery. The mass which attracted and held me up to now is suddenly gone, and I feel that I am hanging in airless space without a goal. At the same time I have the

feeling that it is absolutely impossible to be able to produce anything ever again. (Schiller to Goethe, March 19, 1799, Dieckmann 266)

Ich habe mich schon lange vor dem Augenblick gefürchtet, den ich so sehr wünschte, meines Werks los zu seyn; und in der That befinde ich mich bei meiner jetzigen Freiheit schlimmer als der bisherigen Sklaverei. Die Masse, die mich bisher anzog und fest hielt, ist nun auf einmal weg, und mir dünkt als wenn ich bestimmungslos im luftleeren Raume hienge. Zugleich ist mir, als wenn es absolut unmöglich wäre, daß ich wieder etwas hervorbringen könnte. (*Schillers Werke* 30:38–39)

What issues did the making of *WALLENSTEIN* raise for its brilliant, troubled, and now seriously ill author? It is tempting to speculate that the very act of creating this work about trauma was itself therapeutic for Schiller and that the process itself may have functioned as a both exhausting and invigorating writing "cure." The loss of such an opportunity may have felt devastating indeed, and Schiller suggests as much when he comments that the weight of the work seems to have anchored him psychologically. But whether or not writing worked in this way for the author, the completion of the text of *WALLENSTEIN* marked the definitive end to Schiller's brief vacation from financial care. Economic concerns were returning to the fore, and were now joined with serious ongoing health worries. Schiller would be, like Max Piccolomini, reconsigned to the monotonous clocks, not of the army but of literary labor for money, while his body experienced increasing discomfort and actual pain. And while after *WALLENSTEIN* Schiller turned resolutely toward dramatic writing about women, rather than men, he would not write so easily again, or with so much pleasure.

Seen in dialogue with the letters, Schiller's Wallenstein project may then be understood as a series of fragmented self-portraits linking him at once to Wallenstein the traitor (an identification that he earlier made with Franz Moor and Don Carlos), Max the idealist, and Octavio the Machiavellian collaborator—the three most prominent voices in the cacophony of war—a trio similar to the primary voices of *Line*. We have already seen that Schiller continually struggled between the opposing forces of his own idealism and his more pragmatic concerns with money, success, and reputation. Placed in this context, Max's love for two enemy "fathers" certainly resonates with Schiller's ongoing strenuous effort to reconcile these opposites.

We have also seen Schiller struggle—in *The Robbers,* in *Don Carlos,* and here—to express and resolve the complexities of the love between men, a love repeatedly established as a set of transgressive, erotically charged, and passionately felt experiences that must be overcome through heterosexuality.[18] In *WALLENSTEIN* this process of "overcoming" succeeds and yet, arguably, something else—a residue—remains. Is there really no such thing as "real" love between men? Do the patriarchal and the hierarchical always taint that love? These questions are never fully resolved in *WALLENSTEIN*, and after this project, Schiller would abandon this arena of dramatic investigation. Inter-male love is both thematized and repressed in the hero worship of the male citizens of *Wilhelm Tell*, but otherwise it is forgotten or transformed into mere competition—as it is in *Maria Stuart* and the *Bride of Messina*. The problem of male love is a mystery whose depths Schiller would no longer have the psychic and physical energy to plumb.

But to the work's credit, and to the author's, the *WALLENSTEIN* trilogy is also about so much more. Schiller's peculiar genius was the ability to understand (his own) personal pain, to give it voice, to translate it into large dimensions, and to articulate the connections between the psychological sufferings of the individual and the greater pathology of the society in which he lived and that we have inherited. *WALLENSTEIN* makes all those connections, etching light on the darkness of personal and collective trauma through words, "In the love stirred by Photography, another music is heard, its name oddly old-fashioned: Pity" (Barthes 116).

◀ CHAPTER 4 ▶

The Picture Palace of Dr. Schiller

Classicism, Commerce, and Silence
in *The Bride of Messina*

The choruses stand like echoing pillared halls . . . the whole is almost
architectural and made of stone; but they are sounding stone monuments
. . . The whole thing was immensely strange but you were soon reconciled
[to it] as with all well balanced architecture.

> *Brentano on a performance of* Bride

Sometimes the more nearly normal characters in their unnatural surroundings give an impression of incongruity, but this wears off after a time, and
in most of the scenes there is unity and vitality.

> New York Times *review of "The Cabinet of Dr. Caligari," April 4,
> 1921*

The rejection of an idea from consciousness is obstinately maintained, because it ensures abstention from action. . . . So the final form of the work
of repression . . . is a sterile and never-ending struggle.

> *Freud*

COMING ATTRACTIONS: CLASSICISM, EXPRESSIONISM, AND CALIGARI

In the famous German expressionist film, *The Cabinet of Dr. Caligari*, a
handsome somnambulist is held enthralled by an evil magician who displays
him like a puppet at fairs and carnivals. Once awakened, Cesare abducts a
beautiful woman, carrying her amidst the twisted rooftops of a pasteboard city.
The cramped quarters of the cityscape and Cesare's coffin give way at the end
of the film to the brilliant white neoclassical courtyard of the mental institution. The actors of the drama we have been witnessing prove to be inhabitants
of a beautiful and spacious sanatorium, and the evil magician proves to be the
wise and ever vigilant psychoanalyst, who hopes in the film's final sequence to
cure his beleaguered male patient, Francis, the seemingly sane teller of the tale
we have just viewed. Melodrama and the extreme emotional affect of the actors

105

PICTURE PALACE

are symbolically anesthetized and calmed by being housed within the architecture of psychiatry and a benevolent science, as well as within a cinematic master narrative in which even the strangest phenomena do, in the end, achieve coherence.

In his cogent reading of the film and the texts that surround it ("The Moments of *Caligari*"), Mike Budd argues that while *Caligari* has been characterized as an avant-garde work, the movie was in fact produced in the classic Weimar studio system and was consequently molded by that creative paradigm. Consequently, while the film negotiates a contradictory space between the discursive systems of modernism and expressionism, the film's narrative structure actually follows the rules and conventions of classical narrative; the plot includes such features as a search, a mystery, resolution, exchange of women, and narrative omniscience (Budd 11).

Moreover, the film's conclusion makes its "commitment" (in both senses of the word) to the classical through a telling articulation of the space to which the insane characters have themselves been consigned. The sanitorium scene serves several important purposes. It explains the story, contains madness, remarks distinctions between public and private, and erases the potentially subversive potential of female desire.[1] But equally significant is the fact that the courtyard of the sanitarium (the sanitarium is the only setting that appears in both frame and internal stories [Budd 46]) proposes a resplendent neoclassical architecture, grounded on a solar patterned flooring whose illuminating rays shoot out from the center. Thus, the final sequence of *Caligari* radically repositions the avant-garde, expressionist aesthetic of the film's narrative, placing it under the aegis of the grand and the traditional. Plot, visuals, filmic sequencing, and the film's highly successful exhibition in the grandiose neoclassical "picture palaces" of the 1920s situate *Caligari* within a narrative and spectatorial architecture that is neither expressionist nor modernist, but neoclassical.

Budd's reading of *Caligari* implies the strong connection between evocations of the classical and the emergence of mass media narrative—narratives meant to be desired and consumed by vast numbers of people. In order to attract a middle-class audience, the cinema had to insist relentlessly on cultural "value"—a legitimacy that could be posited through the invocation of the classical past. Siegfried Kracauer suggests as much in his observations of the New Berlin Cinema in his essay "Cult of Distraction: On Berlin's Picture Palaces" (1926): "To begin with, the architectural setting tends to emphasize the dignity which used to inhabit the institutions of high culture. It favors the lofty and the *sacral,* as if designed to accommodate works of eternal significance. . . . The show itself aspires to the same exalted level, claiming to be a finely-tuned organism, an aesthetic totality as only an artwork can be" (71). Later in this same essay, Kracauer astutely notes the connection between the cinema's "thespian" nostalgia and the—for him—insidious return of a "new idealist culture":

"Distraction—which is meaningful only as improvisation, as a reflection of the uncontrolled anarchy of our world—is festooned with drapes and forced back into a unity that no longer exists. Rather than acknowledging the actual state of disintegration which such shows ought to represent, they glue the pieces back together after the fact and present them as organic creations" (71). Kracauer sees the movies in Germany as part of a complicated cultural dynamic that makes money by two related maneuvers: the movies invoke the high art of the theater, and thereby appeal to a bourgeois audience; the movies then hermeneutically remove the viewers (through the process of watching the film) from the very real and pressing social problems in the public, political world that the audience inhabits. The appeal to the theater—in particular, a classically unified one—brings audiences out of the real, in Kracauer's opinion, and into an illusory and potentially paralyzing "idealist culture."

While Budd regards Kracauer's view of *Caligari* as simplistic in some ways, the former concurs with the latter's tracing the roots of the culture of distraction to the German philosophical movements of the late eighteenth and early nineteenth centuries. Moreover, Budd links Kracauer's critique of the movies with Herbert Marcuse's notion of "affirmative culture":

> By affirmative culture is meant the culture of the bourgeois epoch which led in the course of its own development to the segregation from civilization of the mental and spiritual world as an independent realm of value that is also considered superior to civilization. Its decisive characteristic is the assertion of a universally obligatory, eternally better and more valuable world that must be unconditionally affirmed: a *world essentially different from the factual world of the daily struggle for existence, yet realizable by every individual for himself "from within," without any transformation of the state of fact.* (Marcuse quoted in Budd 100, my italics)

The implications of Budd's argument are important and surprising: the consumption of cinema by bourgeois audiences is, according to Budd (relying on Kracauer), predicated upon a nostalgia for the classical theater and upon a desire for a hermeneutic of aesthetic values, which are independent of the workaday world in which modern people are increasingly enmeshed. Therefore, far from being antithetical, modern (the new, the original) and classical (the unified, the harmonious, and the old) aesthetics would appear to go hand in hand; they operate together to form a culture of consumerized forgetfulness for an upwardly mobile audience that seeks at once class—in the form of aesthetic "value"—and distraction from the pernicious realties of a life devoted to the pursuit of capital. In this manner, mass media intervene to at once vent and severely control and contain emotion—a dynamic already signaled by the events in the film.

PICTURE PALACE

FEATURE SHORT: FRIEDRICH SCHILLER AT WORK

The unlikely connections between mass media, classicism, modernism (in its extreme form of expressionism), Schiller's most relentlessly neoclassical play, and the texts that surround it anticipate German idealism, capital, and control. *The Bride of Messina* [*Die Braut von Messina*] and its con-texts stress concerns about finances, property, and acquisition, which are all forcibly contained within Schiller's obsession with establishing artistic legitimacy of a specific kind. Schiller's texts also concretize a problem only hinted at in Kracauer's and Marcuse's commentaries, and which *Caligari* thematizes through its passive and silenced mad characters. Both critics and the film itself gesture toward the muffled, halting, and eventually mute personal despair that lurks on the margins of consumer society. Capitalism, both Kracauer and Marcuse suggest, hurts. Schiller's efforts during this period of his life corroborate this impression and paint a portrait of a mature artist struggling against a silencing despair.

Schiller took up work on *The Bride of Messina* in 1802, in the wake of his mother's death and concerns about the distribution of her property. The reasons for working on this project were overtly material, as he explained to Körner:

> Instead of the long vacillation here and there between one subject and the other, I grabbed at this one first and for the following three reasons: (1) I was furthest along with my intention for the plan, which was very simple; (2) I needed a certain stamp of newness in the form and such a form that took a step nearer to ancient tragedy—which was really the case here, because the play really lends itself to Aeschylean tragedy; (3) I had to choose something that would not take a long time to finish, since I absolutely had to once again see something finished before my eyes after such a long pause. In any case, I must have the thing ready by the end of the year, because it is set to be performed at the end of January in honor of our Duchess's birthday. (September 9, 1802)

> Ueber dem langen Hin und HerSchwanken von einem Stoffe zum andern habe ich zuerst nach diesem gegriffen und zwar aus dreierlei Gründen: (1) war ich damit, in Absicht auf den Plan, der sehr einfach ist, am weitsten; (2) bedurfte ich eines gewißen Stachels von Neuheit in der Form und einer solchen Form die ein Schritt näher zur antiken Tragödie wäre, welches hier, wirklich der Fall ist, denn das Stück läßt sich wirklich zu einer äschylieschen Tragödie an; (3) mußte ich etwas wählen, was nicht de longue haleine ist, weil ich nach der langen Pause nothwendig bedarf, wieder etwas fertig vor mir zu sehen. Ich muß auf jeden Fall am Ende des Jahres damit zu Stande seyn, weil es Ende Januars zu Geburtstag unsrer Herzogin aufgeführt zu werden bestimmt ist. (*Schillers Werke* 31:159)

Schiller's explanation is curious; he enumerates three reasons but there seem to be four—all of which have to do with being in a hurry. Three of the four stress marketing and quick and easy production: he has made the most progress with this play, whose structure is simple—making it easy (and fast) to compose; it proposes something "new"; and it can be finished in time to be produced in honor of the duchess's birthday. In these moments, Schiller sounds indeed like a studio head, hoping to put out the latest spectacle in time for the Christmas holidays, and thereby increase both the play's intrinsic "value" (it achieves status as "art" because it was performed for the local ruling family) and its media hype. This sense is reinforced by Schiller's prompt enumeration in the following parts of the letter of his production schedule for the foreseeable future; here he articulates his excitement about *Wilhelm Tell*—an enthusiasm mixed with anxiety. Schiller is convinced that the work will please his audience, provided it can be constructed in the right way (*Schillers Werke* 31:160).

Throughout this period, Schiller's writing concerns itself with questions of money, the best venues for publication and distribution of his work, as well as negotiations as to how much he can now charge. As early as 1801, Schiller wrote Körner telling him that he was determined to demand greater financial compensation for his creations. But now he faced a new problem:

> But whatever I can gain in the way of bigger honoraria, I lose again through my thoughtfulness and slowness in working, and even at this instant what I should write about first hangs in the balance. (October 19, 1801)

> Aber was ich an größeren Honararen gewinnen könnte, das verliere ich wieder durch meine Bedenklichkeit und Langsamkeit im Arbeiten, und selbst in diesem Augenblick steht die Waage bei mir noch ein, was ich zuerst schreiben soll. (*Schillers Werke* 31:66)

This new trouble returns us to Schiller's cited third reason for working on *Bride*—the personal, urgent need to see something finished. Indeed, while Schiller's attitude toward his work seems to have developed into that of skilled salesman, it has also become that of a laborer on an unending assembly line. Even as his anxiety with a production schedule and details of publishing (including the type of paper to be used for printing) manifests itself in his correspondence to Cotta, Schiller's other letters repeatedly emphasize the onerous character of his own labor:

> The main thing is diligence; because this not only provides the means to live, but it also gives life its only value. I have worked for six weeks with zeal and I think with success. 1500 lines of The Bride of Messina are already finished. (Schiller to Körner, November 15, 1802)

> Die Hauptsache ist der Fleiß; denn dieser giebt nicht nur die Mittel des Lebens, sondern er giebt ihm auch seinen alleinigen Werth. Ich habe seit

sechs Wochen mit Eifer und mit Succeß, wie Ich denke, gearbeitet. Von
der Braut von Meßina sind 1500 Verse bereits fertig. (*Schillers Werke*
31:172)

Not inspiration but diligence has now become Schiller's watchword; this practice provides not only money but meaning as well. The poetic zealot [*Eiferer*]
has become a day laborer, a man who unceasingly works not only to make a
living but to *live* meaningfully at all. But, as this letter makes plain, meaning
and means have become hopelessly entangled; the playwright extols diligence
as "worth"—a monetary category inextricably connected to the spiritual and
the existential. This obsession with "worth" appears again in Schiller's dismis-
sive reaction to finally obtaining his patent of nobility; it matters little, he tells
Körner, ostensibly because it will not help him monetarily (November 29,
1802, *Schillers Werke* 31:177).

The style of Schiller's letters has visibly and dramatically changed. Once
florid and agitated, his sentences are more ordered, controlled, but also terribly
sad. No attainments seem to make him happy. Nothing matters but the anxious compulsion to work and earn. The lack of joy is palpable in places:

> It doesn't go so quickly on my end, because I am interrupted much too
> often by my uncertain health and insomnia and because of my incapaci-
> tated head, often must pause for weeks at a time. (Schiller to Körner,
> January 7, 1803)

> Bei mir geht es so rasch nicht, weil ich gar zu oft durch meine unstäte
> Gesundheit und Schlaflosigkeit unterbrochen werde und wegen zerstörten
> Kopfs oft Wochenlang pausieren muß. (*Schillers Werke* 32:1)

Even to Goethe, to whom he had written six months earlier of the pleasantness
of the writing exercise vis-à-vis *Bride* (to Goethe, August 18, 1802), he finally
admits, "I have a misbegotten and unhappy business, namely I have to fill in
the many still remaining holes in the four first acts" (to Goethe, January 26,
1803) [Ich habe ein mißliches und nicht erfreuliches Geschäft, nehmlich die
Ausfüllung der vielen zurückgelaßenen Lücken in den 4 ersten Akten] (*Schillers
Werke* 32:5).

In contrast to the massive blockage that Schiller encountered in the creation of *Don Carlos,* Schiller now suffers from the opposite problem; this play is
not a piled and blocked textual body with too much crammed into it but rather
a leaky and hole-ridden corpse that does not have all its vital organs. This body
must be filled up, as though Schiller were a mortician faced with the bullet-
ridden remains of a gangster whom he must somehow make aesthetically pleas-
ing in time for the funeral. Schiller, for the first time, appears to be at a literal

loss for words; he must struggle to find language, rather than throw it away, to bridge the gaps, to fill in the emptinesses.

In her book on depression and melancholy, Kristeva links sadness with both a profusion of traumas—physical and emotional (*Black Sun* 21)—and a declining ability to speak and use language. While linguistic creation, and particularly artistic creation, can work as a therapeutic device in resisting and triumphing over sadness (24), language can also work with and as sadness, revealing odd characteristics and tendencies. Often rhythmically and repetitively driven by what Kristeva calls "a denial of negation" (43), the language of perpetually sad people may manifest an obsessive, idealized relationship to the past:

> Massive, weighty, doubtless traumatic because laden with too much sorrow or too much joy, a *moment* blocks the horizon of depressive temporality or rather removes any horizon, any perspective. Riveted to the past, regressing to the paradise or inferno of an unsurpassable experience, melancholy persons manifest a strange memory: everything has gone by, they seem to say. But I am faithful to those bygone days, I am nailed down to them, no revolution is possible, there is no future. (60)

Certainly, such an "unsurpassable" past experience sets the wheels of *Caligari* in motion (the bulk of the film is a flashback), and the lost past—the utopian rule of the king and the lost daughter—drives the plot of *Bride* as well. But even more important, Kristeva's notion of the sad person's obsessed relation with an utterly lost past gives an insightful account for Schiller's self-conscious aesthetic turn to such a rigid form of neoclassicism at this point in his career. This aesthetic shift can be read—particularly in the context of the letters—as a desperate endeavor to find and use language derived from some other source. The sad artist will often do this, as Kristeva notes, when discussing the poetry of Nerval: "Sublimation is a powerful ally of the Disinherited, provided, however, that he can receive and accept another one's speech. As it happened, the other did not show up at the appointment. . . . Without a lyre this time, but alone in the night, under a street lamp" (172). Kristeva's evocation of Nerval as the poet on the modern street corner waiting in vain for a classical poet to meet him with a lyre—the instrument of Ancient Greek poetry—easily applies to Schiller's own efforts to absorb the ancients, particularly Aeschylus, during this period. The exchange between the playwright and Wilhelm von Humboldt regarding *Bride* talks about precisely such appropriation and reveals the complicated psychological dynamics underlying Schiller's supposed "affinity" with the classical:

> I have never forgotten, that you once called me the *most modern* of all new poets and that you also thought me to be in the greatest possible opposition to all that which is called ancient. It should therefore please me

111

doubly, if I could force from you the admission, that I can make even this foreign spirit my own. (Schiller to Humboldt, February 17, 1803)

Ich habe es nicht vergessen, daß Sie mich den *modernsten* aller neuern Dichter genannt und mich also im größten Gegensatz mit allem was antik heißt, gedacht haben. Es sollte mich also doppelt freuen wenn ich Ihnen das Geständniß abzwingen könnte, daß ich auch diesen fremden Geist mir habe zu eigen machen können. (*Schillers Werke* 32:11)

In this long letter (composed between February 17 and March 16, 1803) Schiller issues an aggressive and resentful challenge to his friend and admirer who was visiting Rome at the time. Insinuating that the appellation "modern" is insulting, Schiller insists—with no little hostility—that his friend change his mind, admit his error, and recognize Schiller's mastery of the Greek antique spirit. It is striking that Schiller cannot accept what is clearly meant as a flattering and sincere compliment; he must control the very terms by which he is artistically regarded.

Clearly, the writing of *Bride* was inspired by the desire to prove—among other things—that Schiller could work with the tenets of German neoclassicism.[2] But equally apparent are the vested interests in ownership and image-management that emerge from the letter to Humboldt. Schiller implies that he has paid his dues and has now earned full rights to an appropriation of classical identity, much as subscribers to the Weimar consumer catalogues could purchase and own copies of classical works of art. He is, he argues, literally entitled, to be called a classicist, and he demands to be considered such (and *only* such). In a clear rejection of the Bloomian anxiety of influence formula (whereby the son must kill the father [Bloom 36–37]), Schiller wants not to kill off the ancients but actively to merge identities with them: he wants to make their art his own ("daß ich auch diesen fremden Geist mir habe zu eigen machen können"), as though he were a New Age channeler, trying to call up the wisdom of the past, which will then speak *through* and *as* him. Through this absorption of the classical, the author claims he has become rejuvenated, "This new form has rejuvenated me, or rather the more Ancient has made me myself more old-fashioned, for true youth is nonetheless in olden times" (to Körner, November 15, 1802) [Die ganz neue Form hat mich verjüngt, oder vielmehr das antikere hat mich selbst alterthümlicher gemacht; denn die wahre Jugend ist doch in der alten Zeit] (*Schillers Werke* 31:172). By using the style of others, Schiller hopes to regain his youth, thereby recapturing his own past, and becoming the poet he once was.[3]

Tellingly, Schiller delays sending and almost withholds this letter, declaring its tone too "sad" to share.[4] Humboldt's affectionate response praises the author, while maintaining the modernist viewpoint and astutely critiquing the drama's aesthetic and the author's aim. He asks a key question:

The Bride of Messina

I long incredibly for it [the manuscript of Bride]. I am certain in advance
that your wrestling with the ancients was not in vain. But why do you
want to achieve only what the others have achieved? It is at once obvious
that we have more than they, and it is possible, to poetically express this
More. They *were* merely what they were.

Ich sehne mich unglaublich danach [the manuscript of Bride]. Ich bin im
voraus sicher, dass Ihr Ringen mit den Alten nicht vergebens gewesen
wird. Aber warum wollten Sie nur leisten, was jene leisteten? Es ist einmal
verkennbar, wir haben mehr als sie, und es ist möglich, dies Mehrere
poetisch darzustellen. Sie *waren* bloß, was sie waren. (Humboldt to Schiller, March 1803, Kraft 2:572–73)

While he seems to misunderstand Schiller's relation to the ancients (although
the image of the neurasthenic Schiller attempting to pin the likes of Sophocles
and Aeschylus to the ground is ludicrous enough to be playful), Humboldt
expresses his amazement at Schiller's desire to repeat classical accomplish-
ment—an aesthetic that he sees as severely lacking, as having and expressing
less than the modern. Humboldt understands that Schiller's classicism strips his
art down in certain ways and that the result is going to be less rather than
more.

The exchange between Schiller and Humboldt aptly highlights the problematic nature of *The Bride of Messina*; this work derives from the author's own
desperate contest to prove himself a classicist practitioner, to acquire and possess classicism, and to fill up his own empty artistic identity with the rhetoric
of Ancient writers. As Schiller attempts, more and more obsessively, to exert
control over his finances and schedules, so do creative words elude him. Appropriately, controlling both fate and the meaning of language will become the
operative problems in the play. *Bride* will procure Schiller his desired professed
identity as classicist, but at a high price: the private man himself disappearing
into the professional one, the man without qualities, frozen in stone.

PLEASE, No TALKING: A PALACE OF PICTURES, A THEATER OF STONE

Schiller performs this disappearing act in the strange essay that accompanied the publication of *The Bride of Messina*.[5] "On the Use of the Chorus in
Tragedy" [Ueber den Gebrauch des Chors in der Tragödie] is Schiller's last
significant theoretical discussion of the theater (Sharpe 283). It proposes the
retrieval of the classical aesthetic as a pharmakon for the German audience;
classical theater provides the aesthetic means to contain and control a depressed
bourgeois sensibility in retreat from the unfixable stresses of public life. Clearly
informed by the aesthetic stance enunciated by Lessing in his seminal essay

113

PICTURE PALACE

"Laocoon," Schiller's own essay is nonetheless a departure from Lessing's nostalgia for the pure art of the ancients, and reveals itself to be peculiarly modern in its proto-pharmaceutical approach to drama and the ways in which the theater may be deployed to act therapeutically upon an audience's psyche.[6]

Throughout the essay Schiller enlists not the rhetoric of classical drama—for all that this is what he claims to be doing—but rather the imagery of visual art and architecture. In these pages, tragedy emerges not as theatrical process but as visual result; not as action but as artifact that fixes movement through stasis, solidity, and the articulation of space: it is a naked sculpture, a richly colored painting, and, most important, a building, an edifice made of living material that closes in on itself, thanks to the crucial wall provided by the chorus. With these appeals to plastic and architectural arts, Schiller likens drama to an imaginary palace long closed and now restored and reopened by the poet. The condition of the palace has not only aesthetic but also indeed social and political ramifications, as the following description makes plain:

The palace of the kings is now closed; the judges have retreated from the gates of the city to the interior of houses; the letter has crowded out the living word; the people themselves, that materially living mass, has become the state,—unless it is acting as a raw force,—and hence has become an abstract principle; and the gods have returned to the bosoms of men. The poet must reopen the palaces, he must once again bring the judges forth beneath the open skies, he must establish the gods anew, he must restore everything that is direct and which has been abolished by the artificial arrangements of actual life, he must cast off all artificial contrivances in man and around man which hinder the manifestation of his inner nature and his original character, just as sculptors cast away modern garments and accept nothing of all external surroundings except what renders visible the highest of forms—the human form. (Passage, *Bride of Messina* 8)

Der Pallast der Könige ist jetzt geschlossen, die Gerichte haben sich von den Thoren der Städte in das Innere der Häuser zurückgezogen, die Schrift hat das lebendige Wort verdrängt, das Volk selbst, die sinnlich lebendige Masse, ist, wo sie nicht als rohe Gewalt wirkt, zum Staat, folglich zu einem abgezogenen Begriff geworden, die Götter sind in die Brust des Menschen zurückgekehrt. Der Dichter muss die Palläste wieder aufthun, er muß die Gerichte unter freien Himmel herausführen, er muss die Götter wieder aufstellen, er muss alles Unmittelbare, das durch die künstliche Einrichtung des wirklichen Lebens aufgehoben ist, wieder herstellen, und alles künstliche Machwerk *an* dem Menschen und *um* denselben, das die Erscheinung seiner innern Natur und seines ursprünglichen Charakters hindert, wie der Bildhauer die modernen Gewaender, abwerfen, und von allen äussern Umgebungen desselben nichts aufnehmen, als

114

was die Höchste der Formen, die menschliche, sichtbar macht. (*Schillers Werke* 10:11–12)

Schiller's palace is not only the architecture of princely art, but also indeed a site that houses governmental authority, the law, the gods, the nation, and the people as collective entity. Art, as Schiller has suggested already in the *Aesthetic Letters* [*Briefe über die ästhetische Erziehung des menschen*], changes reality; it drastically shapes and affects public life as well as public identity.

The reopening of the palace of art based on principles of classicism should promise to open up a utopian social creative space; the references to the law and the people and the pluralized repetition of the word "palace" indicates a successive unlocking of a multitude of grandiose spaces. But interestingly, as Schiller's argument approaches that possibility, his own writing retreats before it. The image of the poet as master builder immediately shrinks into an image of the sculptor. Likewise the palace dissolves into a row of emphatically human but imagistically undifferentiated statuary. During the course of this passage, Schiller's palace suddenly changes into a dusty warehouse of classical objects, a museum, and a mortuary. The festive reopening of the palace, and the reawakening of vital public life inaugurated by this newly unbarred architecture, literally retracts as the author writes, into the contemplation of sculptural detail, not of human beings, but of human forms (literally—forms that make the human visible).

The jerky movement of Schiller's imagery, which moves us triumphantly outward only to yank us back and in, anticipates Schiller's eventual explanation of the function of the chorus that is to provide the audience with—of all things—a sense of tranquility:

> Just as the chorus brings life to language, so does it bring calm into action—but the beautiful and lofty calm which must be the character of a noble work of art. For the spectator's feelings must retain their freedom even amid the most vehement passion; they must not be the victim of impressions, but rather they must come away serene and clear from the agitations sustained. (Passage, *Bride* 10)

> So wie der Chor in die Sprache *Leben* bringt, so bringt er *Ruhe*, in die Handlung—aber die schöne und hohe Ruhe die der Charakter eines edeln Kunstwerkes seyn muß. Denn das Gemüth des Zuschauers soll auch in der heftigsten Passion seine Freiheit behalten, es soll kein Raub der Eindrücke seyn, sondern sich immer klar und heiter von den Rührungen scheiden, die es erleidet. (*Schillers Werke* 10:14)

Thus, the "real" freedom that Schiller claims to want for his viewers consists not in political freedom but in a psychological self-control that literally rests

115

PICTURE PALACE

upon calm, an emotional serenity that "frees" the individual from the "blind power" of affect.[7] In "On the Use of the Chorus" Schiller proposes tragedy without pain, a theater not of cruelty or alienation but of relaxed quietude in the face of catastrophe and human suffering.[8] The drama's characters are likewise to incarnate such quiescence:[9]

> The tragic persons likewise have need of this respite, this calm, to collect themselves, for they are not real beings that merely obey the force of the moment and represent mere individuals, but ideal personages and representatives of their class. (Passage, *Bride* 11)

> Auch die tragischen Personen selbst bedürfen dieses Anhalts, dieser Ruhe, um sich zu sammeln; denn sie sind keine wirkliche Wesen . . . sondern ideale Personen und Repräsentanten ihrer Gattung . . . (*Schillers Werke* 10:14)

This model of audience response differs radically from that articulated by Aristotle and the Aristotelian tradition—of fear, pity, and catharsis. Similarly, while the ancient Greek chorus functioned as a literal and figurative intermediary in Greek drama—a human bridge that would integrate the audience with the noble characters on stage through the communication of key ideas—Schiller sees the chorus producing not identification but alienation.

In this manner, the invocation of classical architecture for the theater serves to impel the audience not toward public activity but rather in the opposite direction—toward a life of increased and renewed private repose. Thus, Schiller advocates the reintroduction of the ancient Greek chorus and neoclassical drama in general as a means to create an aesthetic experience that is meant to function something like a tranquilizer, which is meant to control and "manage" psychological pain.[10]

The necessity of the theater as pharmakon has already been posited in advance by the discussion in the first portion of the essay, which we can now reread as an examination of a suffering patient—the German audience—who is troubled by a vague but nagging psychological deficiency, "Audiences come before the curtain with an undefined longing and with a many-sided capacity" (Passage, *Bride* 3) [Es (das Publikum) tritt vor den Vorhang mit einem unbestimmten Verlangen, mit einem vielseitigen Vermoegen] (*Schillers Werke* 10:7). Schiller's viewer hopes and needs to *forget*—to distract himself from the smallness, the petty concerns of his everyday life:

> From the arts of the imaginative faculties everyone expects a certain liberation from reality; he wants to delight in the possible and give free rein to his fancy. The man with the least expectations still wants to forget his business, his everyday life, his individual self; he wants to feel himself in

116

extraordinary situations, to revel in the odd vagaries of chance. If he is of a more serious nature, he wants to find on the stage that moral government of the world which he misses in actual life. (Passage, *Bride* 4)

Jeder Mensch zwar erwartet von den Künsten der Einbildungskraft eine gewisse Befreiung von den Schranken des Wirklichken, er will sich an dem Möglichen ergötzen und seiner Phantasie Raum geben. Der am wenigsten erwartet, will doch sein Geschäft, sein gemeines Leben, sein Individuum vergessen, er will sich in ausserordentlichen Lagen fühlen, sich an den seltsamen Combinationen des Zufalls weiden, er will, wenn er von ernsthafterer Natur ist, die moralische Weltregierung, die er im wirklichen Leben vermißt, auf der Schaubühne finden. (*Schillers Werke* 10:8)

Schiller's language stresses constriction, a lack of space that is at once physical and psychological; the viewer literally has no room even to fantasize. He is caught, hemmed in, and thwarted by ordinary circumstances. But, as the second clause of the last sentence makes clear, Schiller's viewer is not only oppressed by smallness, he is also really morally and politically oppressed, hoping for an aesthetic experience that will compensate for the lack of justice in everyday life.

Therefore, classical art must be marshaled because more realistic art forms cannot control the theatergoer's ailment:

Yet he himself knows perfectly well that he is only carrying on a pointless game, that in the last analysis he is only indulging in dreams, and when he comes away again from the stage into the actual world, the latter will once again beset him with all its oppressive constriction; he will be the world's victim as before, for that has remained what it was and nothing in him has been altered. (Passage, *Bride* 4)

Aber er weiß selbst recht gut, daß er nur ein leeres Spiel treibt, daß er im eigentlichen Sinn sich nur an Träumen weidet, und wenn er von dem Schauplatz wieder in die wirklich Welt zurück kehrt, so umgiebt ihn diese wieder mit ihrer ganzen drückenden Enge, er ist, ihr Raub wie vorher, denn sie selbst ist geblieben was sie war, und an ihm ist nichts verändert worden. (*Schillers Werke* 10:8)

Returning to earth, as it were, from the illusion of art and theater, the viewer feels more distressed than ever; after his respite in the theater, the workaday world now presses in upon him all the more forcefully; he experiences a sense of violation and bereavement; his very dreams have been stolen from him, and the world he lives in circumvents some crucial, essential need that cannot be filled. This turns loss into actual pain "and we find ourselves painfully thrust back into common and narrow actuality by the very art which was to have set

PICTURE PALACE

us free" (Passage, *Bride* 5) [. . . wir sehen uns durch die Kunst selbst, die uns befreien sollte, in die gemeine enge Wirklichkeit peinlich zurück versezt] (*Schillers Werke* 10:9). Thus, *Bride* aims to deliver a homeopathic series of gestures based on the notion of similars: the theatergoer will vent his own frustration from the viewing of Eros eternally frustrated, find freedom through the treatment of the characters' imprisonment within a fate they cannot escape, find his authentic, dynamic personhood through the static statuary of neoclassicism, feel refreshed and joyous, connected, and whole through the depiction of fatal tragedy.

It is remarkable that Schiller, in his role as poet/diagnostician, makes no recommendations for any social mode of action, or for any activity that might alter or impact upon the outside world. The prescription outlined in "On the Use of the Chorus" does not entail therapy—which aims for resolution of the problem and a renewed return to a full and active life—but rather pain management—the aesthetic equivalent of Prozac.[11] Reforms other than that of the theater—the delivery system for calm—appear so out of reach that they do not even bear mentioning. The gods, judges, and *Volk* of the palace gates can be invoked but they will—it seems—never return. They are specters of the bourgeois imaginary, relegated to the private life of fancy, of which the Weimar theater is to be the extended living room, and the play a soothing pre-television soap opera of terrible suffering, to be contemplated calmly over a defrosted frozen dinner.

Few people would call "On the Use of the Chorus" a commercial work, and yet its very aesthetic plays into the complex relays of consumer culturalism. Its peculiar insistence on physical human forms that are and are not bodies, on the control of affect, and on the freezing up of motion all signal its participation in what Mark Seltzer has called the "aesthetics of consumption." This system disavows material and natural bodily needs by appealing to the model of the natural body (Seltzer 121), creates an asceticism that calls itself "disinterestedness" (125), and assigns class (and racial) privilege by a "relative disembodiment . . . [which makes] the body an artifact."

"But what most strikingly belongs to the privileged body is its radically and aesthetic formality. . . . The aestheticized body that belongs to the gentleman reappears in terms of what the psychoanalyst Jacques Lacan calls 'this *belong to me*' aspect of representations, so reminiscent of property" (137). Seen from this point of view, the prescription that Dr. Schiller writes out for his melancholy patient is *precisely* consumption of (his) cultural goods, for which the essay is itself a brilliant marketing ploy. The bodies displayed on stage incarnate the ultimate in bourgeois self-possession, just as the architecture implicitly advertises the neoclassical decor and accouterments that make for a gracious home.[12]

118

The Bride of Messina

AND NOW FOR OUR FEATURE PRESENTATION

The play's spatial organization literally buttresses the essay's image of classical architecture as model for the domestic; the staging obsessively controls the agonies the play depicts by rigidly demarcating public and private spaces and placing male and female characters within them, respectively. The stage directions perfectly mimic Schiller's notion of the chorus as wall of a virtual edifice:

(Enter the chorus)
>   *(It consists of two semi-choruses that enter simultaneously from opposite directions, one from the rear, the other from downstage. Each of them forms in a row on the side where it entered, after making the circuit of the stage.)*

FIRST CHORUS:
Reverent greetings I give you,
Mansion resplendent,
You my ancestral
Cradle of Princes,
Roof upon columns loftily borne.
Deep in its scabbard
Let the sword rest,
Chained outside of the gates
Let Discord be left, the serpent-haired monster.
For inviolable thresholds
Of welcoming houses
Are guarded by Oath, the Erinyes' son,
Most dread of the gods of the underworld realm.
>   (Passage, *Bride* 18)

Chor tritt auf.
>   *Er besteht aus zwey Halbchören, welche zu gleicher Zeit, von zwey entgegengesetzten Seiten, der eine aus der Tiefe, der andere aus dem Vordergrund eintreten, rund um die Bühne gehen, und sich alsdann auf derselben Seite, wo jeder eingetreten, in eine Reihe stellen.*

ERSTER CHOR
>   Dich begrüß ich in Ehrfurcht
Prangende Halle,
Dich meiner Herrscher
Fuerstliche Wiege.
Säulengetragenes herrliches Dach.

119

Tief in der Scheide
Ruhe das Schwert
Vor den Thoren gefesselt
Liege des Streits schlangenhaarigtes Scheusal.
Denn des gastlichen Hauses
Unverletzliche Schwelle
Hütet der *Eid,* der Erinnyen Sohn,
Der furchtbarste unter den Göttern der Hoelle!

(*Schillers Werke* 10:25–26)

The introduction of the chorus marks the classical self-consciousness of the piece while also operating as a survey team that differentiates space.[13]

Notably, most of the action in *Bride* takes place within this palatial hall, and within this arena the author repeatedly draws clear, gendered boundary lines: between the feminine domestic sphere of family and the home on one side, and the masculine polis on the other—the public space of government and war. Tellingly, both Queen Isabella and her daughter Beatrice live gladly in the sequestered spaces of the women's apartments and the convent, while the sons have been banished from the home by the father, and they range freely outside of it with their rival armies.

The masculine geography of war present in *The Robbers* and in *Wallenstein* also provides the spatial template in the passage cited above. The chorus represents the opposing armies of Don Cesar and Don Manuel who roam "outside" the home, be it the house or the homeland, and contend with each other for the power of domination (*herrschen*) so prized by Schiller's early hero, Fiesko. A later disgruntled choral reaction to the prospect of peace between the brothers signifies how much of masculine, social identity is invested in war, and how much the notion of living leads men toward aggressive adventure beyond the bounds of the domestic. The men are, in turn, literally out of place in the palace and must surrender a crucial aspect of their collective identity, the phallic sword, in order to enter.

Likewise Donna Isabella and her daughter Beatrice stress the pleasures of the feminine retreats they call home. This is particularly clear in Beatrice's speech describing the convent life that she has abandoned irrevocably, merely by stepping briefly outside of its bounds:

Why did I leave my tranquil convent nook?
There I lived free of yearning, free of harm!
My heart was quiet as a meadow brook,
Without desire, yet full of comfort warm.

(2.1.45).

Warum verließ ich meine stille Zelle,
Da lebt ich ohne Sehnsucht, ohne Harm!

Das Herz war ruhig wie die Wiesenquelle,
An Wünschen leer, doch nicht an Freuden arm.

(10:55)

Beatrice's speech concretizes the spatial problem of the play, for the home proves tenuous, at once easily penetrated from without and easily abandoned from within, since its threshold is hazy:[14]

I was rejected, suffered exile's ban,
In tender years a cruel destiny
(I may not lift its darkling veil) began,
from mother's arms it snatched me ruthlessly
I saw her only once—or so it seems—
But, vanished is her image like my dreams.

(2.1.46)

Denn ausgesezt ward ich ins fremde Leben,
Und frühe schon hat mich ein strenges Los
(Ich darf den dunkeln Schleier nicht erheben)
Gerissen von dem mütterlichen Schoss.
Nur einmal sah ich sie, die mich geboren,
Doch wie ein Traum gieng mir das Bild verloren.

(10:56)

Donna Isabella—a maternal and commanding figure new to Schiller's pantheon of characters (and who will appear later in *Demetrius*)—corroborates the tenuous nature of home, for while she has not been formally exiled, she inhabits a domicile that has been emptied of the characteristics that *make* it home. As she herself recognizes at the outset, Isabella's royal establishment is no more a home than Beatrice's because it lacks the principal actors of home life—the children, and most particularly the father, who "ruled this city with his mighty power / Protecting you with his strong arm against / A world that hemmed you hostilely about" (14). [Der mächtigwaltend dieser Stadt gebot / mit starkem Arme gegen eine Welt / Euch schützend, die euch feindlich rings umlagert] (Schillers Werke 10:21) Not coincidentally, Schiller begins the play with Isabella's announcement that it is the absence of the father that drives the mother out of her seclusion in search of her scattered children, and later Beatrice is easily uprooted from her refuge by the presence of masculinity: the promise of patriarchal love and protection by Don Cesar; and the opportunity to view and mourn the dead body of the father-king. It would seem that neither the convent nor the palatial residence can function properly as proper domestic sites without the presence of the male head. Thus, the play suggests it is precisely because home constitutes a domestic, feminine space that a male authority must oversee it. Isabella summarizes the ramifications of this lack by noting that her husband was the protecting father not only of the family but also of the nation, which becomes an extended larger family of children under his strong arm, and Beatrice uses this same image to describe Don Cesar's abduction of her.

The rigid spatial arrangements described here do indeed refer to a political and social architecture—albeit not that of classical Greece. Schiller is literally laying down a floor plan—consciously or unconsciously—that anticipates by only a small margin of time the theory of separate spheres put forward by evangelical activist Hannah More (Hunt 58). Opposed to the feminist egalitarianism of her contemporary Mary Wollstonecraft, More envisaged different roles and realms for women and men that look very much like they do in Schiller's neoclassical play:

> The fin was not more clearly bestowed on the fish, nor the wing given to the bird that he should fly, than superior strength of body, and a firmer texture of mind was given to man, that he might preside in the deep and daring scenes of action and of council; in the complicated arts of government, in the contention of arms, in the intricacies and depths of science, in the bustle of commerce, and in the professions which demand a higher reach, and a wider range of powers. (Hunt 58)

Men are by nature suited for public pursuits, argued More, while woman's place is literally and symbolically in the home as mother and wife. Such distribution is not merely patriarchal but indeed fits into both bourgeois and Protestant mindsets. The man of the house is, according to such a view, also a man of business—furthering the links between work, monetary acquisition, and predestination discussed by Weber and originating in the notions of Luther, Calvin, and Zwingli.

These ideas as articulated by spatial distribution are more fully evident in *Wilhelm Tell*, which is an ideological pageant of the virtues of private life. In *Bride* on the other hand, it is the failure of this spatial arrangement that provides the "tragic" focus. When father is absent the separate spheres collide and collapse. This collapse is signaled both rhetorically and spatially in the play's obsessive references to the Father's unseen funeral. Here, at this very moment of patriarchal absenting, everything falls apart.

The funeral marks the beginning of the play's action and is the event that causes the women to cross the boundary of the domestic; the death of the king/father literally *moves* them out of their proper sphere. Donna Isabella's first speech (1.1) justifies her very appearance on stage in terms of the time span that has elapsed since that death, while Beatrice explains her fear at having for one time only left the perimeter of the convent cell in order to view the funeral of the king (2.1).

The Bride of Messina

But the most important invocation of the funeral is reserved for Don Cesar, the younger of the two sons. In a lengthy speech whose detail recalls the narrative of Mortimer at St. Peter's, Don Cesar describes the crucial and fatal moment of seduction that literally occurs over the father's dead body:

> But as
> I turned my eyes, there she was standing at
> My side, and with a dark and wondrous power
> Her presence seized upon my inmost being.
>
> (2.2.62).

> Als ich
> Die Augen wandte, stand sie mir zur Seite,
> Und dunkel mächtig, wunderbar, ergriff
> Im tiefsten Innersten mich ihre Nähe . . .
>
> (10:71–2)

Like his expressionist namesake, Cesare, Don Cesar too is mesmerized by a beautiful stranger.

Thus, it is the feminine transgression of the domestic boundary that causes catastrophe. This notion is reinforced by the information that Donna Isabella has also violated the hierarchical power structure within the family. Although her husband, the ostensible head of the family as well as of the state, commanded the death of his infant daughter (because of a dream that predicted the downfall of the dynasty should the infant live), the queen disobeys the directive, on the basis of her own dream-vision.[15] The father's dream is fulfilled, assigning the ultimate blame to the mother, who like the misguided African Othello, loved not wisely but too well. At the end of the play, the two sons are dead, their funerals reiterating each others' as well as the father's. The transgressive mother and daughter are left to mourn the ruin of the family, to return—rightfully—to the seclusion from which they willfully emerged.

Read from this point of view, *Bride* articulates Schiller's most conservative dramatic view thus far on the relation between the sexes; the play ostensibly shores up the strict gendered divisions of separate spheres and ushers a grim warning of what will happen to the family whose women disobey orders. The warning addresses itself to both sexes in the Weimar audience. The female members of Schiller's audience are warned explicitly against leaving the strictly defined parameters to which they are assigned, even under the direst circumstances. More important, they are warned against sentimentality and the rule of the emotions. The play's language emphasizes that both women are "unable" to control themselves at key moments. Like a naughty child caught with

her hand in the cookie jar, Beatrice confesses to her fiancé that despite his
orders, she could not stop herself from attending her father's funeral:

> Curiosity compelled me.
> Forgive me. I confessed that wish to you:
> But with a sudden somberness you left
> My plea unanswered, nor did I speak either.
> And yet I do not know what evil star
> Forced me with irresistible desire.
> I had to satisfy my heart's strong impulse.
> The aged servant lent me his assistance.
> And thus I disobeyed you, and I went.
>
>   (3.76)

> Die Begierde war zu mächtig!
> Vergieb mir! Ich gestand dir meinen Wunsch,
> Doch plötzlich ernst und finster liessest du
> Die Bitte fallen, und so schwieg auch ich.
> Doch weiß ich nicht welch bösen Sternes Macht
> Mich trieb mit unbezwinglichem Gelüsten.
> Des Herzens heißen Drang mußt ich vergnügen,
> Der alte Diener lieh mir seinen Bestand,
> Ich war dir ungehorsam und ich gieng.
>
>   (10:89–90)

Schiller suggests that even a daughter's "natural" and therefore understandable love for her father is dangerous when left uncontrolled and undi-
rected by a paternal authority; Schiller uses the words that connote instinctual
drive, rather than filial loyalty, of sensual pleasure rather than the urge to
mourn, and a passion resembling lust rather than a more suitably feminine
longing, to describe Beatrice's emotional motivations. These are even more
negatively marked by the fact that Beatrice has expressly disobeyed the order
of her beloved.

The mother reveals herself to be no more self-controlled than the daughter. At the beginning of the play, Isabella explains matter of factly that she
could not "bring" herself to obey the king's command to kill her third child,
despite the fact that the king's dream and its interpretation suggest that this
child represents a variation of the Oedipal curse: according to the prediction, a
daughter will destroy the two sons and destroy the patrilineal line of the family
(the only one that matters). Isabella simply invalidates the order in her own
attempt to control fate. She mistakenly places a superior truth value on her
own dream and its interpretation:

I thwarted that
Inhuman order and preserved my daughter
Through silent service of a trusted henchman.
(2.2.56)

Ich vereitelte
Den blutgen Vorsatz und erhielt die Tochter
Durch eines treuen Knechts verwschwiegnen Dienst.
(10:65)

Schiller's play puts forth a line of reasoning that is patently paternalistic, and not so subtly misogynist.[16] Woman appears to be the container of all manner of drives that must be contained and controlled at all costs. Beautiful, desirable, but weak, women in a given household must be supervised and tightly controlled at all times, else they will necessarily stray. Above all, women must not want things for themselves; their desires are dangerous, and as Beatrice herself suggests, women are happier when they give up desire altogether.

On the other hand, the play offers itself as medicating consolation and as validation to the male viewers and readers. It proffers them with both a relaxant and a stimulant, reminding them that, while their freedom in the world of the public may be constricted, they are indeed the *only* free agents in the domestic sphere—a place where they are indeed mandated to wield authority over their wives and children, both male and female. Failure to wield power successfully, to see that their every wish is carried out, leads to catastrophe for male and female children alike as well as for the wife. But the danger of an early-nineteenth-century bourgeois wife listening to dream prophecies and calling in soothsayers seems remote, and so as promised in "On the Use of the Chorus," the male viewer can contemplate danger from a considerable remove, all the while feeling exceedingly comfortable and safe within the walls of the domestic world he has established and governs.

In this manner, the play produces a deeply conservative and ideologically freighted message, marking out gendered separate spheres for an increasingly bourgeois audience of viewers and readers—themselves presumably engaged in similar negotiations in their own families. Schiller's ability to vent, displace, and capitalize upon contemporary, repressed anxieties goes a long way to account for this strange play's initial and subsequent success both on stage and in print (Brandt 276, Thompson 329).

But is this all that *Bride* says?

Even as it dramatizes its deeply conservative, bourgeois, and consumerist message, Schiller's play also makes it clear that the matter with this family may not be its *mater,* and her problematic legacy to her daughter, after all. Indeed the question as to feminine weakness as well as the ambiguity of the

contradictory dream messages have already been preempted at the end of act
1 by a much more fatal factor—the fault of the father—a by-now familiar and,
for Schiller, always tragically resonant concern.

There are indications throughout the play that this family is dysfunctional for reasons that have nothing to do with the women. Even before the
father dies, the household is in complete disarray. No one seems to remember
what initiated the brothers' hatred for each other (and if Donna Isabella
knows—which she might—she is unwilling to say), and the all-powerful king
proves surprisingly powerless to persuade or command the sons to resolve their
dispute. Instead, he behaves as a tyrant, banishing both sons from their rightful
homes (Atkins 556), after having—it seems with perfect equanimity—
condemned his own infant daughter to death as well.

But most important is the information slipped in at the end of act 1 by
the chorus. They mention in passing a criminal act of great proportions, one
that is never even mentioned by the principals of the play but that in fact
completely predetermines the tragic outcome (Sharpe 290):

> Theft was it also, as we all know,
> When the former Prince's bride was brought
> To a sinful bride-bed long ago,
> For she was the bride his father sought.
> And the family's founder, fierce in his wrath,
> Poured ghastly curses upon the same,
> Strewing that bride-bed with seeds of crimes . . .
> It is no chance, no blind work of fate,
> That these brother in fury destroy each other,
> For conceiving of strife and bearing of hate,
> That was the curse on the womb of their mother.
> But in silence I shall beshroud the fact:
> In silence the gods of vengeance act;
> It is time enough to lament mischance
> When it onward comes in actual advance.
>
> (1.44)

> Auch ein Raub wars, wie wir alle wissen,
> Der des alten Fürsten ehliches Gemahl
> In ein frevelnd Ehebett gerissen,
> Denn sie war des Vaters Wahl.
> Und der Ahnherr schüttete im Zorne
> Grauenvoller Flüche schrecklichen Saamen
> Auf das sündige Ehebett aus . . .
> Es ist kein Zufall und blindes Loos,
> Daß die Brüder sich wüthend selbst zerstören,
> Denn verflucht ward der Mutter Schooß,

126

The Bride of Messina

Sie sollte den Haß und den Streit gebähren . . .
Denn die Rachgoetter schaffen im Stillen,
Zeit ists, die Unfälle zu beweinen
Wenn sie nahen und wirklich erscheinen.

(10:53–54)

This crucial information is delivered as a suspense-building throwaway, but this revelation also completely shifts the meaning of the play. The curse on the father contextualizes both father's and mother's dreams as strategies of fate (Weigand 180), and shifts the blame away from mothers and daughters and most emphatically toward fathers and sons—that familiar tragic nexus so beloved by Schiller. The figure of the kingly father, so mourned by his family, emerges now as himself a rebellious and disrespectful son, who, in the manner of Schiller's earlier would be wife-stealer, Don Carlos, hopes and actually succeeds in stealing the sexual object of his own father. The tragedy, as in so many of Schiller's plays, proves to be always already Father's fault.

TRAUER, SPIEL

Despite these tragic twists and turns, *The Bride of Messina* culminates neither with agony nor with heroic renunciation, but rather with profound disenchantment and silent resignation. Discovering at last how much her plans have gone awry, Donna Isabella reacts not with anguish but with a kind of detached aggravation as though she has received a piece of bad news that she has already expected. Her speech does not disclose her horror at the fatal fulfillment of the father's prophecy; instead she is struck by the meaninglessness of all and any prophecy. Strikingly, Isabella declares the lack rather than the acquisition of knowledge—tragic or otherwise—and her speech emphasizes the utter absence of transcendence, as it issues a blanket condemnation of dream as the artistry of self-delusion:

About the future no truth can you know
. . . To what end do we visit holy houses
And raise our pious hands aloft to Heaven?
Good-natured, simple fools, what do we gain
By all our faith? It is impossible
To reach the gods who dwell on high, just as
One cannot shoot an arrow to the moon.
The future is from mortals walled apart
And nor prayer penetrates the iron sky.
Let birds fly to the right or to the left,
Let stars stand this or that way in the sky,

127

There is no sense in Nature's book, the art
Of dreams is dreams, and all portents lie.

(4.93–94)

Nichts wahres laeßt sich von der Zukunft wissen . . .
. . . was gewinnen wir
Mit unserm Glauben? So unmöglich ists,
Die Götter, die hochwohnenden, zu treffen,
Als in den Mond mit einem Pfeil zu schießen.
Vermauert ist dem Sterblichen die Zukunft,
Und kein Gebet durchbohrt den ehrnen Himmel . . .
Nicht Sinn ist in dem Buche der Natur,
Die Traumkunst träumt, und alle Zeichen trügen.

(10:108–9)

Donna Isabella's words reiterate and shift the architectural language of
Schiller's essay. Her building is no haven but a semiotic prison, which walls
humanity away from meaning, from truth, from self-understanding, from control, and from comfort. The speech bewails the end of possibility and signals the
failure of religious faith, of visionary imagination, and, even more important, of
logos; there is literally no "sense" in the world of the play.[17]
    The play corroborates this disenchantment in two important ways. After
killing his brother, Don Cesar matter-of-factly stabs himself, more depressed
than agonized, and even hints that he may actually prefer death to life. His
final speech too is revealing:

You want to drive me back into the struggle
And make the sunlight dearer still to me
Upon my journey to eternal night?

(4.107)

In neuen Kampf wills du zurück mich stürzen?
Das Licht der Sonne mir noch theuer machen
Auf meinem Wege zu der ewgen Nacht?

(10:123)

Here the distressed mother is momentarily upstaged by her masochistic,
suicidal son, who actively desires release from life's "struggle." He does not so
much argue with his mother and sister as ignore them, plunging the dagger
into himself as the chorus chatters, falling at their feet.
    Equally important is the way the two surviving characters are literally
struck dumb by the final events; they are displayed to us in the final moments
of the play much like the figures of Caligari's sanitarium: as mute sufferers in

a columned courtyard. Like the playwright, the characters too are at a loss for words. The coda to the play is only belatedly delivered by the chorus's terse commentary after a long pause:

> *(Don Cesar plunges a dagger into himself and, dying, sinks down beside his sister, who throws herself into her mother's arms.)*

> THE CHORUS *(after a profound silence)*
> I stand here overwhelmed, uncertain whether
> To laud or to lament his destiny. . . .
>
> (4.109)

> *(er durchsticht sich mit einem Dolch und gleitet sterbend an seiner Schwester nieder, die sich der Mutter in die Arme wirft.)*

> DER CHOR *(nach einem tiefen Schweigen)*
> Erschüttert steh ich, weiß nicht, ob ich ihn
> Bejammern oder preisen soll sein Loos . . .
>
> (10:125)

In her analysis of Holbein's painting "Dead Christ," Kristeva observes what she calls a "melancholy moment" in which "an actual or imaginary loss of meaning, an actual or imaginary despair, and actual or imaginary razing of values, including the value of life" occurs (*Black Sun* 128). This sensual cooperation of depression and artifice (125) would seem aptly to describe the procedure of *The Bride of Messina* that proceeds toward an "eventual collapse of meaning," which renders the characters speechless and fades away into a static tableau—a living painting of death (53).[18] Its pharmaceutical aims shattered, the play can do nothing but offer us in its closing moments the spectacle of silent disenchantment, a beautiful despair.[19] "The picture seems to give expression to the idea of a dark, insolent, and senseless eternal power, to which everything is subordinated, and which controls you in spite of yourself. The people surrounding the dead man . . . must have been overwhelmed by a feeling of terrible anguish and dismay . . . *which had shattered all their hopes and almost all their beliefs in one fell blow*" (109).

Unlike Schiller's earlier, more overtly agonized plays, *The Bride of Messina* proves to be a "Trauerspiel" in the truest sense of the word. Through its invocation of classical beauty, the plot refers to but does not actually perform mourning, just as it plays with but does not actually dramatize trauma, and formally imitates but does not actually reproduce tragedy.[20] Its aesthetic practice already announces the degree to which extreme pain has been dis-placed and re-pressed onto a flat surface. Like classical bas-relief, the drama carves out tragedy against a shallow background, its structure ensures stasis, and its indifferent manner of

PICTURE PALACE

reporting awful occurrences establishes distance. Thus flattened, pain is man-
aged and forcibly faded into silence—into the mute tableau that marks the end
of the play as an odd forbearer of the silent film.[21]

French surrealist filmmaker Jean Cocteau once complained that cinema
has attempted from the beginning to *photograph theater* (cited in Budd 55).
Schiller's neoclassical aesthetics do just this; his stated desire to "frieze" the
theatrical into neoclassical architecture, to make actors into figures operating
on a surface already anticipates both the aesthetic and the technical apparatus
that made *Caligari* possible.

From this point of view, *Bride*'s dramatic descendants may not belong to
the realm of stage drama at all. Are not the static, beautiful, and despairing
images of Schiller's drama reiterated in such screen masterpieces as *Metropolis*,
The Children of Paradise, Citizen Kane, Open City, and *Cries and Whispers*? Inflected
by a tension between the architectural and the personal, between language and
silence, and negotiating a fine line between expressing, elevating, calming, and
selling bourgeois melancholy, this tradition finds its culmination and correction
in Wim Wenders's *Wings of Desire* [*Der Himmel über Berlin*], where the familiar
Schillerian spectacle of opposed brothers plays out against the black and white
of Berlin's new and old buildings, and where—at last—all voices are heard.[22]

Is There a Doctor in the House?

Schiller's own correspondence during the period of *Bride*'s composition
suggests that the play represented a turning point in his own oeuvre and, more
interestingly, in his own understanding of himself as an artist. It is evident that
Schiller constructs himself, self-consciously and obsessively, around the creation
of this play, as a professional man, as a professor, as a practicing classicist—a
role that he seems to regard as similar to that of his first profession—that of
doctor. His triumphant remark to Körner concerning the cheers issued by his
own students at the play's first performance (Letter, March 28, 1803; Letter
33 of *Schillers Werke* 32:25) bears out the degree to which Schiller the Stürmer-
und-Dränger has been contained and replaced by Dr. Schiller the academic
luminary and classical playwright.

But such containment kills. Writing has now become drudgery, a project
of filling in, rather than creating, of atomized supplement rather than a grand
scheme. *The Bride of Messina* testifies to the efforts of this physician-turned-
playwright to rejuvenate his own artistic sensibility through the making of
wordplay, to heal himself and his imagined audience, and to earn a living
through a classical cure. This aesthetic medication is to be administered in a
templelike inner sanctum that will function like an ethereal sanitarium—the
quintessence of Marcuse's "affirmative culture." But the palace and the peace

130

it offers prove false. The patient escapes—if only through his imagination—and the cure proves fatal, as the dead bodies and the muteness of the survivors on the stage and on the screen would seem to suggest.

Likewise, Schiller's classical cure masks but does not alleviate the symptoms of his own malady, and the new persona of the classical Dr. Schiller only partially represses the agonized Schiller of Sturm und Drang, just as the mad doctor and his eventually rebellious somnambulist lurk behind the kindly visage of Caligari and his now docile charge, Francis. As the old adage already warns, the treatment never fails to fail the expert. The doctor is dying. *The Bride of Messina* is Schiller's most carefully controlled drama;[23] as such it sounds his death knell, "Think, from your mild climate, about our iron sky;[24] from where I write, all lies buried under the snow, and it looks as if, in all eternity, summer could never come again" (Schiller to Humboldt, February 17, 1803) [Denken Sie in Ihrem milden Clima an unsern eisernen Himmel, indem ich Ihnen schreibe liegt alles von Schnee begraben und es sieht aus, als wenn es in Ewigkeit nicht wieder Sommer werden könnte] (*Schillers Werke* 32:11).

CHAPTER 5

Unfinished Business

Trauma, Mother, and
Acquisition in *Demetrius*

> I want to write the story of a pair joined by the same blood and every kind of difference . . . She silent most of the time, with only a few words at her disposal to express herself; he constantly talking and unable to find in thousands of words what she could say with a single one of her silences . . . Mother and son.
>
> *Albert Camus*

> For what I have lost is not a figure (the Mother), but a being (my mother); and not a being, but a quality (a soul): not the indispensable, but the irreplaceable. I could live without the Mother (as we all do, sooner or later); but what life remained would be absolutely and entirely unqualifiable (without quality).
>
> *Roland Barthes*

> I want my mommy.
>
> *Art Spiegelman*

"WORK IN THIS NEIGHBORHOOD WAS NOT A VIRTUE BUT A NECESSITY, THAT, IN ORDER TO SURVIVE, LED TO DEATH."[1]

In 1787 Schiller arrived in Weimar, poised to begin a new phase of his life as part of the important circle of writers and intellectuals who were gathering there. Sixteen years later he was dead, having expired with the fragment of a play called *Demetrius* lying unfinished on his desk, and the dreams of future projects to be forever unfulfilled. Schiller died at both the midpoint and a turning point of his career; he was finally achieving recognition and had hopes of turning the corner on his considerable financial woes. But artistic creation had now become an arduous and unending task—a pressure to produce plagued him and was heightened by his concern with providing for his family, as this letter to Körner considering a possible move to Berlin testifies:

133

But my salary is small and I lose just about everything that I earn in a year, so that little is put aside. In order to contribute to my children's fortune, I must press on, so that the output of my scribbling can be turned to profit. (May 28, 1804)

Abes meine Besoldung ist klein und ich setze ziemlich alles zu, was ich jährlich erwerbe, so daß wenig zurück gelegt wird. Um meinen Kindern einiges Vermögen zu erwerben, muß ich dahin streben, daß der Ertrag meiner Schriftstellerei zum Kapital kann geschlagen werden. (*Schillers Werke* 32:133)

Indeed, Schiller regarded his own failing health as an expensive luxury until the end, "I am indeed quite diligent now, but my long break from work and my ever-lingering weakness permit me to make only slow progress" (Schiller to Körner April 25, 1805). [Ich bin zwar jetzt ziemlich fleißig, aber die lange Entwohnung von der Arbeit und die noch zurückgebliebene Schwäche lassen mich doch nur langsam fortschreiten] (*Schillers Werke* 32:218). In this final letter to his dearest friend, Schiller regards the upcoming months with fear and trepidation rather than anticipation, viewing a seemingly unending mass of work to be done—in order to make good, to compensate for and pay back the time that he has lost in being ill.

But Schiller was not entirely misguided to think in such brutal fiscal terms. The people who knew and loved him best saw their own existence, as well as his, in similar fraught ways. The problematic social status of artistic production for a primarily Protestant society moving into capitalism becomes evident in Christophine Schiller's (now Reinwald) last letter to her brother. Here an unwilling awareness of the importance of material goods and a deep ambivalence vis-à-vis art go hand in hand with an extremely perspicacious understanding of how Schiller created his plays:

It is very expensive to live in Weimar—that I have certainly noticed during my short stay. . . . Especially wood, which became a big item this winter. . . . You can not live as withdrawn from the world as we can; surely you have more sources of struggle with all this than we do. . . . May God send you back your full health, which however you must not strain through too much mental work, for I believe very definitely that your more frequent illness are the result of this, and I feel afraid, whenever I read something new of yours—which must have cost you great effort, for it is impossible that something like that can let itself be written without imagining oneself entirely in the situations of the persons that one is handling—and this exhausts one's energies, as it does mine, when I even read your writing. (Christophine Reinwald to Schiller, March 30, 1805)

In Weimar ists sehr theuer zu leben das habe ich bey meinem kurzen Aufendhalt wohl gesehen. . . . Besonders das Holz was diesen Wintter

ein Groser Artikel ist. . . . Du kanst in deiner Lage nicht so zuerükgezogen
leben wie wir, freilich hast Du auch mehr Quellen zur Bestreittung alles
dieses als wir. Gott schenke Dir nur Deine völlige Gesundheit wieder die
Du aber ja nicht durch zu viel GeistesArbeit anstrengen mußt, denn ich
glaube ganz gewiß daß Dein öfteres Krankseyn nur Folge davon ist und
mir ist bang wenn ich wieder etwas Neues von Dir lese welche Anstren-
gung es Dir gekostet haben mag, denn unmöglich läßt sich so etwas
schreiben ohne sich ganz in die Lagen der Personen hinein zu denken die
man handeln läßt und daß zehrt die Kräfte auf, ist mirs doch so, wenn
ich Deine Schriften nur lese . . . (*Schillers Werke* 40 I:305)

Christophine's letter suggests strongly that unremitting financial pressure played at least some role in Schiller's untimely death, and, read retrospec-
tively, the letter impresses us with its—now poignant—psychological
awareness of and devotion to her brilliant brother. But the letter also betrays a
great reluctance to regard financial concerns as the significant matters that
they were for Schiller, or indeed for anyone.

Noting how expensive it is to live in Weimar, Christophine veers between two different notions of "economizing"—first in regard to physical comfort (wood for the winter) and second in regard to spiritual/emotional
management. This passage comes very close to saying (without directly expressing the criticism) that Schiller spends too much money to run his household; Christophine's implication is that her brother "should" in fact live more
removed from the worldly, ambitious social space that is Weimar. In like fashion, Christophine indirectly suggests that he exercises his imagination in a
spendthrift manner. In order to create as he does, Schiller has had to mortgage
his physical health. In this way, Christophine—for all her sympathy—reveals a
Protestant-inflected view of her brother's physiological difficulties as deriving
from the spiritual excess that makes art. Such a view once again resonates with
Max Weber, who notes:

Combined with the harsh doctrines of the absolute transcendality of God
and the corruption of everything pertaining to the flesh, this inner isolation of the individual contains . . . the reason for the entirely negative
attitude of Puritanism to all the sensuous and emotional elements in culture . . . because they are of no use toward salvation and promote sentimental illusions and idolatrous superstitions. (Weber 105)

The young Schiller frequently agonized over whether his art was a vocation or
a business. But now, he no longer had the time. The author did not respond to
his sister's letter from the end of March; he was too busy working, and by May
he was dead. But *Demetrius*, as we shall see, explores the relationships between

the psyche and material possessions, and probes the ways in which the family may become at once the greatest acquisition and the greatest liability of all.

"I WANT TO TELL THE STORY OF AN ALIEN. . . ."

Schiller's untimely death was a tragedy for all that knew and loved him; it marked an already distinguished body of work as somehow sadly incomplete. This sense of unfinished artistic business resonates with many other artists of the turn of the eighteenth century—with Mozart, Shelley, Keats, Novalis, and Kleist, to name but a few. But, on closer inspection, Schiller's death and his unfinished manuscript connect in curious, provocative ways with an author who wrote almost two hundred years later: namely the French modernist writer and Nobel prize winner, Albert Camus (1913–60).[2]

The two had a great deal in common. Like Schiller, Camus was a troubled but famous genius, as well as a neurasthenic writer plagued by ill health; like Schiller, he favored the modes of theater and philosophy, although he became well known primarily as the composer of three breathtakingly original and disturbing novels: *The Stranger, The Plague,* and *The Fall.* Like Schiller, Camus died in his midforties; the French writer was killed in a dramatic car accident, although his lungs might have killed him shortly after, being, as he described them, "full of holes."

Camus was not a scholar, in comparison to his Goethean competitor-mentor, Jean Paul Sartre, and yet the contradictions of Camus's writing point to a deep affinity with Schiller—an affinity based on psychological suffering and an ambivalence toward commercial success—an ambivalence that may have contributed to his demise as indirectly and as surely as Schiller's own painful contradictions weakened him, making him vulnerable to the disease that took his life.[3] Like Schiller, Camus was a provincial, an exile from his true homeland, French-speaking Algeria—a place he would never truly leave, spiritually or politically. And like Schiller, Camus saw himself as an outsider trying to move in, a regional trying to make it in the big city. Paris was Camus's Weimar—a place he longed for but never felt at home in; Camus's writing is imbued with a sense of inner exile—which we can see working so forcefully, particularly in Schiller's early plays.

There are other disconcerting points of comparison between Schiller's and Camus's career trajectories. Camus's first important work is the famous absurdist novel *The Stranger* [*L'Etranger*]. In this odd book a strangely indifferent young French man named Meursault murders a native Algerian on the beach and is eventually convicted, not for the murder but for another "crime" altogether (Tarrow 82). The racist jury is swayed to convict the white Frenchman only because it is discovered that Meursault did not cry at his mother's funeral. Failure to mourn the mother in the socially accepted, proper, exterior-ized way condemns the son (Tarrow 82). But, in his jail cell, Meursault affirms a fleeting, surprising solidarity with his mother, and the closing pages of the novel make the fleeting implication that the true personality of this modern man without qualities is linked to his mother's in ways that the novel will not or cannot share.

To the Schiller scholar, Meursault's philosophical transformation even as he anticipates his walk to the gallows sounds a bit like the ending of *The Robbers,* another story of a rebel without a cause, and the novel certainly hints at a link between mother, son, and trauma in a manner not dissimilar to Schil-ler's first play. Yet, the problem of longing for a lost mother is a difficulty that overtly attends not Schiller's and Camus's first works but rather their last ones.

On one of the seats of Camus's wrecked automobile was found a manu-script for a novel, entitled *The First Man.* In this incomplete text what begins as a forty-year-old man's quest for the history of his dead father rapidly meta-morphosizes into an attempt to reunite with and fully remember Mother, at the same time as the protagonist struggles to come to terms with his uncertain personal, moral, political, sexual, and national identities. Making his first, over-due visit to his father's grave, the protagonist, Jacques Cormery, makes the traumatic realization that his father died at an age far younger than he himself now is—making the discovered dead father younger than the son. Everything falls apart for the protagonist at that moment: personal and collective history and psychological wholeness collapse under the weight of this discovery. The novel's protagonist finds himself reduced to one emotion: "anguish."

> The course of time itself was shattering around him while he remained motionless among those tombs he no longer saw, and the years no longer kept to their places in the great river that flows to the end . . . in the strange dizziness of that moment, the statue every man erects and then hardens in the fire of the years, into which he then creeps and there awaits its final crumbling—that statue was rapidly cracking, it was already col-lapsing. All that was left was this anguished heart, eager to live, rebelling against the deadly order of the world that had been with him for forty years, and still struggling against the wall that separated him from the secret of all life, wanting to go farther, to go beyond, and to discover before dying, discover at last in order to be, just once to be, for a single second, but forever. (Camus 27)

Following that emotional shattering, Camus's language bursts into an explo-sion of words, which peter out, leaving in the wreckage only one primal, auxil-iary infinitive: "to be" [*être*].

But intimately connected to the suffering of the orphaned adult son is the repeated image of the traumatized mother:

And immediately she turned away, went back into the apartment, and seated herself in the dining room that faced the street; she no longer seemed to be thinking of him nor for that matter of anything, and she even looked at him from time to time with an odd expression, as if—or so it seemed to him—he were now in the way, were disturbing the narrow, empty closed universe which she circled in her solitude. What was more, once he was seated by her, she seemed on this day to be seized with some sort of anxiety, and occasionally she would glance furtively out at the street with her lovely melancholy expression, her eyes feverish until she turned to Jacques. (Camus 56)

Almost completely deaf, illiterate, and possessing only a limited vocabulary, Jacques's mother fulfills the melodramatic function played by the mute; she represents the quintessential incarnation of trauma—a pain beyond words. Unavailable, because she can neither hear nor literally "read" him, she and her adult son carry on a tortured, poignant dance of longing and distance. Indeed it is the wish to bridge the enormous, painful gap between him and mother that haunts Camus's final, deeply autobiographical text. But the title itself points to the impossibility of ever truly mending that rift: the "first man" is necessarily—according to biblical legend—the first (and as it turns out, the only) man without a mother.[4]

In the notes to the unfinished novel, Camus makes it clear that the mother he has in mind is in fact his own; in the novel itself he repeatedly calls the fictional mother by the name of his own real mother: Catherine. Schiller, in contrast, never wrote much about his mother. He barely ever mentions her in his correspondence and has little to say about her until she becomes ill and dies.[5] In fact, it is the absence rather than the presence of mothers that is striking both in Schiller's letters and in his early plays, all of which feature motherless protagonists: Karl and Franz, Fiesko, Ferdinand von Walter, Don Carlos. Many of the later plays follow this same pattern: Max Piccolomini has no mother, nor do Elizabeth Regina or Beatrice of *Bride*.

But while absent mothers are common in the German theatrical work of the eighteenth century (again, Schiller's important predecessor, Lessing has paved the way here), even more significant (and surprising) is their sudden reemergence in Schiller's final plays.[6] In her powerful reading of *The Maid of Orleans* [*Die Jungfrau*], Gail Hart points to a new and crucial character development in Schiller's dramaturgy;[7] here we have yet another fearful, traumatized son named Karl (the third in Schiller's dramatic oeuvre) escaping, not from father but from a castrating, killer mother whose Amazonian features mark her as the slippery and highly disturbing counterpoint to Joan herself. In the later plays, it seems as though for the first time in Schiller's dramas, the figure of the mother rears her head: and what a strange set of hydra heads it is: the murderous Isabeau, the grief-stricken but manipulative Isabella of *Bride*, the restrained but very reluctant Hedwig (Tell's taciturn domestic angel), and finally, Demetrius's alleged mother, the incarcerated Marfa. Remarkably, Schiller's final plays focus increasingly on maternal characters—who occur as objects of rage, objects of mourning, or both. In his last work, Schiller, like Camus, seems to be, at last, directly exploring the relation between the child—specifically the male child—and the difficult, troubled mother.

These explorations connect powerfully to Julia Kristeva's work on this subject. In *Black Sun*, Kristeva discusses the loss of the *thing*—the love of mother. Lost very early, the primal and irreplaceable connection to mother becomes, according to her, "an unsymbolizeable unnamable narcissistic wound, so precocious that no outside agent (subject or agent) can be used as referent" (13). Those unable to triumph over their need for the *thing* through the therapeutic creation of artistic and linguistic supplements suffer from a depression so all-encompassing that it eventually destroys belief in the logos, resulting in the loss of language and in eventual silence, leading to death.

But in her more recent book, *New Maladies of the Soul*, Kristeva goes further in her analysis of the mother-son relation and how the loss of maternal love may manifest itself. Here, she argues that constant exposure to a "depressed" mother is, in and of itself, particularly traumatizing for the son, who often represses the relationship altogether, and who subsequently talks about fathers and brothers and lovers but only rarely about his "buried mother" (*Maladies* 53ff.). Such sons internalize the pain of their physically present but emotionally absent mothers by "assimilat[ing their] mother's helplessness" (63).

Not coincidentally, the male children of the difficult mothers in Schiller's late plays tend to be melancholic at best and disturbed at worst. The Dauphin in *Maid* is paralyzed and weak, while mysterious sibling hatred and what proves to be an incestuous lust drive the sons to their demise in *Bride*. And the orphaned Demetrius is haunted by a traumatic memory that propels him not toward glory but toward imposture and destruction. Along the way, he will find a deeply distressed and depressed mother, enraged by her exile and longing for revenge.

Following Kristeva's lead, Juliet Mitchell's discussion of trauma and orphans argues for the crucial role played by writing in the therapeutic process of coming to terms with trauma: "When one writes with a sense of aliveness, one commonly discovers that one didn't know that one had such ideas and perceptions. . . . To be able to write in a sustained, active way necessitates a new positioning. Or, in reverse, trying to write may facilitate this positioning" (131). Camus's unfinished masterpiece may certainly be understood as a linguistic struggle to reposition the (his) mother and the adult son (himself) through writing and thereby to overcome the inaccessibility/loss of his female parent. In theatrical fashion, *Demetrius* may be read as a less fully realized but equally compelling attempt to confront the same problem.[8]

Moreover, as though bearing out Kristeva's observation that an apparent obsession with the paternal may *mask* the far greater anxiety with mother (*Maladies* 52–53), both Camus's novel and Schiller's unfinished drama employ a seemingly patriarchal premise in order to uncover what is—at the root—a quest for Mother. Like Jacques, Demetrius desperately seeks Mother because he is uncertain who he is, and she alone, as the survivor of his missing parents, can guarantee his identity (he claims to be the missing son of Ivan the Terrible). Connected to the quest for Mother are also questions of national identity and allegiance. Like Camus's hero, Demetrius is "alien" in the sense that he possesses dubious national affiliations; just as Jacques is at once Algerian and French, so is Demetrius at once Polish and Russian. Both characters are at once national foreigners and strangers to both others and themselves. Without Mother, Schiller and Camus suggest, the son is cast adrift into a diasporic existence that is at once internal and external:[9] One of Kristeva's patients appropriately acts out his kind of nomadic self-construction: "He directed himself toward other people, he moved about and became agitated. Yet, he remained tentative, hesitant, and weary from having assimilated . . . his mother's wounded narcissism" (*Maladies* 60).

"REMEMBRANCE OF THINGS PAST IS ONLY FOR THE RICH"

In *The First Man*, financial concerns play an enormous role. Money, Camus tells us sardonically, determines whether and how much we remember, and the degree to which we must repress the unbearable, "To begin with, poor people's memory is less nourished than that of the rich; it has fewer landmarks in space . . . and fewer reference points in time throughout lives which are grey and featureless . . . And besides, in order to bear up well one must not remember too much" (Camus 80). If *The First Man* suggests that only the rich and powerful can afford to remember trauma, *Demetrius* makes a somewhat different but equally disturbing suggestion about the relationship between pain and finance; the play implies that the convincing performance of trauma may be indeed fruitfully employed as a means to acquire wealth and power. In the opening acts, Schiller establishes complex connections between the relating of unbearable memories and acquisition, by repeatedly displaying and rhetorically invoking the importance of possessions, and the proprietary negotiations necessary to obtain them, even as traumatic memory asserts itself directly. Not coincidentally, in *Demetrius* the business of creation—in both literal and figurative senses, as birth and as commercial product—looms large, and the play features a character who is literally a "self-made man"—a man who hopes to make his fortune by creating an identity through narrative.

We should remember that self-invention as a means for material gain is at this point in Anglo-European culture something of a commonplace—a phenomenon that marks once again that complex relation that Weber remarked between emerging capitalism and Protestant notions of radical individuality. Self-invention marks the narrative trajectory of Marivaux's early-eighteenth-century French novel *The Successful Peasant* [*Le Paysan Parvenu*]; the failure to reinvent himself as the various social venues require is what precipitates Werther's downfall—he cannot play multiple parts—whereas it is precisely this performative flexibility that ensures the eventual success of Wilhelm Meister.

This practical, material importance of self-invention becomes even more central to Realist and Modernist drama. On one hand, the practical matter of self-creation and the careful managing of the story, and on the other hand, the chaos that ensues when the story gets mixed up or forgotten, drive such very different modernist plays as Pirandello's *As You Desire Me*, Synge's *The Playboy of the Western World*, Anouilh's *Traveler without Baggage*, and Wilde's *The Importance of being Ernest*. These are all plays about legitimacy, about financial inheritance, and about returns to family and to family origin, as well as about amnesia and pretense. In all of them, identity gets worked out through alternating narrative schemas and the performances of self, which derive from them. The wished-for result always includes a new birth of self accompanied by possessions—both sexual and financial. In these plays the desire for the "truth" and the anxieties of imposture are superceded by the more material (and pressing) desires of ownership and social status.

Looking forward to these dramas, *Demetrius* also deals with questions of legacy and a self from a point of view that seems bourgeois, insofar as it is linked overtly to questions of acquisition. "I am the story I tell"—a model that Ziad Elmarsafy has argued becomes a hallmark of modern sensibility—and one might add here, "particularly if it will get me something."[10]

The beginning of *Demetrius* would seem to bear out such an understanding of self. The opening scenes unfold as a complex dance of mergers and acquisitions; everyone in the drama comes to the table wanting to get something and ready to do whatever it takes to get it (Martini 323): The Polish court wants more land from Russia, the Polish king wants more power over his fiefs. The main characters are more specific: Maryna wants to be Tsarina, Demetrius wants Russia and his mother, Marfa wants out of the convent, she wants power (Martini 324), and of course, she wants her baby, her creation, back.[11]

Accordingly, the title character himself is careful to emphasize how much profit the Polish court stands to make by supporting his claim, and he himself comes equipped with the emblems of property. It is, after all, the material possession of numerous affidavits that enables Demetrius to be heard by the court in the first place. Evidence is described in terms of visible matériel in the possession of the claimant:

> Give us proof of that.
> Whereby do you attest that you are he?
> And by what signs can you be recognized?
>
> (Passage, *Demetrius* 1.1.8)

> Davon gebt uns Beweise.
> Wodurch beglaubigt ihr, daß ihr *der* seid?
> An welchen Zeichen soll man euch erkennen?
>
> (*Schillers Werke* 11:11)

That proviso being accomplished, there is the strong sense in the opening scene that the court is willing to use any excuse to make war on Russia in order to acquire and reacquire territory, and that Demetrius could say just about anything to them. Small wonder then that Demetrius is able to convince this throng; he speaks their language—the lingo of acquisition, as his clearly stated agenda shows: "I stand here to claim / An empire and a royal scepter" (5). [. . . ich stehe hier, ein Reich / Zu fodern und ein koenigliches Scepter] (11:9). A page later he affirms his right to such possessions by placing himself as a victim of theft: "I am a prince despoiled" (6). [Ich stehe vor euch ein beraubter Fürst] (10).

But in terms of hard evidence, Demetrius does not give the Polish court much to work with. Instead of actual material, he tells them a story—a narrative that is as precociously contemporary as it is strange:[12]

> I tell you what I know.
> If any rumor spread of my existence,
> Some god officiously had made it current.
> I did not know myself. In the house of
> The Palatine and lost among his servants
> I lived out youth's obscure and cheerful time.
>
> (1.1.9)

> Ich erzähle was ich weiß.
> Gieng ein Gerücht umher von meinem Daseyn
> So hat geschäftig es ein Gott verbreitet.
> Ich kannt' mich nicht. Im Hauß des Palatins
> Und unter seiner Dienerschaar verloren
> Lebt ich der Jugend froehlich dunkle Zeit.
>
> (11:12)

Ignorant of his true birth, Demetrius commits a crime of passion and find himself (as do so many of Schiller's heroes) on the brink of execution. Recognized at the last moment by a cross he wears and a religious Psalter he carries, Demetrius's memories—as though legitimized by others— miraculously flow back to him:

> All of a sudden memories revived
> In the remotest depths of my past life,
> And in the furthest depths of my past life,
> And as the furthest towers of the distance
> Will gleam amid the gold of sunlight, so
> Within my soul two images shone forth.
> The sunlit pinnacles of consciousness.
> I saw myself in *flight* in dark of night
> And I beheld a flashing flame blaze up
> As I looked backward through the black night's horror.
> It must have been a distant, early image,
> For what preceded it and what came after
> Was blotted out in distances of time;
> Disjointed only, solitary gleaming,
> That picture had stuck in my memory.
>
> (1.1.11)

> Errinerungen belebten sich auf einmal
> Im fernsten Hintergrund vergangner Zeit;
> Und wie die lezten Thürme aus der Ferne
> Erglänzen in der Sonne Gold, so wurden
> Mir in der Seele zwey Gestalten hell,
> Die höchsten Sonnengipfel des Bewußtseyns.
> Ich sah mich *fliehn* in einer dunkeln Nacht,
> Und eine lohe *Flamme* sah ich steigen
> In schwarzem Nachtgraun, als ich rükwärts sah.
> Ein uralt frühes Denken mußt es seyn,
> Denn was vorhergieng, was darauf gefolgt,
> War ausgelöscht in langer Zeitenferne;
> Nur abgerissen, einsam leuchtend, stand
> Dieß Schreckensbild mir im Gedächtnis da.
>
> (11:14–15)

As the ultimate truth, Demetrius, and Schiller with him, proposes an experience of trauma and repressed memory—the hotly disputed psychological phenomena often used now in the furtherance of child abuse and incest lawsuits by adult survivors.[13] Demetrius claims to be a trauma survivor, whose memory unexpectedly came back, ostensibly because of his near brush with death, which operated as a trauma trigger that in turn releases the memory, but he emphasizes that it was his recognition by others that facilitated this sudden upsurging of memory.[14]

Thus, in *Demetrius*, Schiller places trauma in the central and originating position of dramatic action, and trauma relates less to Father than to Mother. In contrast to his other plays, Schiller's final work introduces traumatic memory at the very outset and then proceeds to demonstrate how the performance of traumatic memory supersedes all other concerns—including acquisition—through a claim to absolute, undeniable truth. In turn, traumatic truth legitimizes the rememberer in his own drive to acquire rights and territories, through the insistance on traumatic loss as the first formative moment of Demetrius's identity (the implication being "I have lost everything and so deserve everything"). The king suggests as much when he observes, after having encouraged Demetrius to pursue his claim, that Demetrius has been born a second time in Poland through the recovery of his traumatic origin:

> Remember you first found yourself in Poland,
> And love this country which bore you a second time.
>
> (1.1.22)

> Denkt daß ihr euch in Pohlen selbst gefunden
> Liebt dieses Land, das euch zum zweitenmal gebohren.
>
> (11:27)

Recovering the lost traumatic moment allows for a symbolic second birth. And this birth validates the quest for acquisition.

Second, and equally important, it is mother who emerges as crucial to trauma and to its resolution, as the astute, fiercely ambitious Maryna suggests when she creates the following metaphor:

> Let him believe himself: the world will then
> Believe in him. Let him retain that darkness
> Which is the mother of all great achievements.
>
> (1.2.25)

> Er glaub an sich, so glaubt ihm auch die Welt.
> Laß *ihn* die glükliche Dunkelheit bewahren
> Die eine Mutter großer Thaten ist.
>
> (11:29)

Maryna understands that Demetrius's trauma replaces the maternal as the creatrix of his identity and activity. But if trauma "mothers" the identity

144

and the role, it is the "real" mother who will legitimize this self through the verification of traumatic memory and thereby enable the fulfillment of its plans for action. Once lost and soon to be restored, mother will make Demetrius a whole man and allow him to fulfill his destiny.

"O MOTHER, O LOVE . . . GREATER THAN THE HISTORY THAT SUBJECTED YOU TO ITSELF"

Demetrius uses a tension-building technique that Schiller has consistently used, from *The Robbers* to *Marya Stuart*; he withholds a key character for as long as possible while building up the character's importance through description and reference. In this manner, the opening of Schiller's drama makes it clear that everything depends on the recovery of the absent mother. But the mother proves as traumatized as the son, if not more so—a suffering queen incarcerated in a prisonlike convent. While her interlocutors address her as though she were supposed to have achieved the proper degree of Christian renunciation, Marfa quickly dispels any illusion that she is the patient, resigned pious widow. Instead she speaks in the flat yet resonant voice of the trauma survivor—for whom the past is not past but present, and for whom the pain is an open, uncloseable, and yet strangely indescribable wound:

> I do not want to be at peace, nor to
> Forget. It is a coward soul that will
> Accept its healing and its cure from time,
> Replacing something irreplaceable.
> Nothing shall buy my grief away from me.
> As heaven's arch walks always with the walker,
> Surrounds him totally and endlessly
> Wherever he directs his fleeing step,
> So does my grief walk with me where I walk,
> Surrounding me as with an endless sea;
> My endless tears have not exhausted it.
>
> (2.1.33)

> Ich will mich nicht beruhigen, will nicht
> Vergeßen. Das ist eine feige Seele,
> Die eine Heilung annimmt von der Zeit,
> Ersatz fürs unersetzliche! Mir soll
> Nichts meinen Gram abkaufen—Wie des Himmels
> Gewölbe ewig mit dem Wandrer geht,
> Ihn immer unermeßlich, ganz, umfängt,
> Wohin er fliehend auch die Schritte wende,

145

So geht mein Schmerz mit mir, wohin ich wandle,
er schließt mich ein wie ein unendlich Meer,
Nie ausgeschöpft hat ihn mein ewig Weinen.

(11:40)

Marfa paints herself as the epitome of the melancholic, the person who mourns but cannot get over, the person whose grief has become so enormous it becomes exterior to her and engulfs her like the sea. Once again, this state of affairs is reminiscent of Kristeva's empty self, for whom sadness is the only, the ultimate belonging. Marfa is also the "desperate mother" of *New Maladies of the Soul*; no longer an object of the father's desires, Marfa has also broken a bond with language, one that through the miraculous apparition of the son she is trying at last to reforge (53–54).

But Marfa also speaks her pain in terms of financial exchange. Since she has been deprived of all her material possessions, Marfa's one remaining object is her grief, whose resolution she perceives as a sale she will not make to the world, for to do so would make a bad bargain—leaving her with nothing at all. "Grief" [*Gram*] is the one thing that can't be bought or sold—that transcends the process of acquisition. Or does it? For with this gesture, Marfa also appears to recognize that as former Tsarina she has fallen out of the system of exchanges that governs the world of the play, and she understands rightly that her sorrow isn't worth anything on the open market. There is more than a grain of political and economic truth to her seemingly purely psychological statement.

Having embraced this narrative of the self in pain, Marfa is not pleased but angry to hear that Demetrius may still be alive; such doubt threatens to pull her out of narcissistic depression and into the realm of caring—a move which she deeply resents. "Am I to turn my glances back toward life / On which I had pronounced farewell forever?" (2:1.36). [Soll ich den Blick zurueck ins Leben wenden / Von dem ich endlich abgeschieden war?] (443). This resentment turns quickly—during the course of her conversation with the Archijerei Hiob—into a manic presentiment of Demetrius as an avenging force who will procure revenge for the downtrodden Marfa. This too has narcissistic overtones; in this dream of salvation, it is Marfa's woes that will be made good, her losses restored, and so on. At the same time, though, Marfa's reaction also marks her rebellion against Goudonow, the present Tsar, and her refusal to be the passive object of his tyrannical directive. She immediately understands that Hiob has come on political, not moral, grounds, and she refuses point-blank to be his pawn:

Can terror blind your Tsar to such degree
That he hopes for deliverance from me—

146

From me, who was immeasurably offended?
That he sends you to me,—
To wrest . . .

(2.1.40)

Kann deinen Czar der Schrecken so verblenden,
Daß er Errettung hofft von mir—von mir!
Der unermeßlich schwer beleidigten?
Daß er dich an mich sendet—
—abzulisten . . .

(11:49)

This extreme and precipitous emotional progression culminates with a Marfa who feels the entire weight of her imprisonment but who also, like so many of Schiller's heroes, glimpses herself fleetingly as spiritually creative, rhetorically restored, and potentially powerful:

Eternal sun that moves about the globe
Of earth, be messenger to my desires!
O unrestricted circumambient air
That swiftly finishes its furthest course,
Convey my eager, ardent longing to him!
Supplication and prayer are all I have,
I draw them up in flames out of my heart
And speed them winged to the heights of heaven,
I speed them toward you like a warrior host!

(2.1.43)

Du ewge Sonne, die den Erdenball
Umkreißt, sei du die Botin meiner Wünsche!
Du allverbreitet ungehemmte Luft,
Die schnell die weitste Wanderung vollendet
O trag ihm meine glühende Sehnsucht zu!
Ich habe nichts als mein Gebet und Flehn,
Das schöpf ich flammened aus der tiefesten Seele,
Beflügelt send ichs in des Himmels Höhn
Wie eine Heerschaar send ich dirs entgegen!

(11:52)

Addressing the goddesslike—and, of course, pagan—figures of the sun and the air, Marfa again speaks in terms of possession but this time adds to it her sense of personal creativity. She figures herself literally as the mother of desire—of prayer and supplication—which she sends to her son in an act of imaginative transformation, metamorphosing her wishes into an army, a magical, heavenly host that will bring him victory and bring him to her as well.

The curious envisaged twists and turns in Schiller's plot outlines suggest that Demetrius's repressed memory will prove to be a false one, and yet the reality of his own trauma remains. And, although Demetrius and Marfa are not, as it turns out, biologically related, the opening scenes of the play establish a clear psychic relation between them through their shared access to trauma; it is this shared experience that enables Demetrius to declare that Marfa should regard him as her son in fact (although both realize that he is not who he thought he was), and it makes psychological (as well as political) sense that she should accept such an offer. Finally, while the accuracy of Demetrius's memory may not guarantee his rights as king, the memory does, Schiller seems to suggest, possess an emotional veracity, which cannot be denied, although its objective correlative cannot be established.

The *Demetrius* fragment implies that trauma may be real and yet not reducible to a single event and that memory, while significant, may not represent a *literally faithful,* linear narrative re-production of what actually happened. In so doing, Schiller's unfinished play promises a highly sophisticated, nuanced understanding of trauma and memory that looks forward to the recent work of John Frow:

> To say that memory is of the order of representation rather than a reflex of real events, and that its temporality is that of the reworking of earlier material rather than that of a causality working as a line of force from the past to the present, is not to deny the reality of traumatic experience . . . and its working through in present suffering; but it is to say that this experience is always reconstructed rather than recalled; that reconstruction takes place within the specific and formative circumstances of the present; and that causes are always attributed rather than known. (234)

Similarly, practicing psychiatrist and cultural psychiatry researcher Laurence Kirmayer observes, "Although we do not know the effects of trauma on registration and recall, most of the arguments about narrowing of attention and affect state-dependence and defensive dealing with emotional context would make traumatic memories *more*, not less, malleable and influenced by imagination and context-sensitive reconstruction" (181).

Do we ever definitively know ourselves? What do our memories signify? How and according to what measure of truth do we interpret them? How can psychic pain be healed? And how do we conduct ourselves—socially, politically, ethically—in the meantime? Writing one hundred years before Freud, Schiller anticipates and articulates questions about the unconscious, memory, and interpretation that the father of psychoanalysis will repeatedly confront and spend a lifetime tackling,[15] and that we are still struggling to make sense of at the turn of the twenty-first century.

Moreover, in this drama, which focuses on the performative recapitulation and working out of trauma, Schiller may have precociously glimpsed a connection between psychoanalysis and theater. Cynthia Chase argues that Freud seems to have partially understood the essentially *dramatic* nature of psychoanalysis; this would account for the emphasis in Freudian theory on the Oedipus complex and, more important, for Freud's own interest in the actual Sophoclean play:

> We should make the attempt to read . . . Freud's remark . . . that the "process of revealing" that constitutes "the action of the play . . . can be likened to the work of a psychoanalysis." . . . In the context of his practice and writing . . . Freud's comparison meant that Oedipus Tyrannus successfully dramatizes the activity of repression and unrepression—the "abnormal defense" that characterizes "psychoneurosis" and the peculiar "process of revealing" that constitutes interpretation of dreams, or psychoanalysis. (178)

Freud, then, saw the classical tragedy as both enacting and undoing repression—the latter being the cure toward which analysis moves. Chase also speculates that Freud's writing constitutes a performative supplement to his own practice (189). Through invoking a group of *readers* who would witness the trials and tribulations of the analysand and the analyst, Freud constructed psychoanalysis as both internal drama and belated spectacle (for the readers have access to the therapy in writing only after it has actually taken place).

Such an understanding of psychoanalysis and the drama leads back in turn to the dramatic action and trauma depicted in *Demetrius*. Like the orphaned Oedipus, Demetrius also proceeds in twists and turns to the discovery of who he really is; as shattering as this discovery proves to be, it is precisely this unearthing of identity that is the goal of psychoanalytic therapy. By making his audience witness to Demetrius's performance of traumatic memory and to the tortuous process of self-understanding that unfolds from it, Schiller is tentatively exploring an epistemological paradox that Freud will elaborate upon a hundred years later. The theater is the site par excellence for the representation of trauma, but it is no less crucial as a site for its cure, for its very dynamic at once performs repression and encapsulates the possible mode of recovery from trauma—its unveiling: "We could also put it another way: as writing, and reading, psychoanalysis is an endlessly recited tragedy. For it is generated . . . by the aspiration to a cure, whether conceived as resembling laughter or a catharsis of pity and fear" (190).

Arguably all of Schiller's plays have been concerned with this very process; they all proceed dramatically through the veiling and unveiling of trauma,

149

making their audiences witnesses and potential partners in the emotional passages that Schiller depicts; the psychological depth and emotional intensity of those navigations mirror and, to some degree, explain the very intense emotional reaction that the original audiences had to the plays (and that contemporary audiences still have). Indeed, the construction of the plays suggests that—long before *The Bride of Messina* and after it—the medically trained Schiller conceived of drama not only as a *pharmakeia* but also as *therapeia*—that which heals.

But in most of Schiller's dramas the process of healing is aborted. The protagonists are never entirely able to know who they are; for the most part they are unable to break beyond the various repressions and traumatic aftereffects that bind them into destructive and self-destructive behaviors. Franz never consciously knows his trauma, and neither does Karl. Don Carlos remembers but cannot attach emotional significance to trauma; rather the emotions drift off in other, perverse directions. Wallenstein blocks trauma within the depth of paranoia and depression. The triad of siblings of *Bride* displace trauma onto incest and fratricide, and the play as a whole freezes trauma into classical aesthetics. The protagonists of the other plays—Fiesko, Ferdinand von Walter, Maria Stuart and Elizabeth I, and, arguably, Joan of Arc—are likewise unable to come fully to grips with the traumatic memories that haunt them. Only Max Piccolimini is able to see beyond and act against his dehumanizing experience of the war machine.

Seen against the other plays that make up Schiller's theater of trauma, *Demetrius* becomes all the more striking. The fragment emerges clearly as the playwright's most psychologically self-aware and informed play, incomplete though it may be. It self-consciously foregrounds and depicts trauma as both distorted, unreliable memory and as the center of spectacle. In a similarly complex fashion, the play's envisioned culmination in the protagonist's full comprehension of the truth of his past points to the cruciality of self-revelation as well as to the disruptive consequences that such self-revelation incurs. Indeed, from a psychological point of view it is difficult *not* to read the imagined end of *Demetrius* in this light. According to Schiller's notes, Demetrius was to be murdered and another man would call himself Demetrius and try to take his place.[16] But what is the difference between the two? Is it not possible to think of the second Demetrius as the new man who rises from the ashes of the old? Moreover, isn't the second Demetrius—the man who dares to name himself with the name of a king and who proceeds to fulfill his destiny and win his desires—similar to the analysand after the drama of therapy? The analysand must also eventually name him/herself with a name of his/her own choosing, and, finally free, pursue adventure beyond the realms of the analyst's stage.

"THE VERY GREAT VISION I HAVE OF ART"

The unfinished business, which is *Demetrius*, is a road map in progress that indicates other exciting directions that Schiller's creative work was heading in when he died. In this last, fragmentary theatrical composition Schiller seems to be renewing the effort—evident particularly in *Don Carlos*—to think of his art and the role of the artist as something more and other than as a product and producer within the financial system in which he found himself increasingly enmeshed and with whose power he found himself constantly negotiating. Social agents may all be "performers" of one fiction or another, but there are nonetheless, he suggests in Marfa's speeches, feelings and experiences that are more than the market. These feelings are neither quantifiable nor qualifiable, and these emotions are linked in profound ways with the relationship the child has with his mother. And yet, Marfa's declaration "I will not sell my pain" must strike us as ironic, for as Schiller's own work testifies, pain does indeed sell, and we in the early twenty-first century are also, like Schiller's audiences, for the most part very eager traders in its futures.

Schiller did not resolve that paradox—that trauma is at once outside of economy and a crucial cog, which turns the wheels of entertainment within an emerging cultural market. Rather the fragment of *Demetrius* poses that paradox as the ground for any productive thinking about trauma. Trauma is now, the play suggests, inseparable from a society of acquisition in which any meaningful, individual activity must somehow confront the imperatives of buying and selling. In his final play Schiller suggests that we—audience and artist alike—are no different from these characters that construct themselves in terms of what they can get, sell, and trade for the articulation of their personal misery. At the same time the author suggests—particularly through his imprisoned former queen—that such a state of affairs is unacceptable and intolerable.[17] And here for the first and last time in his theatrical work, Schiller directly posits the central role—both psychologically and socially—of that foundress of the bourgeois self: the elided, domestically imprisoned mother. Herself in the grip of patriarchal and economic forces, herself a powerless pawn in the game of men and of money, Marfa looks forward to the ubiquitous "madwoman in the attic" of nineteenth-century Anglo-European writing as well as to the problematic mothers who, like Catherine Camus, inhabit the work of so many famous male writers of the twentieth century: Tennessee Williams, Peter Handke, Roland Barthes, Jack Kerouac, and graphic novelist Art Spiegelman. Within the oeuvres of these melancholy, troubled authors stands the woman who inspired them—herself a sad and sorry object of acquisition and an unwilling subject who experiences terrible loss.

While he could not quite outstrip the melancholy that seems to have

151

dogged the steps of his own life, in *Demetrius* Schiller seems to have also intuited something about the relationship of traumatic experience to gender and class. Looking forward to contemporary theories of transgenerational trauma, he suggests that pain may be something that the child inherits from the mother; he suggests here that under patriarchal conditions it is the son who is best positioned to receive and act upon his mother's pain and that her loss inaugurates his (Kristeva, *Maladies* 54), an emptiness he attempts to pay back through power, lands, money and the possession of people and things.[18]

In this light, Schiller's theatrical corpus may be seen as an ingenious form of traumatic compensation, an artistic creation that imperfectly and provisionally mothered the self who made it by selling itself off as a commodity and making Schiller the Weimar great we now know and study. That this construction of self never seems to have pleased Schiller, and that it may even have played a role in the author's early death, serves as a sobering indicator of how much artists and intellectuals are both created and undone by the cultural market we at once critique and serve. At the same time, Schiller's oeuvre, prematurely interrupted though it is, testifies to the power of creative cultural activity that—at its most courageous—strives to work out, work through, and eventually overcome the personal pathology and social ideology that gave it birth:

> And in the end we are really both Idealists, and we would be ashamed of ourselves if people were to say of us—after our passing—that things formed us, rather than that we formed things. (Schiller's last letter to Humboldt, April 2, 1805).

> Und am Ende sind wir ja beide Idealisten und würden wir uns schämen, uns nachsagen zu lassen, daß die Dinge uns formten und nicht wir die Dinge. (*Schillers Werke* 32:206)

> Who can live with his own truth? But it is enough to know it is there, it is enough to know it at last and that it feeds a secret and silent [fervor] in the self, in the face of death. (Camus 307)

Notes

1. Pioneering psychiatrist Judith Herman (the author of the definitive work *Trauma and Recovery*) argues that the early study of trauma was broken off by Freud himself, when he discovered that the syndrome was linked at once to gender and femininity, and that it seemed related to a startling preponderance of sexual abuse in the families of the patients he was treating (12–14).

2. As will be seen, Kristeva's work with trauma spreads itself out over the course of several books—the most intriguing of which are *Powers of Horror,* which discusses trauma in terms of the "abject," and *Black Sun,* a study of aesthetics and depression.

3. Herman notes "traumatized people relive as though it were continually recurring in the present . . . It is as though time stops at the moment of trauma" (37).

4. Psychologist Ellen McGrath stresses the crucial importance of "trauma triggers"—seemingly innocuous events that "trigger" a post-traumatic episode, a feeling of reliving the original, repressed event (conversation, March 20, 1996).

5. Scattered sensations and a few vivid images are constitutive of traumatic memory, according to Herman (38).

6. This tenuousness looks forward in turn to the increasingly politicized plays of the German theater—from Büchner to Brecht, and to Müller—dramas that foreground the unclean political dealings of our own time. Numerous critics have stressed the contemporary, political aspect of Schiller in recent years, and this perspective is particularly evident in two collections of essays from the 1980s: Wolfgang Wittkowski's *Friedrich Schiller: Kunst, Humanität, und Politik in der späten Aufklaerung* (1982) and Alexej Ugrinsky's *Friedrich von Schiller and the Drama of Human Existence* (1988). See in particular the essays by Reinhold Grimm and Donald Crosby (Ugrinsky 310–25 and 341–50), as well as those by Steven Taubeneck, Karin Barnaby, and Hans Joachim Bernhard (Ugrinsky 103–8, 119–28, and 155–62).

7. Sturm und Drang and its English equivalent Storm and Stress will be used interchangeably in this book.

8. The importance of Lessing for the development of European realist drama cannot be overstated. Lessing was, according to F. J. Lamport, the first important practitioner and theorist of realist drama (31) and was a significant contributor to the ongoing discussion of audience psychology and the theatrical experience.

9. See Susan Gustafson's compelling reading of the Gerstenberg play as a crucial bridge from Enlightenment to Storm and Stress Aesthetics ("Sadomasochism, Mutilation, and Men"). Indeed, her reading suggests that *Ugolino* is an important precursor to *Die Raueber,* for it foregrounds a hysterical insistence on wounded "men under siege" (199).

10. See *Powers.*

11. See Gustafson's psychoanalytic interpretation of Lessing's aesthetics and dramas, *Absent Mothers and Orphaned Fathers.* See in particular her discussion of Lessing's aesthetics, 51–117.

12. Zelle notes that, in the end, "pleasurable terror" could be represented only when it was safely contained within the scheme of a reasonable, theologically inflected world order, where fear could serve a conservative, art affirming, ethical, quasi-religious purpose (412).

13. See Simon Richter's remarkable study of writing around the issue of this famous statue, *Laocoon's Body and the Aesthetics of Pain.*

14. At moments like these one wonders if Thomas Mann's vision of Schiller in "die Schwere Stunde" does not have some validity. In that short story Mann sees Schiller as a homoerotic figure possessing deeply closeted but passionate inclinations. It seems possible that homoeroticism may comprise at least part of the secret and frightening "Kräfte" referred to in the latter part of the letter, especially given Schiller's history of and interest in passionate male friendships.

15. Schiller "acts out" his resentment of his relentless work schedule most tellingly in a histrionic set of letters describing his illness to his rival—the prolific and financially successful Goethe. See in particular their correspondence regarding Schiller's visit to Weimar during August and September of 1794.

CHAPTER 1

1. I am referring to the "unexpurgated" 1781 version of the play, which contains some wording later cut by the Mannheim Intendant, Dahlberg.

2. In his "Supplement to the Performance of The Robbers" [Anhang über die Vorstellung der Räuber]—a review written by the author himself in the guise of a letter received from a friend (Brandt 250)—Schiller remarks "It seemed to me that there were too many realities dragged in together . . . One could have made three plays out of the thing" [Mir kam es auch vor, es waren zu viele Realitäten hieneingedraengt . . . Man hätte drei Theaterstücke daraus machen können] (Grawe 174). Translations of the correspondence and occasional papers are mine, unless otherwise indicated.

3. English quotations from *The Robbers* (ch. 1) are from *The Robbers and Wallenstein* translated by F. J. Lamport. English quotations from *Don Carlos* (ch.2) are translated by Charles Passage from *Don Carlos. Plays.* by Schiller. All English quotations from the Wallenstein trilogy (ch. 3) are from *WALLENSTEIN* by Passage. In chs. 4 and 5, all English quotations are from *The Bride of Messina, Wilhelm Tell, and Demitrius by Friedrich von Schiller* by Passage. German quotations from all the plays are from *Schillers Werke.*

4. For a full discussion of the problem of masculinity in the play, see Hammer, *Sublime Crime* 83–97, and "Schiller, Time and Again."

5. In this way, Schiller's play makes "good" on the threat of masculine fragmentation, which Susan Gustafson sees as crucial to the theatrical and critical oeuvre of Lessing—Schiller's most important (and most influential) predecessor in the German theater. See *Absent Mothers* 110.

6. Criticism of the play has stressed the opposition between the two brothers. See my discussion in *Sublime Crime,* 188 n. 2.

7. See Alan C. Leidner's discussion of audience reactions to *Die Räuber* in " 'Fremde Menschen fielen einander schluchzend in die Arme.' "

8. In his role as deprecator, Spiegelberg closely resembles Diderot's satiric spokesman, Rameau's Nephew.

9. Stage director Erwin Piscator made Spiegelberg the focal point of his ironic, politicized postwar production of the play in 1926 (Grawe 198ff.).

10. Dahlberg cut the first line (variant, *Schillers Werke* 3:359).

11. Nietzsche himself saw this connection when he reread the play and commented in his journal entry of August 24, 1859: "The characters are almost superhuman; one believes that one is watching a struggle of Titans against religion and virtue" [Die Charaktere sind mir fast übermenschlich, man glaubt einen Titankampf gegen Religion und Tugend zu sehen] (in Grawe 195).

12. This line was cut by Dahlberg for the Mannheim production.

13. Viewers seem to have been aware of the curious use of humor in the play. One early reviewer comments: "So is his use of wit sometimes forced and odd" [So ist sein Witz zuweilen gesucht und abenteuerlich] (Review of Christian Friedrich Thimme in Grawe 181).

14. Recent performances of the play appear to foreground the comic-satiric, as in the 1997 production in Oberhausen, where Franz Moor intones the pop song "What a Wonderful World" ("Zeitgenosse Schiller").

15. John Simon sees a direct connection between Schiller and Dostoevsky in this regard. See "The Nature of Suffering in Schiller and Dostoevsky."

16. Freud argues that jokes and other forms of humor work like dreams to break through repression and, as a result, provide a brief access to a "mood of our childhood . . . when we had no need of humor to make us feel happy in our life" (Freud, *Jokes and Their Relation to the Unconscious* 293).

17. This is particularly true if we factor in Otto Rank's theory of "birth trauma." See Rank in Kristeva, *Powers* 33.

18. Similarly, Lacan notes, "It wouldn't surprise you if I told you that, first and last, we're actually dealing with the mother" (*Seminar* 251).

19. Kristeva makes this connection imagistically at the outset of the study, "In the dark halls of Auschwitz, I see a heap of children's shoes, or something like that, something I have already seen elsewhere, under a Christmas tree, for instance, dolls, I believe. The abjection of Nazi crime reaches its apex when death, which, in any case, kills me, interferes with what, in my lived universe, is supposed to save me from death: childhood, science, among other things" (*Powers* 4).

20. Tellingly, such emotions may involve food, particularly that first kind:

> Along with sigh-clouding dizziness, nausea makes me balk at that milk cream, sepa-
> rates me from the mother and father who proffer it. "I" want none of that element,
> sign of their desire, "I" do not want to listen; "I" do not assimilate it; "I" expel it. But
> since the food is not an "other" for "me," who am completely in their desire, I expel
> *myself, I* spit *myself* out . . . it is thus that *they* see that "I" am in the process of becoming
> an other at the expense of my own death . . . I give birth to myself amid the violence
> of sobs and vomit. (Kristeva, *Powers* 3)

21. Freud notes, "If one has the occasion as a doctor to make the acquaintance of
one of those people who . . . are well known in their circle as jokers and the originators
of many viable jokes, one may be surprised to discover that the joker is a disunited
personality, disposed to neurotic disorders" (*Jokes and Their Relation to the Unconscious*
174).

22. See Harald Steinhagen's fine analysis of the similarities between Schiller and
Sade.

23. Narcissism stems, Kristeva reminds us, from a severe wound to the early
mother-child relationship (*Powers* 62).

24. Correspondingly, in the nightmare of divine condemnation that drives him to
suicide, Franz finds the complement of and punishment for his own murderous desires—that which he would like to do and fears will be done to him. See Freud, "Beyond
the Pleasure Principle" 157.

25. The similarity between Franz Moor's pathology and that of Hitler, as articulated in *Mein Kampf* is eerily striking, and German Jews in the 30s were apparently
sensitive to the play's connection to fascism—as the following joke implicitly suggests:

> Shortly before World War II, a British travel bureau takes a number of men and
> women on a tour of Germany. The party includes an English Jew. While in Dresden,
> the group visits Schiller's study.
> "Here the great German national poet expressed the soul of his people," says the
> Nazi guide.
> "Pardon the correction," said the Jew. "Schiller was not a national, but an inter-
> national poet. You know that he wrote *Maria Stuart* for the English, the *Maid of Orleans*
> for the French, and *Wilhelm Tell* for the Swiss.
> "Hasn't he done anything for the Germans?" asks the Nazi indignantly.
> "Schiller did not neglect you," replies the Jew. "For the Germans he wrote *The
> Robbers*." (Lipman 169)

26. Kristeva notes that the abject self wishes to throw away both himself and all
others (*Powers* 47).

27. Similarly, Freud notes, "no neurotic harbors thoughts of suicide which are not
murderous impulses against others redirected upon himself" ("Mourning and Melancholia" 133).

28. Despite Karl's nimble facility with the language of Enlightenment fraternity
and freedom as well as the masochistic, virtue-laid-low language of melodrama, the
robber captain proves to be the play's killer par excellence (Hammer, *Sublime Crime* 92).
Moreover, his "repentance" at the end of the drama is rendered dubious by a consistent
pattern of violent acts, denial of responsibility, and attempted flight that governs all of
his actions in the play.

29. Schiller is also, in very crucial ways, taking on and attempting to unpack what

Gustafson sees rightly as Lessing's utter refusal to inaugurate any possible connection between audience emotive reaction and the abject. Schiller's aesthetic practice in *The Robbers* dramatically explodes the viewer's "narcissistic confirmation of self as complete, as distanced from and thereby protected from the deficiencies/loss of the suffering object/body" (*Absent Mothers* 102).

30. In this way, Schiller's first play also implicitly questions the possibilities of emerging bourgeois dramatic forms. See Helmut Schmiedt's discussion of how Storm and Stress both deployed and interrogated drama in "Wie revolutionär ist das Drama des Sturm und Drang?"

31. Such an account explains Schiller's appeal in England to such psychologically troubled artists as Wordsworth, Blake, Coleridge, and Shelley, who were also committed to political and social change through art. See Meller.

32. Seen from this point of view, the play's critique of patriarchy is not ultimately "ambivalent" as Richard Koc argues.

33. Having left town without leave to attend a performance of his play in Mannheim, Schiller was put under fourteen days' arrest. He was further instructed by the duke that he was forbidden to write anything other than medical treatises or to communicate with foreigners (Sharpe 29–30). For a good description of Schiller's studies and life under the ducal regime in Württemberg, see Sharpe 6–9.

34. Karl Eugen apparently cast his relations between himself and his subjects in precisely these paternal-filial terms. See Reed 64.

35. The understanding of the Karl Eugen incident in traumatic terms would account for why, in T. J. Reed's words, "the dialogue" between Schiller and the Duke continues in both *Intrigue and Love* and in *Don Carlos* (66–67).

36. Again, see Lacan, who tells of a writer suffering with writer's block because of a deep psychological suspension deriving from his childhood inability to understand an article of the (in this case, Islamic) law (Lacan, *Seminar* 129–30).

CHAPTER 2

An early version of this chapter was presented at the Davidson College symposium on Weimar (Feb. 1997) and published in *Unwrapping Goethe's Weimar,* ed. Burkhard Henke, Suzanne Kord, and Simon Richter (Camden House, 2000).

1. See Passage's description of the different phases of composition, *Friedrich Schiller* 63–66, and Sharpe 80–82.

2. Charlotte von Kalb (von Wiese 224) facilitated this meeting.

3. The translations of the *Rheinische Thalia* and the letters are mine unless otherwise indicated.

4. Freud, "Rat Man" 12.

5. Thus what Kirtz describes as Schiller's declaration that "business [is] unreconcilable with literary dignity" may be understood as the author's accurate assessment of the paradoxical roles of cultural production and the cultural producer within emerging capitalist/Protestant confines.

6. With some reason, Wieland called the work a "dramatic novel" (von Wiese 246).

7. Feminist psychiatrist Judith Herman notes "traumatized people relive as though it were continually recurring in the present . . . It is as though time stops at the moment of trauma" (37).

8. This description in terms of sensation and a few vivid images are constitutive of traumatic memory, according to Herman (38).

9. The horror of the memory suggests obliquely that more than the back has been revealed to the throng.

10. "The trauma, instead of being forgotten, is deprived of its affective cathexis; so that what remains is nothing but its ideational content, which is perfectly colourless and is judged to be unimportant." Freud, "Rat Man" 38.

11. Literally, the translation reads, "God! Here I feel I am becoming bitter— Away, away, away from this place!"

12. Herman aptly describes the quality of this encounter when she notes, "There is something uncanny about reenactments. Even when they are consciously chosen, they have a feeling of involuntariness . . . they have a driven, tenacious quality" (41).

13. Von Wiese suggests that this relationship may reflect the tensions of the troubled passion between Schiller and Charlotte von Kalb (Von Wiese 226–27), a passion blocked effectively by the fact that she was—albeit unhappily—married.

14. In this sense, the play clearly derives from bourgeois tragedy traditions in which "sexual yearnings are inherently illicit" (Gustafson in Kuzniar 112). Here the state replaces the family, and *Don Carlos* gestures toward "disciplining" and normalizing desire through enlisting it as duty to the fatherland, rather than the *father*. But desire sublimated into duty doesn't fare well either, and while the notion of "the love for the State" (*Staatsliebe*) will eventually culminate in the heterosexual father-hero of *Wilhelm Tell*, it remains deeply problematic for Schiller up through *The Maid of Orleans*.

15. Freud's final footnote to the Rat Man case study suggests a tragic dimension to the therapy, for the patient has been cured only to be killed: "Like so many other young men of value and promise, he perished in the Great War." Freud, "Rat Man" 81.

16. Occasional writings composed ten years later bear out such a reading of *Don Carlos* (Sauder 224). Schiller critiques both his historical moment and his homeland when he observes in a letter to Johann Suevern in 1800: "Our tragedy, if we had one, must wrestle with the impotence, the sleepiness, and the characterlessness of the spirit of the times" [Unsere Tragödie, wenn wir eine hätten, hat mit der Ohnmacht, der Schlafheit, der Charakterlosigkeit des Zeitgeistes . . . zu ringen] (Sauder 224).

17. Von Wiese hints fleetingly at such a reading when he notes the psychological similarities between Carlos and Schiller during his Mannheim stay (von Wiese 247). See also Friedrich Kittler's intriguing reading of the play as a displaced description of the Karlsschule in terms of discipline and psychiatry. Kittler's analysis suggests that *Don Carlos* represents several layers of traumatic experiences in Schiller's own life— originating perhaps with traumatic experiences in his own home as a child.

18. Schiller made a direct and visceral connection between himself and his creation early on, writing Reinwald that Carlos had Hamlet's soul but that his *"pulse"* comes from *"me"* (Schiller to Reinwald, 1783, in von Wiese 247–48).

19. Such a reading of the play is supported by the valuable stylistic analysis of Arnd Bohm, who notes a recurring obsession with property exchanges and with problems of giving, taking, and earning. Bohm's reading suggests once again *Don Carlos*'s deep indebtedness to such homosocial/mercantilist bourgeois tragedies as *The London Merchant* (see my analysis in *Sublime Crime*), but while Bohm sees the play as a shoring up of mercantilist values, I tend to see it rather as what Alan Sinfield calls an ideological "fault-line story" (4), where notions of gender, libidinal economy, power relations, and modes of artistic production all break down.

20. Thus, in the ubiquitous Goethe-Schiller pair we can see the template for a powerful bifurcation of male cultural work (in Anglo-Europe and the United States), which seeks to join the figure of the best-selling, virile man of literary business with his effete, professorial, and/or spiritual partner even as it sets the two apart. Contested and complicated versions of this already problematic binary may be seen in such couples as Byron/Shelley, Sartre/Camus, Washington/Du Bois, Hemingway/Fitzgerald, and even McCartney/Lennon.

21. A preliminary reading suggests that the letters are ironic and bitterly parodistic, indicating the leakage of yet another of Schiller's repressed interests—namely satire, theorized later in *Über naïve und sentimentalische Dichtung*.

22. One can also see that the various Goethe properties were already in the process of being transformed to the authorial shrines that they now are.

CHAPTER 3

1. With justification, David Ng argues in his review that the film can only be understood as a cinematic "poem." See his "Review of *The Thin Red Line*."

2. The subtitles are all lines from the film *The Thin Red Line,* which significantly alters the James Jones novel by the same name.

3. Lacan implies as much in his linking of mimicry, mask, travesty, and play (see in particular *Four Fundamental Concepts* 107) and by his appeals to gestures in theatrical performance (116–17).

4. See Gisela Berns's study of the influence of the *Iliad* on WALLENSTEIN.

5. While Schiller did not begin active work on the trilogy until 1796, the subject matter and plan to make a poem out of the Thirty Years War material was a subject of constant conversation between him and his correspondents from 1791 on.

6. In a compelling conversation in February 1999, Reinhold Grimm remembered driving through a forest with his grandparents when he was a child. At one point they stopped and told him that "this" was where the town was that their family was from, and that it had been utterly destroyed during the Thirty Years War. They were standing on completely deserted and empty ground, where no trace remained. This was, Professor Grimm observed, what happened to families. They could not remember past the Thirty Years War, and the war marked the loss of cultural memory of what had happened before.

7. Such an awareness is hinted at in Schiller's observations: first, that a rewriting of *the Iliad* was simply not possible any longer (Schiller in Berns 48), and second, that

even if it were possible it was not desirable because Homer's poetry, as moving as it was, lacked real depth (49).

8. Recent criticism of the play cycle recognizes the importance of memory in *WALLENSTEIN* but tends to regard the act of memory itself as unproblematic and more or less direct. See Jens Dwars, who observes that the plays are an act of "social remembering" (152), and Burkhard Henke who—building on Dwars—argues for a process of remembering deriving from political, intellectual, and dramatic traditions (313).

9. In the citations *WC* refers to *Wallenstein's Camp* [*Wallensteins Lager*], *TP* to *The Piccolomini* [*Die Piccolomini*], and *DW* to the *Death of Wallenstein* [*Wallensteins Tod*] translated by Passage from *WALLENSTEIN*.

10. See Theweleit's account of the stick—which the members of Freikorps all carried—as an "ocnophile object"—a post-transitional object that signals at once a repressed longing for the mother, a fear of being swallowed up, and a sense of being reduced, objectified, of being partly an object (2:263–65).

11. Rightfully, Karl Guthke calls Wallenstein a master manipulator, who moves the other characters with finesse as though they were playthings or chess pieces (181).

12. Small wonder that, as Walter Hinderer notes, Hegel had problems with the ending of *WALLENSTEIN*, and the reviews of the cycle were mixed (Hinderer 258–62).

13. See Dieter Borchmeyer's intriguing discussion of Wallenstein's character in terms of Renaissance notions of the four temperaments—a set of theories that the young Schiller had enthusiastically studied (9–11). The book's argument that Wallenstein is a quintessential melancholic further substantiates how very interested in psychology Schiller was, and continued to be.

14. Melancholy is therefore only a symptom of a larger and deeper psychological issue. See my in-depth discussion of repetition and circularity in *WALLENSTEIN* in "Schiller, Time and Again."

15. Thus it is not time that is Wallenstein's enemy—as David Richards (relying on Oskar Seidlin's earlier essay) has argued (241)—rather it is his trauma-driven (mis)-understanding of time that destroys him.

16. Seen in this light, Schiller's trilogy undertakes a dramatization and literalization of the implied critique of civilization (and a call for a new one) that Herbert Marcuse sees Schiller's "Aesthetic Letters" as implicitly performing. The outlining in drama of a profoundly "alienating society" (Marcuse 169) testifies to the both "explosive" and "radical" power of Schiller's aesthetic vision (173–74).

17. Several critics refer to the difficulties that Schiller encountered with this project. Elfriede Heyer notes, "No material caused Schiller more agony, no language presented more challenge than the Wallenstein trilogy" (Heyer 77). See also Zeyringer's intriguing discussion of passages excised from the work.

18. This is Robert Gross's observation.

CHAPTER 4

1. Catherine Clément remarks that the issue of female desire is raised and answered negatively in the final moments of the film and reminds us that the mad Jane observes tellingly "queens may never choose as our hearts dictate" (214).

2. Kluge sees this as a struggle on several levels with several people—notably Goethe and the Schlegelians (251). Ultimately however, as the following discussion suggests, Schiller's principal struggle—as always—was with himself and his finances.

3. Schiller admits as much to Humboldt, telling him that a new translation of Aeschylus's *Prometheus* greatly facilitated the present work (February 17, 1803), and playfully calling himself a contemporary of Sophocles.

4. In a March 3 addendum to the February letter, Schiller wrote: "This letter has a dejected tone; I would do better perhaps not to send it" [Dieser Brief hat eine schwermüthige Stimmung, ich thäte vielleicht besser ihn nicht abzusenden] (Letter 15, *Schillers Werke* 32:12).

5. "On the Use of the Chorus in Tragedy" was written after the play (Sharpe 283), and as such may be read as Schiller's interpretation (and theoretical defense) of it.

6. See Gustafson's astute analysis of Lessing's aesthetic theory, and of the "Laokoon" in particular, *Absent Mothers* 41–71.

7. See Michael Böhler's tackling of this vexed question through reader-response approaches and the lively argument that follows in Wittkowski 273–94.

8. Thus, if Lessing's aesthetics are concerned with "protection, preservation, and presentation of beautiful bodies" (Gustafson, *Absent Mothers* 45), Schiller's preoccupations here are with the calming, repression, seclusion, and radical internalization of the "beautiful" (read bourgeois) psyche.

9. Goethe gave the actors of the production very specific instructions, which were to form the basis for his 1803 "Rules for Actors" (Brandt 276). The following suggest how very much the actors were to imitate sculpture: "(35) First, the actor must consider that he should not only imitate nature but present it in an idealized form, and thus unite the true with the beautiful in his presentation. (36) Therefore every part of his body should be completely under his control. . . . (43) A beautiful contemplative pose (for a young man, for example) is this: the chest and entire body held erect, standing in the fourth dance position, the head turned somewhat to the side, the eyes fixed on the ground" (Brandt 162).

10. From this point of view, Schiller's approach to the psychology of the theater as palliative rather than as curative for depression recasts the German attitude toward tragedy articulated more than a century before. Zelle cites a seventeenth-century text, Sandart's *Teutsche Academie,* which touts the positive effect of tragedy on the melancholy person—making him "refreshed and cheered" (Zelle, *Angenehmes Grauen* 122).

11. Seen from this point of view, "On the Use of the Chorus" represents a radicalization of the views proposed in the Aesthetic Letters and gives a retroactive explanation of the psychological desperation underlying Schiller's move into "a narrowly aesthetic project" (Woodmansee 59). See Woodmansee's reading of the Aesthetic Letters, 58–86.

12. *Bride* marketed itself to its Weimar audience, not only through "values" (such as the notion of separate spheres), but also through its use of decor. Here classical ornamentation was presented in such a way as to shore up mass wants class bourgeois values and also covertly advertise certain objects for the home. This connection is—perversely—made clear in the March 31, 1803, edition of the *Journal for the World of Elegance* [*Zeitung für die elegante Welt*], which discusses the lighting for the play: "In the last act the major lighting . . . is from a twelve-branched candelabra above the action

which has a lovely effect, giving a chiaroscuro of heavy shadows and painterly light, particularly in the striking scene where the brother's corpse is bought in" (Brandt 276).

13. Lines of demarcation are rendered even more distinct by Schiller's use of different kinds of prosody for the chorus than for the rest of the characters: pentameter for the action and other meters for the chorus, such as dimeter and tetrameter—the latter, when Don Manuel's bier is brought on stage (Clark 1143).

14. In this same speech, Beatrice's home is revealed to be a surrogate for the lost real thing. She, like Schiller's other heroes, is haunted by a traumatic abduction.

15. The problem of fate and the concomitant issue of character motivation have preoccupied critics of this play. See Frank Fowler's summary of the debate in "Matters of Motivation" as well as Stuart Atkins's discussion in "Gestalt als Gehalt."

16. In particular vis-à-vis the mother. See Kluge 257.

17. This loss of logos elaborates on Atkins's astute observation that in this and the other later dramas the rhetoric becomes "empty"—a mere display of verbal splendor (Atkins 554).

18. Such a reading makes sense of what critics call the "ambivalence" of the dream meanings (see Kluge 258 and Weigland 195).

19. Aptly, Sharpe observes, "the serenity and stylization of *Die Braut von Messina* mask a savage and treacherous world" (293).

20. In an uncanny way, Schiller's play recapitulates and develops both the theoretical writing and dramatic efforts of Herder to account for the problems of representation posed by the wounded Greek hero Philoctetes. Described by Herder as a "Bildsäule" (a sculpture), the character of Philoctetes, according to Liliane Weissberg, "does not represent a body of marble that is without any reactions" but rather "reproduces" inner pain with "silence" (Weissberg 565). Like Schiller's tragedy, Herder's play of 1774 also retells a story of pain through traumatic gaps and silences rather than through lucid, consistent speech (577–78), reducing truncated language down to a series of raw exclamations, much as Schiller would do in *The Robbers*. In *Bride,* however, the mature Schiller attempts to cover the gaps of pain over with the "beauties" of classical poetics, and with artistically rendered tableaux that attempt to show that which cannot be voiced. See Weissberg's cogent and intriguing reading of Herder in her essay, "Language's Wound."

21. Weigland also notices a "lurid discrepancy between Schiller's infernal plot, the working out of the ancestral curse, and the magnificent, stately, superbly rhythmical language of Schiller's chorus that draws upon every device of baroque pomp and classical rhetoric." He observes further that "without question, Schiller counted upon the chorus and the sustained lofty style of the dialogue . . . to offset . . . the bloodcurdling thrills of the plot, and make a mood of solemn edification prevail" (196).

22. Robert T. Clark argues for *Bride*'s relationship to opera and—by implication—to the musical, but the stasis of the work argues against this, unless one enlists such unusual musical productions as Brecht's *A Threepenny Opera* and Sondheim's *Sunday in the Park with George*.

23. Gerhard Kluge rightly assesses *Bride* as Schiller's most controversial and challenging play (Kluge 242).

24. Note the identical expression in Isabella's speech.

CHAPTER 5

1. Subtitles are all citations from Camus's *The First Man.*

2. The importance and influence of Albert Camus on postwar writing and thought in Anglo-Europe cannot be overemphasized. For an introduction to his work, see Bettina Knapp's *Critical Essays on Albert Camus,* Phillip Thody's *Albert Camus,* and Susan Tarrow's *Exile from the Kingdom.*

3. Note the similarity between Schiller's comments and Camus's: "The worst is that I no longer have the time, nor the interior leisure to write my books, and I spend four years writing what, with freedom would have taken two years. For several years now my work hasn't freed me, it has enslaved me" (Camus in Lottman 539).

4. Significantly, the original title for the novel was *Adam* (Lottman 8).

5. Schiller's mother died in the spring of 1802. See the correspondence between Schiller and his sister, in particular his letter to her of May 10 (*Schillers Werke* 31:131).

6. At the outset of her important book on the development of the bourgeois tragedy in Germany, Gail Hart notes the consistent process of removal of female protagonists from the German stage so as to facilitate the homosocial bonding of the men, in a world "without women" (*Tragedy in Paradise* 126).

7. See "Re-dressing History."

8. It seems likely that—at bottom—Schiller was undertaking in *Demetrius* the same kind of personal, autobiographically grounded "repositioning" that Camus was attempting—in response to an emotionally unavailable, depressed, or troubled mother. Camus—writing after both Freud and Marx—seems to have been quite aware of how both problematic and crucial his relationship to his mother was (his mother, incidentally, survived him by only nine months). Schiller, writing before psychoanalysis and Marxism, probably was not. But it is impressive to see how much he intuitively understood about family dynamics, gender, and trauma.

9. Mother was to have played an even more important role in the plans both authors had for the finished product. Camus's notes for his novel indicate that he contemplated writing alternating chapters in which the mother would give her own point of view (with her sparse vocabulary of four hundred words), and that there might be an eventual apotheosis of bonding between the two wherein the son would ask the mother for forgiveness (Camus 313–17). In the plans for *Demetrius,* a reunion with Mother would take place, but only in the wake of Demetrius's tragic discovery of his own imposture—a realization that would make the anticipated reunion a travesty for both "mother" and "son." See Passage's discussion of Schiller's plan for acts 3–5, 49–61.

10. Conversation, spring 1995.

11. Maryna particularly thinks in terms of financial exchanges. Her own happiness is something to be thought of as daily interest that must accrue in order to be valuable: "What new gain would accrue from that exchange? / Can I rejoice in what the next day brings / If it brings nothing other than today?" (1.3: Passage, *Demetrius* 30) [Was wächst mir neues zu aus diesem Tausch / Und kann ich mich des nächsten Tages freuen / Wenn er mir mehr nicht als der heutge bringt!] (*Schillers Werke* 11:36).

12. The emphasis that Demetrius places on the performance of an arresting story anticipates in curious ways the manner in which dramatic narratives supercede "truth"

in such pseudojuristic television shows as *People's Court* and *The Blame Game*, and particularly in the ubiquitous *Jerry Springer* confrontations.

13. See John Frow's useful summary of this phenomenon as well as the furor and the problems that it raises (230–38).

14. See Laurence Kirmayer's account of this process, 178.

15. See for example, Freud's disclaimer at the beginning of "Mourning and Melancholia" (124) as well as the opening paragraphs of *Civilization and Its Discontents*.

16. See Passage, *Demetrius* 60–61.

17. In this sense, the "value" of trauma as articulated in *Demetrius* looks forward to the current uncertainty that John Frow sees as peculiar to "advanced capitalist societies [where] it has now become difficult to separate the commodification of material from that of immaterial goods, including such 'services' as knowledges and feelings" (145). Other objects of uncertain relation to commodification include—significantly— female reproductive capability and *ova* (145).

18. Transgenerational trauma—at time of writing—represents the latest direction in trauma studies. See Yael Danieli's compilation of research approaches, *International Handbook of Multigenerational Legacies of Trauma*.

Works Cited

Atkins, Stuart. "Gestalt als Gehalt in Schillers 'Braut von Messina.' " *Deutsche Vierteljahresschrift für Literaturwissenschaft und Geistesgeschichte* 33.4 (1959): 529–64.

Bach, Sheldon, and Lester Schwartz. "A Dream of the Marquis de Sade: Psychoanalytic Reflections on Narcissistic Trauma, Decompensation, and the Reconstitution of a Delusional Self." *Journal of the Psychoanalytic Association* 20:3 (1972): 451–75.

Barthes, Roland. *Camera Lucida: Reflections on Photography*. New York: Hill and Wars, 1993.

Beckett, Samuel. *Molloy. Three Novels*. New York: Grove, 1955. 7–176.

Benjamin, Jessica. *The Bonds of Love: Psychoanalysis, Feminism, and the Problem of Domination*. New York: Pantheon, 1988.

Berns, Gisela N. *Greek Antiquity in Schiller's WALLENSTEIN*. Chapel Hill and London: U of North Carolina P, 1985.

Bloom, Harold. *The Anxiety of Influence*. 2nd ed. New York and Oxford: Oxford UP, 1997.

Böhler, Michael. "Die Zuschauerrolle in Schillers Dramaturgie. Zwischen Außendruck und Innenlenkung." *Friedrich Schiller: Kunst, Humanität und Politik in der späten Aufklaerung*. Ed. Wolfgang Wittkowski. Tuebingen: Max Niemeyer Verlag, 1982. 273–94.

Bohm, Arnd. " 'Ich will den Käufer nich betrügen': Give and Take in Schiller's *Don Carlos*." *Seminar* 27.3 (1991): 203–18.

Borchmeyer, Dieter. *Macht und Melancholie: Schillers* Wallenstein. Frankfurt: Athenaeum, 1988.

Brandt, George W. *German and Dutch Theater, 1600–1848. Theatre in Europe: A Documentary History*. Cambridge: Cambridge UP, 1993.

Brooks, Peter. *The Melodramatic Imagination*. New Haven: Yale UP, 1976.

Budd, Mike. "The Moments of *Caligari*." *The Cabinet of Dr Caligari: Texts, Contexts, Histories*. Ed. Mike Budd. New Brunswick and London: Rutgers UP, 1990. 7–120.

Burns, Rob, ed. *German Cultural Studies: An Introduction*. Oxford: Oxford UP, 1995.

The Cabinet of Dr. Caligari. Dir. Robert Wiene. 1920.

Camus, Albert. *The First Man*. Trans. David Hapgood. New York: Knopf, 1995.

Caruth, Cathy. "Unclaimed Experience: Trauma and the Possibility of History." *Yale French Studies* 79 (1991): 181–92.

Chase, Cynthia. *Decomposing Figures: Rhetorical Readings in the Romantic Tradition*. Baltimore and London: Johns Hopkins UP, 1986.

Works Cited

Clark, Robert T. "The Union of the Arts in *Die Braut von Messina." PMLA* 52.4 (1937): 1135–46.

Clement, Catherine B. "Charlatans and Hysterics." *The Cabinet of Dr. Caligari: Texts, Contexts, Histories.* Ed. Mike Budd. New Brunswick and London: Rutgers UP, 1990. 191–204.

Danieli, Yael. *International Handbook of* Multigenerational Legacies of Trauma. New York: Plenum, 1998.

Dieckmann, Liselotte, trans. *Correspondence between Goethe and Schiller, 1794–1805.* New York: Peter Lang, 1994.

Dollimore, Jonathan. *Sexual Dissidence: Augustine to Wilde, Freud to Foucault.* Oxford: Clarendon, 1991.

Dwars, Jens-F. "Dichtung im Epochenumbruch. Schillers *Wallentstein* im Wandel von Alltag und Oeffentlichkeit." *Jahrbuch der deutschen Schillergesellschaft* 35 (1991): 150–79.

Fowler, Frank M. "Matters of Motivation: In Defence of Schiller's *Die Braut von Messina." German Life and Letters* 39.2 (1986): 134–47.

Freud, Sigmund. "Beyond the Pleasure Principle." *A General Selection from the Works of Sigmund Freud.* New York: Anchor Books, 1989. 141–68.

———. *Civilization and Its Discontents.* New York: Norton, 1989.

———. *Jokes and Their Relation to the Unconscious.* New York: Norton, 1989.

———. "Mourning and Melancholia." *A General Selection from the Works of Sigmund Freud.* New York: Anchor Books, 1989. 124–40.

———. "The 'Rat Man.' " *Three Case Histories.* Intro. Philip Rieff. New York: Collier, 1993 [1963]. 1–81.

———. "Repression." *A General Selection from the Works of Sigmund Freud.* New York: Anchor Books, 1989. 87–97.

———. "The Wolf Man." *Three Case Histories.* Intro. Philip Rieff. New York: Collier, 1993 [1963]. 161–280.

Frow, John. *Time and Commodity Culture: Essays in Cultural Theory and Postmodernity.* Oxford: Oxford UP, 1997.

Gaiman, Neil. "Imperfect Hosts." *The Sandman: Preludes and Nocturnes.* New York: Vertigo/DC Comics. 43–67.

Gordon, Mel. *The Grand Guignol: Theatre of Fear and Terror.* New York: Amok Press, 1988.

Grawe, Christian, ed. *Friedrich Schillers die Räuber: Erläuterungen und Dokumente.* Stuttgart: Reclam, 1977.

Grey, Margaret E. "Beckett Backwards and Forwards: The Rhetoric of Retraction in *Molloy. French Forum* 19:2 (1994): 161–74.

Gustafson, Susan. *Absent Mothers and Orphaned Fathers: Narcissism and Abjection in Lessing's Aesthetic and Dramatic Production.* Detroit: Wayne State UP, 1995.

———. "Goethe's *Clavigo:* The Body as an 'Unorthographic' Sign." In *Body and Text in the Eighteenth Century.* Ed. Veronica Kelly and Dorothea von Mücke. Stanford: Stanford UP, 1994. 229–46.

———. "Sadomasochism, Mutilation, and Men: Lessings *Laocoon,* Herders' *Kritische Waelder,* Gerstenberg's *Ugolino* and the Storm and Stress of Drama." *Poetics Today* 20:2 (1999): 197–218.

Works Cited

Guthke, Karl S. *"Wallenstein als Spiel vom Spiel." Wirkendes Wort* 43:2 (1993): 174–95.

Hammer, Stephanie. "Schiller, Time and Again." *German Quarterly* (Spring 1994): 153–72.

———. *The Sublime Crime: Fascination, Failure, and Form in the Literature of the Enlightenment.* Carbondale: Southern Illinois UP, 1994.

Hart, Gail. "Re-dressing History: Mother Nature, Mother Isabeau, the Virgin Mary, and Schiller's Jungfrau." *Women in German Yearbook* 14 (1998): 91–107.

———. *Tragedy in Paradise: Family and Gender Politics in German Bourgeois Tragedy, 1750–1850.* Columbia S.C.: Camden, 1996.

Henke, Burkhard. *"Wallenstein* und *Macbeth:* Schillers Neugestaltung des Usurpatorenmotivs." *Journal of English and Germanic Philology* 94:3 (1995): 313–31.

Herman, Judith Lewis. *Trauma and Recovery.* New York: Harper Collins, 1992.

Heyer, Elfriede. "The Genesis of *Wallenstein." Friedrich von Schiller and the Drama of Human Existence.* Ed. Alexej Ugrinsky. New York: Greenwood, 1988. 71–80.

Hill, Phillip. *Lacan for Beginners.* New York and London: Writers and Readers, 1997.

Hinderer, Walter. *Von der Idee des Menschen: Über Friedrich Schiller.* Würzburg: Königshausen & Neumann, 1998.

Horkheimer, Max, and Theodor Adorno. *The Dialectic of Enlightenment.* New York: Herder and Herder, 1972 [1944].

Hunt, Lynn and Catherine Hall. "The Sweet Delights of Home." *A History of Private Life,* vol. 4. Ed. Michelle Perrot. Cambridge and London: Belknap and Harvard, 1990. 47–93.

Jameson, Fredric. *The Political Unconscious: Narrative as a Socially Symbolic Act.* Ithaca: Cornell UP, 1981.

Kirmayer, Laurence J. "Landscapes of Memory: Trauma, Narrative, Dissociation." *Tense Past: Cultural Essays in Trauma and Memory.* Ed. Paul Antze and Michael Lambek. New York: Routledge, 1996. 173–98.

Kittler, Friedrich. "Carlos als Karlsschüler." *Unser Commercium: Goethes und Schillers Literaturpolitik.* Ed. Wilfried Barber et al. Stuttgart: Cotta, 1984. 241–74.

Kluge, Gerhard. "Die Braut von Messina." *Schiller Heute: Neue Interpretationen.* Ed. Walter Hinderer. Stuttgart: Reclam, 1979. 242–70.

Knapp, Bettina L., ed. *Critical Essays on Albert Camus.* Boston: G. K. Hull, 1988.

Knowlson, James. *Damned to Fame: The Life of Samuel Beckett.* New York: Simon and Schuster, 1996.

Kostka, Edmund K. *Schiller in Russian Literature.* Philadelphia: U of Pennsylvania P, 1965.

Kracauer, Siegfried. "Cult of Distraction: On Berlin's Picture Palaces." *New German Critique* 40 (Winter 1987):91–96. A translation by Thomas Y. Levin of "Kult der Zerstruung." *Frankfurter Zeitung* 70, 167 (14 March 1926).

Kraft, Herbert, ed. *Schillers Werke.* Frankfurt: Insel, 1966.

Kristeva, Julia. *Black Sun: Depression and Melancholia.* New York: Columbia, 1989.

———. *New Maladies of the Soul.* New York: Columbia, 1995.

———. *Powers of Horror: An Essay on Abjection.* New York: Columbia UP, 1982.

Kuzniar, Alice, ed. *Outing Goethe and His Age.* Stanford: Stanford UP, 1996.

Lacan, Jacques. *The Four Fundamental Concepts of Psycho-Analysis.* New York: Norton, 1981.

————. *The Seminar of Jacques Lacan, Book II.* New York: Norton, 1991.

Lamport, F. J. *German Classical Drama: Theater, Humanity, and Nation.* Cambridge: Cambridge UP, 1990.

Leidner, Alan C. " 'Fremde Menschen fielen einander schluchzend in die Arme': *Die Räuber* and the Communal response." *Goethe Yearbook* 3 (1986): 57–71.

Lipman, Steve. *Laughter in Hell: The Use of Humor during the Holocaust.* Northvale and London: Jason Aronson, 1991.

Lorant, Andre. "Oedipus, Hamlet and Don Carlos: Fathers and Sons in Dramatic Literature." *Neohelicon* 12:2 (1985): 115–45.

Lottman, Herbert R. *Albert Camus: A Biography.* Corte Madera: Gingko Press, 1997 [Doubleday, 1979].

Marcuse, Herbert. *Eros and Civilization: A Philosophical Inquiry into Freud.* New York: Vintage, 1955.

Martini, Fritz. "Demetrius." *Schillers Dramen: Neue Interpretationen.* Ed. Walter Hinderer. Stuttgart: Reclam, 1979. 316–47.

Meller, Horst. "The Parricidal Imagination: Schiller, Blake, Fuseli, and the Romantic Revolt against the Father." *The Romantic Imagination: Literature and Art in England and Germany.* Ed. Frederick Burwick and Juergen Klein. Amsterdam and Atlanta: Rodopi, 1996. 76–94.

Mitchell, Juliet. "Trauma, Recognition, and the Place of Language. *Diacritics* 28:4 (1998): 121–33.

Mücke, Dorothea von. "The Powers of Horror and the Magic of Euphemism in Lessing's 'Laokoon' and 'How the Ancients Represented Death." *Body and Text in the Eighteenth Century.* Ed. Veronica Kelly and Dorothea von Mücke. Stanford: Stanford UP, 1994. 163–80.

Ng, David. "Review of *The Thin Red Line.*" *Images: A Journal of Film and Popular Culture* (Spring 1999). Web address: http://imagesjournal.com/issue07/reviews/thinredline/

Passage, Charles, trans. *The Bride of Messina, Wilhelm Tell, and Demetrius by Friedrich von Schiller.* New York: Ungar, 1962.

————. *Friedrich Schiller.* New York: Ungar, 1975.

————. *WALLENSTEIN.* New York: Ungar, 1965.

Penley, Constance. *The Future of an Illusion: Film, Feminism, and Psychoanalysis.* Minneapolis: U of Minnesota P, 1989.

Porcell, Claude. "Les signes, le mal et l'histoire dans le theatre de jeunesse de Schiller." *Etudes Germaniques* 34 (1979): 22–33.

Reed, T. J. "Talking to Tyrants: Dialogues with Power in Eighteenth-century Germany." *Historic Journal* 33:1 (1990): 63–79.

Richards, David B. "The Problem of Knowledge in *Wallenstein.*" *Goethezeit: Studien zu Erkenntnis und Rezeption Goethes und seiner Zeitgenossen.* Ed. Gerhart Hoffmeister. Bern: Francke, 1981. 231–42.

Richter, Simon. *Laocoon's Body and the Aesthetics of Pain.* Detroit: Wayne State UP, 1992.

Ronell, Avital. *Dictations: On Haunted Writing.* Bloomington: Indiana UP, 1986.

————. "Le Sujet Suppositaire: Freud and Rat Man." *On Puns: The Foundation of Letters.* Ed. Jonathan Culler. Oxford: Basil Blackwell, 1988. 115–39.

Rosenblum, Naomi. *A World History of Photography.* New York: Abbeville, 1997.

Sauder, Gerhard. "Die Jungfrau von Orleans." *Schillers Dramen: Neue Interpretationen.* Ed. Walter Hinderer. Stuttgart: Reclam, 1979. 217–41.

Schiller, Friedrich. *Don Carlos. Plays.* Ed. Walter Hinderer. Trans. Charles Passage. New York: Continuum, 1983. 103–303.

———. *Naïve and Sentimental Poetry.* Trans. Julias Elias. New York: Frederick Ungar, 1966.

———. *The Robbers and Wallenstein.* Trans. F.J. Lamport. New York: Penguin, 1979.

———. *Schillers Dramen.* In 2 vols. Ed. Herbert Kraft. Frankfurt: Insel, 1966.

———. *Schillers Werke.* NationalAusgabe. Ed. J. Petersen et al. 42 vols. Weimar: Böhlaus, 1943–.

Schmiedt, Helmut. "Wie revolutionär is das Drama des Sturm und Drang?" *Jahrbuch der deutschen Schillergesellschaft* (1985): 48–61.

Seidlin, Oskar. "Wallenstein: Sein und Zeit." In *Schillers Wallenstein.* Ed. Fritz Heuer and Werner Keller. Darmstadt: Wissenschaftliche Buchgesellschaft, 1977. 237–53.

Seltzer, Mark. *Bodies and Machines.* New York and London: Routledge, 1992.

Sharpe, Lesley. *Friedrich Schiller: Drama, Thought, Politics.* Cambridge: Cambridge UP, 1991.

Simon, John D. "The Myth of Progress in Schiller and Dostoevsky." *Comparative Literature* 24:4 (1972): 328–37.

———. "The Nature of Suffering in Schiller and Dostoevsky." *Comparative Literature* 19:2 (1967): 160–73.

Sinfield, Alan. *Cultural Politics: Queer Reading.* Philadelphia: U of Pennsylvania P, 1994.

Steinhagen, Harald. "Der junge Schiller zwischen Marquis de Sade und Kant." *Deutsche Vierteljahresschrift für Literatur* 65:1 (1982): 135–57.

Tarrow, Susan. *Exile from the Kingdom: A Political Rereading of Albert Camus.* University: U Alabama P, 1985.

The Terminator. Dir. James Cameron. 1983.

Theweleit, Klaus. *Male Fantasies.* 2 vols. Trans. Erica Carter, Stephen Conway, and Chris Turner. Minneapolis: U of Minnesota P, 1987–89.

The Thin Red Line. Dir. Terence Malick. 1998.

Thody, Phillip. *Albert Camus: A Study of His Work.* New York: Grove, 1955.

Thompson, B. "The Limitations of Freedom: A Comparative Study of Schiller's 'Die Braut von Messina' and Werner's 'Der 24ste Februar.'" *Modern Language Review* 73.2 (1978): 328–36.

Ugrinsky, Alexej, ed. *Friedrich von Schiller and the Drama of Human Existence.* New York: Greenwood P, 1988.

Von Wiese, Benno. *Friedrich Schiller.* Stuttgart: JB Metzler, 1959.

Weber, Max. *The Protestant Ethic and the Spirit of Capitalism.* New York: Scribners, 1958.

Weigand, Hermann. "*Oedipus Tyrannus* and *Die Braut von Messina.*" *Illinois Studies in Language and Literature* 46 (1959): 171–202.

Weissberg, Liliane. "Language's Wound: Herder, Philoctetes, and the Origin of Speech. *Modern Language Notes* 104:3 (1989): 548–79.

Wirtz, Thomas. "The Spirit of Speculation: Hermeneutics and Economic Credit in Weimar." Paper presented at the Second Annual Davidson Symposium for German Cultural Studies: Approaches to the City of Weimar. February, 1997.

Wittkowski, Wolfgang, ed. *Friedrich Schiller: Kunst, Humanität, und Politik in der späten Aufklärung.* Tübingen: Max Niemeyer Verlag, 1982.

Woodmansee, Martha. *The Author, Art, and the Market: Rereading the History of Aesthetics.* New York: Columbia UP, 1994.

"Zeitgenosse Schiller." *Theater Heute* 6 (June 1997): 46–47.

Zelle, Carsten. *Angenehmes Grauen.* Hamburg: Felix Meiner Verlag, 1987.

————. "Physiognomie des Schreckens im achtzehnten Jahrhundert. Zu Johann Caspar Lavater und Charles Lebrun." *Lessing Yearbook 21* (1989). 89–102.

Zeyringer, Klaus. "Beispiel eines Schaffensprozesses: Die unterdrückten Stellen in Schillers *Wallenstein.*" *Études Germaniques* 47 (1992): 19–30.

Index

abjection, definition of, 20, 38; in *The Robbers*, 44, 49
affirmative culture, 107, 130

Barthes, Roland, 73, 74, 104, 133, 151
Beckett, Samuel, 51–52, 64, 69; *Molloy*, 66
Borges, Jorge Luis, 49
Brecht, Berthold, 49
Brentano, Clemens, 105
Bronte, Charlotte, 37
Brooks, Peter. *See* melodrama
Budd, Mike, 106–7
Buechner, Georg, 49
Burgess, Anthony, 36, 49

The Cabinet of Dr. Caligari, 105–7, 128–29, 131
Camus, Albert, 133, 136–38, 163nn. 1–3, 8, 9; *The First Man*, 137–38, 140, 152; *The Stranger*, 136–37
capitalism, 24, 26, 66, 151–52, 159n. 19, 164n. 17
Caruth, Cathy, 13, 15–16
Celine, Louis-Ferdinand, 49
Chase, Cynthia, 149
Cocteau, Jean, 130
commodification, 25, 56, 118, 141, 152, 161n. 12
culture industry, 24, 66–67

displacement in Schiller's plays, 13–14, 122, 140
Dostoevsky, Fyodor, 37, 49

Fascism, 15; and Franz Moor, 36, 45–46, 156n. 25
Freud, Sigmund, 33, 105, 148–49, 155n. 16, 156nn. 21, 27, 163n. 8, 164n. 15; "Beyond the Pleasure Principle," 29; "The Rat Man," 52–53, 55, 60, 64, 66, 67–68, 70, 157n. 4, 158n. 15; "The Wolf Man," 33

Gaiman, Neil, 28, 30; *The Sandman*, 28–29, 34, 44, 49
Goethe, Wolfgang von, 67, 69, 71, 75, 102–3, 110, 154n. 15, 159n. 20, 161n. 9
Gordon, Mel. *See* Grand Guignol
Grand Guignol, definition of, 37
graphic novels, 27–30
Gustafson, Susan, 19–20, 138, 154n. 11, 155n. 5, 157n. 29, 158n. 14, 161n. 6

Handke, Peter, 49, 151
Hart, Gail, 138, 163n. 6
Herman, Judith, 16, 23, 45, 49, 88–89, 90–91, 100–101, 153n. 1, 158n. 7
Herzog, Werner, 49
homosocial attachments, 21, 32, 57, 59, 62, 65
Humboldt, Wilhelm von, 111–13, 131, 152, 161n. 4
humor, 34–37, 52, 155nn. 13, 16

Kafka, Franz, 49
Kalb, Charlotte von, 102, 158n. 2
Kerouac, Jack, 151
Kleist, Heinrich von, 49

171

Books in the Kritik:
German Literary Theory and Cultural Studies series

Walter Benjamin: An Intellectual Biography, by Bernd Witte, trans. by James Rolleston, 1991

The Violent Eye: Ernst Jünger's Visions and Revisions on the European Right, by Marcus Paul Bullock, 1991

Fatherland: Novalis, Freud, and the Discipline of Romance, by Kenneth S. Calhoon, 1992

Metaphors of Knowledge: Language and Thought in Mauthner's Critique, by Elizabeth Bredeck, 1992

Laocoon's Body and the Aesthetics of Pain: Winckelmann, Lessing, Herder, Moritz, Goethe, by Simon Richter, 1992

The Critical Turn: Studies in Kant, Herder, Wittgenstein, and Contemporary Theory, by Michael Morton, 1993

Reading After Foucault: Institutions, Disciplines, and Technologies of Self in Germany, 1750–1830, edited by Robert S. Leventhal, 1994

Bettina Brentano-von Arnim: Gender and Politics, edited by Elke P. Frederiksen and Katherine R. Goodman, 1995

Absent Mothers and Orphaned Fathers: Narcissism and Abjection in Lessing's Aesthetic and Dramatic Production, by Susan E. Gustafson, 1995

Identity or History? Marcus Herz and the End of the Enlightenment, by Martin L. Davies, 1995

Languages of Visuality: Crossings between Science, Art, Politics, and Literature, edited by Beate Allert, 1996

Resisting Bodies: The Negotiation of Female Agency in Twentieth-Century Women's Fiction, by Helga Druxes, 1996

Locating the Romantic Subject: Novalis with Winnicott, by Gail M. Newman, 1997

Embodying Ambiguity: Androgyny and Aesthetics from Winckelmann to Keller, by Catriona MacLeod, 1997

The Freudian Calling: Early Viennese Psychoanalysis and the Pursuit of Cultural Science, by Louis Rose, 1998

By the Rivers of Babylon: Heinrich Heine's Late Songs and Reflections, by Roger F. Cook, 1998

Reconstituting the Body Politic: Enlightenment, Public Culture, and the Invention of Aesthetic Autonomy, by Jonathan M. Hess, 1999

The School of Days: Heinrich von Kleist and the Traumas of Education, by Nancy Nobile, 1999

Walter Benjamin and the Corpus of Autobiography, by Gerhard Richter, 2000

Heads or Tails: The Poetics of Money, by Jochen Hörisch, trans. by Amy Horning Marschall, 2000

Dialectics of the Will: Freedom, Power, and Understanding iModern French and German Thought, by John H. Smith, 2000

The Bonds of Labor: German Journeys to the Working World, 1890–1990, by Carol Poore, 2000

Schiller's Wound: The Theater of Trauma from Crisis to Commodity, by Stephanie Hammer, 2001